THREE HAPPY WANDERERS

This book is dedicated to the memory of our dear friend Mabel, who sadly passed away shortly before it was published.

THREE HAPPY WANDERERS

June Austin, Mabel Pearce, Irene Percy

BREWIN BOOKS

BREWIN BOOKS
56 Alcester Road,
Studley,
Warwickshire,
B80 7LG
www.brewinbooks.com

Published by Brewin Books 2018

© June Austin, 2018

The author has asserted her rights in accordance with the Copyright, Designs and Patents Act 1988 to be identified as the author of this work.

All rights reserved. No part of this publication may be reproduced, stored in a retrieval system, or transmitted in any form or by any means, electronic, mechanical, photocopying, recording or otherwise, without the prior permission in writing of the publisher and the copyright owners, or as expressly permitted by law, or under terms agreed with the appropriate reprographics rights organization. Enquiries concerning reproduction outside the terms stated here should be sent to the publishers at the UK address printed on this page.

The publisher makes no representation, express or implied, with regard to the accuracy of the information contained in this book and cannot accept any legal responsibility for any errors or omissions that may be made.

A CIP catalogue record for this book is available from the British Library.

ISBN: 978-1-85858-583-3

Printed and bound in Great Britain
by Severn Print Ltd.

Contents

	Acknowledgements	6
	Introduction	7
1.	The Cotswolds 1980	9
2.	Eastwood 1981	16
3.	The Malvern Hills 1984	22
4.	Perthy 1987	27
5.	York 1990	33
6.	Derbyshire Dales 1991	40
7.	Derbyshire Dales and Chatsworth 1992	48
8.	Torbay 1993	58
9.	Torbay 1994	71
10.	Torbay 1995	83
11.	York 1996	94
12.	South Woodchester 1997	101
13.	Torbay 1997	109
14.	Torbay 1998	117
15.	Isle of Wight 1999	126
16.	Twynings, Tewkesbury 2000	134
17.	Day Trips (from home) 2001	143
18.	Cromer 2002	150
19.	Ironbridge 2003	156
20.	Anglesey and Dublin 2004	165
21.	Highley, Severn Valley 2005	175
22.	Dolgellau 2007	189
23.	Highley, Severn Valley 2008	197
24.	Highley, Severn Valley 2009	214
25.	Torbay 2010	236
26.	Highley, Severn Valley 2011	258
27.	Highley, Severn Valley 2012	269

Acknowledgements

We realise that we could not possibly have had our 'Adventures' without the co-operation and support of our families and friends, so we would like to thank the following people who made our adventures (and this book) possible.

Irene's husband Buz, who not only transported us to our various destinations, but also minded his own and June's children in the early days whilst we were away.

Rachel, Becky and Mark, Irene's children. Rachel also helped with transport in later years.

John and Sue, June's children. John also accommodated us and gave us lifts.

Doug, Mabel's husband and her children, David who took us to Gloucester and back, and:

Marion who came on our second 'adventure'.

Judy and Clive whose floor we slept on, on our first adventure.

Lannah Coke for welcoming us into her home.

Peggy and Stan for loaning us their cottage.

Sylvia and Ian, who let us stay at Cintra.

Pauline, who stepped in at the last minute and joined us when Mabel couldn't come.

Fred, June's partner who shared the transporting with Buz from 2001.

Brenda and Ray, for letting us use their cabin in Highley.

Pauline and Rob, who loaned us their cottage in Dolgellau.

All the lovely people who accommodated us and added to the fun of our 'adventures' (you know who you are!)

And last but by no means least Betty, who patiently proof-read this epistle and corrected the numerous mistakes!

Introduction

This is the story of the annual adventures (with the exception of a few years) of three friends Irene, June and Mabel, who wanted to have a different kind of holiday together, where nothing was planned and anything could happen. This was in the days before satnavs and mobile phones were in general use. In 2007 they decided to jointly write down their memories so that in future years they could recall their happy times together.

June and Irene had been friends since they were thirteen, when they were in the same class at Erdington Grammar School (later renamed Kingsbury School) and ensured that they kept in close contact during the years after they were married and had children.

This they did by attending some form of 'night school' class once a week in the evenings, and it was at one of these classes, where they went to learn German, that they met Mabel who immediately impressed them, especially when she made mince pies for the whole class at Christmas.

Having sampled her baking, they were resolved to 'adopt' her and they asked her if she would like to go swimming with them. Since Mabel had long wanted to be able to swim but had been put off by an unfortunate incident in her childhood, she agreed to let Irene and June teach her.

Wearing armbands and a rubber ring she entrusted herself to the care of the other two, and before long became a capable swimmer. Mabel felt that this made a lot of difference to her life; she could now swim with her son and daughter on holiday. Eventually the three friends qualified as swimming instructors and went on to join a diving class.

For about thirty years they were volunteers with the Highball Trust, which provides weekend holiday breaks for children from the inner city areas of Birmingham. With a team of volunteers, they regularly took children to the Trust's centre 'Shepherd House' in Hanley Swan near Malvern. They did their utmost to ensure that the boys and girls had a fun packed and adventurous weekend which they would remember for many years to come. Although these weekends were very tiring they enjoyed these trips into the countryside, tramping up the Malvern Hills, cooking, cleaning, organising games, settling children's quarrels and helping to give the children a happy and memorable time.

They continued to do this and thought that it gave them a sense of adventure and of doing something quite different from the usual. In 1980 they decided that they too would like to have an adventure, nothing too daring, you understand, just something a little different from their usual family holidays and without the responsibility of looking after anyone else.

This cemented their friendships and for a further 20 years they did voluntary work together, with the Highball Trust and Home-Start (another charity which supports young children and their families) as well as going on their 'Adventures'.

1. The Cotswolds

15th to 17th August 1980

In the summer of 1980 Irene, June and Mabel decided that the timing was right for an adventure of their own since June's daughter Sue and Irene's youngest daughter Becky were at Sea Ranger Camp in Beaudesert and June's son John was at Scout Camp at Borrowdale in the Lake District. Irene's eldest daughter Rachel was staying at her grandparents in Devon and Buz (Irene's husband) was going to collect her, dropping their son Mark off at the same time. Mabel's children Marion and David were grown up and her husband Doug was quite happy to look after himself, so it was an ideal opportunity for them to take off for a few days. Marion thought that they were all mad and reminded Mabel that she was a bit older than the other two and gave her a packet of energy sweets!!

Enlisting the help of Buz, the friends asked him if he would drop them off somewhere between Birmingham and Paignton on the way to take Mark to visit his grandparents. He agreed to do this, but wanted to call at his younger sister Judy's house in Cheltenham to pay her a visit. Since Judy was happy to accommodate all of them, they thought it would make an interesting beginning to their adventure, so packed their rucksacks in readiness.

Friday
Mabel was working full-time, so when she arrived home late afternoon, Buz collected her and June and with Irene and ten year old Mark they all set out for Cheltenham in his trusty Escort Estate, with the huge Buzby transfer on the bonnet (this was a bird used in British Telecom's advertising). When they arrived in Cheltenham, Buz's sister Judy and her husband Clive made them very welcome and after dinner they spent a pleasant evening chatting and catching up with family news. Eventually they unpacked their sleeping bags and spent the night on the living room floor.

Saturday

After a croissant breakfast they waved goodbye to Judy and Clive and set off travelling along the picturesque lanes through the Cotswolds. Buz asked them where they wanted to go, so when they happened upon Painswick they thought that it looked a very pretty village and decided to start 'the adventure proper' there.

They photographed Mark in the stocks outside the churchyard and Buz, who was a little concerned for their safety, then departed with him for Paignton. After they had waved the boys off they walked around the churchyard and counted the famous 99 yew trees which were originally planted as a deterrent to farmers to keep their cows out, since yew is deadly poisonous to cattle. No doubt the church wardens would have wanted to stop cattle from roaming amongst the graves, making a mess and causing damage. It has long been a mystery as to why only 99 trees ever survive in the churchyard, no matter how many are planted.

They looked around for a shop to buy a map of the area and some padding for Irene and Mabel's straps on their rucksacks as they were cutting into their shoulders. Unfortunately the only shop that was open didn't sell maps, but the lady assistant gave them some polystyrene packing to wrap around the straps making them more comfortable and they bought some safety pins from her to secure it. Having done this they felt in need of sustenance and found a cafe serving tea and scones with cream and jam, which satisfied their inner woman. Since they had failed to buy an Ordnance Survey map earlier, they looked for the post office where they were assured that they could obtain one, but unfortunately due to the scone eating, they were late getting to the post office and as it was a Saturday it had closed at mid-day.

They pondered their dilemma, they had only a small section of a road map which Mabel had cut out and brought with her in case of emergencies, but since they had no other map they resigned themselves to managing with this. Scouring the cards in the window of the post office they espied an advert for bed and breakfast at the romantic sounding Lovers Hall at Pitchcombe, which according to Mabel's scrap of map was just about within walking distance.

Before embarking upon this epic journey they thought it expedient to partake of lunch at The Falcon Inn, where Mabel had it in mind to have a (dry) beef sandwich and orange juice. However, June and Irene had spotted a buffet with a varied selection of delicious hot cooked dishes which they couldn't resist. Watching them pile their plates high, Mabel put her beef

1. THE COTSWOLDS 1980

1980 *Mark in the stocks at Painswick*

1980 *The Cotswolds. Lovers Hall, Pitchcombe*

sandwich back and joined in the feast, all finishing off with apple pie and cream, washed down with lager and lime. For years after June and Irene pulled Mabel's leg about the 'dry beef sandwich'.

After a suitable interval they hoisted their rucksacks onto their backs and trudged slowly up a steep hill towards Painswick Beacon to see if they could get bed and breakfast at Lovers Hall. They headed off towards Pitchcombe and after a while found a footpath which seemed to go in the right direction and after several hours hiking in the heat of the day they eventually came across a farmhouse, where the farmer's wife kindly gave them directions taking them across the fields, until they came to a wooden bridge.

To their surprise, when they crossed the bridge they found themselves in the back garden of a house where two ladies were tending their flower borders. They did not seem at all put out at the sudden appearance in their garden (it must have been a right of way) but of course they wished them 'good afternoon' and apologised for the intrusion into their idyllic haven. They were very pleasant and after chatting to them for a while they gladly gave them further directions to the main road leading to Pitchcombe.

When they eventually got there they had a rest in a bus shelter (hoping that a bus would come along – but it didn't). They were getting very thirsty by this time as it was a very hot day. Continuing on their way, there was nothing but fields on either side for what seemed like miles (if they had seen a house they would have been desperate enough to have knocked on the door and ask for a glass of water).

Eventually, very relieved, they arrived at an inn, however their hopes of liquid refreshment were dashed when they discovered that a wedding reception was in progress and the inn was closed to the general public. Stoically they trudged uphill until they arrived at a dead end and spotting a man by his garden gate they asked him how they could get to Lovers Hall. He generously allowed them to use a short cut, much to the chagrin of his wife who muttered profusely as they walked through their garden and into the grounds of Lovers Hall.

What a lovely surprise when they emerged to find a picturesque Georgian farmhouse, with swimming pool and tennis courts, where they met a young lady named Jocelyn who introduced herself as the daughter of the Hall's proprietors, who it transpired were away on holiday.

They asked Jocelyn if they could stop that night and she said that would be alright if they didn't mind her cooking breakfast, as she wasn't very experienced (she was about 18 years old). Since they were hot and thirsty, she very kindly made them a cup of tea and let them cool off in the outdoor swimming pool. This kind gesture was greatly appreciated as they were getting pretty desperate by this stage, this was after all their first 'Adventure' and they hadn't yet learned to carry drinks with them!

After a lovely dip in the pool, they rested in the garden before having a wash and changing their clothes, then leaving their rucksacks behind they retraced their steps to the inn which they had passed earlier. This was now happily (for them) open to the public and they enjoyed a delicious dinner in the restaurant and long refreshing drinks of lager and lime. Some hours later they wended their way back to Lovers Hall by torchlight where, replete and contented, they fell into their beds exhausted but happy.

Sunday

They awoke refreshed to an overcast morning, and after a beautifully cooked bacon and egg breakfast, they paid their dues and thanking Jocelyn for her hospitality they donned their cagoules, hoisted their rucksacks, and set off once more to see what day two of their adventure held in store.

As they headed off along the main road towards Stroud, the clouds lifted and the sun began to shine upon them again. They waited at a bus stop for a while but no bus appeared, so pressing on towards Stroud they happened upon a leisure centre with a café and as it was time for elevenses, they partook of tea and cakes. Realising that there was a swimming pool they went for a swim, where June and Irene did handstands and raced on their hands underwater, with Mabel looking on and laughing at their antics. June and Mabel then had a session on the sunbeds, while Irene found a quiet spot for a ciggy.

Another mile further along the road they came to Stroud railway station and since it was lunchtime and there was a restaurant in the station hotel, they sat outside looking up towards a hill which Mabel recalled climbing with some friends a few years previously. After a fish lunch, they decided to tackle Rodborough hill, so with rucksacks at the ready they rolled up their trouser legs revealing, to Irene's and June's (mock) horror, Mabel's white socks which became a source of amusement to them all for many years afterwards.

It was very hard work climbing the hill, so half way up they had a lie down (after finding a convenient bush) and surveyed the town of Stroud laid out before them. Pressing on to the summit and exhausted from their efforts they flopped down at the side of a wall and fished out of their rucksacks a small bottle of (medicinal) brandy and a packet of jaffa cakes. After consuming these they lay down on the grass and sunbathed, admiring the view overlooking

THREE HAPPY WANDERERS

Rodborough Common, before meandering back down the hill to the railway station.

They were due to return to Judy's house to meet up with Buz and get a lift back home, so it was fortunate for them that Stroud had a station, since they had not worked out how they were going to get back to Cheltenham. They didn't have long to wait for the train and were soon seated and chatting about the day's events.

At Cheltenham railway station they found a phone box and telephoned Judy and she said that her husband Clive would come and fetch them. He arrived in a red two seater Spitfire sports car and somehow they all crammed in, with June and Irene on the front passenger seat and Mabel squashed into the luggage rack with the rucksacks. In truth Irene was not on the seat but was on the floor between June's legs, where she was delegated to look out for passing police officers. They laughed so much they were in danger of wetting themselves!

They all made a mad dash for the bathroom when they arrived at Judy's house where they sat and drank tea and chatted to Judy while she made a steak and kidney pie for dinner. Later on Buz, who had collected Rachel from her grandparents, joined them. After a delicious dinner with Judy and Clive, Buz and Mabel (who had to be at work the next day) set off home with Rachel, leaving June and Irene behind to continue the adventure.

Irene and June shook out the sleeping bags and spent another night on the dining room floor, bemoaning the fact that Mabel had had to return to work, since they were having so much fun together.

Monday

After breakfast Irene and June squashed into Judy's Spitfire (this time June was in the luggage rack and Irene in comfort in the passenger seat) and like the previous day there was much hilarity. Judy took them to see some of Cheltenham's finest buildings, including the Ladies College, then on to Gloucester where they went to a leisure centre. They played table tennis and badminton, followed by a swim, with Judy sporting a leopard skin bikini and looking quite stunning.

After lunch in the leisure centre Judy took them to the railway station in Gloucester and waved them off as their train headed back to Birmingham. Discussing the holiday on the train June and Irene agreed that the adventure had been great fun and that they had all got to know one another much better. They decided to ask Mabel if she would like to make it an annual event, and later when they asked her she agreed and said that she had greatly enjoyed it too.

When they arrived at New Street Station Buz was waiting and drove them home, reuniting them with their children who had been on their own adventures.

2. Eastwood

29th to 31st August 1981

June heard a programme on the radio about the D.H. Lawrence Society and had made a note of the telephone number of its secretary who, apparently, was prepared to take people on tours of the 'Lawrence Experience'. When she told Irene and Mabel about this, they thought that it sounded like a good idea for their second adventure. When Mabel's daughter Marion, who was a fan of D.H. Lawrence, heard that they planned to go to Eastwood to find out more about his life and works, she asked if she could join them.

They decided in the interest of economy to go in June's faithful old 1962 model Morris Minor Traveller known as 'Mulligatawny Rose' due to the colour being similar to mulligatawny soup and the official name of the colour being 'taupe rose'. For the same reason they decided to camp and hoped to find a site when they arrived in Eastwood, optimistically packing a tent, sleeping bags and enough food to last for a few days.

Saturday
They set off from Irene's house accompanied by Mabel's daughter Marion in June's car, complete with rucksacks and camping gear.

On the way to Eastwood they detoured to Long Eaton to visit Irene's Uncle Bernard and his second wife Edna. Irene had spent many happy holidays in her childhood with her Uncle Bernard and his first wife Auntie Kathleen. Edna and Bernard made the ladies very welcome, considering that they had just called in on spec, and gave them tea and cakes. Afterwards Bernard took them on a tour of the house, showing them some of the furniture he had made and they stopped to admire his paintings.

After thanking them for their hospitality they waved 'goodbye' and continued on their way to visit the birthplace of D.H. Lawrence (born 11th September 1885) at 8a Victoria Street, Eastwood. This was a small Victorian

2. EASTWOOD 1981

shop where his father Arthur was a haberdasher, small wear and lace dealer, who sold the childrens clothes and lace which his wife made.

When they went inside they found that the living room had an iron fireplace with hobs either side and a high black leaded mantelpiece. This would have been the main room of the house, which was quite small and poky. The house had been home to two adults and five children, David Herbert Richards Lawrence, known as Bert, being the fourth. He was a sickly child who was considered to be the hardest to rear, but who went on to gain one of the first county scholarships. This little shop is now a museum and the headquarters of the D.H. Lawrence Society.

They left the first house to visit the second home of the Lawrence family at 28 Garden Road (formerly number 57 The Breach, where in 1888 his dad had returned to work at Brinsley Pit colliery). This was also a museum and they spent more time poring over photographs and details of D.H. Lawrence's life and works. It was administered by the Association for Young Writers; the ground floor was a public museum, the upper floor provided accommodation for visiting students. There was a large mangle and outhouse in the tiny yard, reminding them of the hardships of Victorian life for the lower classes. These locations were the inspiration and settings for his books 'Sons and Lovers', 'Women in Love' and 'The Lost Girl.'

Across the street from his birthplace was the Peacock café which was featured in one of his books (along with many of the local people who were not at all pleased at some of his characterisations). It being lunch time they took themselves off to the café and sampled its wares and once fortified, set off for the third family home at number 8 Walker Street. They could only view this from the outside as it was in use as a family home at the time.

Somehow they got chatting to the lady attendant of the public toilets in the village square, and after a guided tour of the gents (lovely multi-coloured tiles!) and lots of information about the local area, she suggested that they might be able to camp on the 'rec', this being the local park.

They spotted a phone box (old red variety) and June phoned the secretary of the D.H. Lawrence Society only to find that the lady was away at the Edinburgh Festival, but her husband gave June the number of his wife's sister, Lannah Coke, who was the President of the Society and who also conducted tours.

After a quick call they made their way to Lannah's house where she made them welcome, and even invited them to stay at her house after they had explained that they needed to find somewhere to camp for a couple of nights.

1981 *DH Lawrence's childhood home at Eastwood*

1981 *Lannah Coke with Irene, June and Marion*

2. EASTWOOD 1981

They gladly accepted her kind offer and since it was getting close to tea time asked if they might bring in the food from the car, which they had previously cooked, thinking that they would be camping.

She allowed them to set the table in her grand dining room and they laid out the sumptuous feast, consisting of a whole chicken, salad, crusty bread, cheeses and wine. Lannah was quite amazed at the amount of food which kept coming in from the car and could hardly believe what they produced from what must have seemed like thin air. It was a veritable banquet! Lannah must have been wondering what had hit her, when her daughter telephoned. She was apparently quite anxious when her mother told her about four strangers descending upon her. Not surprising really!

After a very pleasant meal recounting stories and getting to know one another, they cleared away the remains of the feast and set about sorting out where they were to sleep. They all had sleeping bags with them and blow up beds, and since there was only one spare room containing a double bed, they all squashed in together, June and Marion in the bed with Irene and Mabel on the blow up beds on the floor.

Sunday

After breakfast (again produced from the car) Lannah's daughter phoned to ask her mother if she could mind her son for the morning. She probably also wanted to check up on these four strange women who her mother had invited to stay in her house. They busied themselves clearing up the breakfast dishes before her daughter arrived with her little boy. They were introduced and must have made a favourable impression since they were invited to stay another night. Leaving Lannah with her grandson, they took off in June's car to look at some other D.H. Lawrence locations which Lannah had told them about, arranging to come back later and take her out for Sunday lunch.

They drove to a small village and looked around the church, where there were plaques showing names which Lawrence had used in his books (apparently he upset many people with his derogatory remarks both about the people and the village).

They then set out for Hags Farm which featured in his book 'Sons and Lovers' as 'Willey Farm'. When they arrived at the farm June and Marion decided to climb over the gate to get a closer look at the farmhouse, whilst Irene and Mabel sat on the gate pretending no knowledge of the trespassers. They were however quite anxious when a policeman cycled past and wishing him a cheery 'good morning' endeavoured to look the picture of innocence!

The two trespassers returned and scrambled back over the gate having escaped the long arm of the law. Happily they all returned to Lannah's house where they piled into her car and went for lunch at the local pub.

Enjoying a pleasant meal and telling her about their adventure at the farm, Lannah then took them in her car on a tour of the area, pointing out places of interest which had been used by Lawrence in his books. They spent a fascinating afternoon soaking up the atmosphere of the area and Lannah's interesting stories, then returned to her house for supper, this being the remains of the previous day's 'feast'. Then after recounting the events of the day and clearing away the supper dishes they retired to their various beds.

Monday

Once breakfast was cleared away, their beds made and bedroom tidied, they realised that it must be difficult for Lannah to do housework as she suffered quite badly with arthritis so, since she had been so kind and hospitable, they offered to clean her house for her. She gratefully accepted so, armed with mops, buckets, dusters and a vacuum cleaner, they all set to work and it didn't take the four of them long to give the place a good old spring clean.

At this point Marion's boyfriend Andy arrived in his car and after a cup of tea and introductions they went in convoy to the mountain cottage at Wirksworth in Derbyshire where Lawrence once lived with his mistress Frieda, the wife of his tutor. Apparently she was a cousin of The Red Baron, Manfred von Richthofen.

The cottage was empty so they were only able to look at it from the outside, where Mabel took a cutting of a fuchsia and June took a small piece of rockery as mementos. Lannah drove them to various places of interest connected with Lawrence's life with Marion and Andy following. They stopped near an old railway line and had a picnic on a patch of waste ground, and then Marion thanked Lannah saying that she had really enjoyed being part of their 'adventure'. Andy and Marion set off back home and the others returned to Lannah's house. She gave them a copy of the book 'Lawrence in Love' a collection of letters from Lawrence to Louie Burrows edited by James T. Boulton.

After packing up their belongings they thanked Lannah for all the trouble that she had taken, showing them around the area, as well as accommodating them at such short notice and she expressed her appreciation for their help in the house and the enjoyment of their company. They bade her a fond farewell before piling their rucksacks into June's Moggy and starting out for home, with a much better understanding of D.H. Lawrence's childhood, life and the inspirations for his books.

    They also took with them many happy memories of their time spent with a very kind, interesting and knowledgeable lady, Lannah Coke.

3. The Malvern Hills

23rd to 25th June 1984

At this time they were taking inner city children for weekends to Shepherd House at Hanley Swan, an old Victorian building which started life as a boys' home and was purchased in the 1960s by the Highball Trust. They wanted to familiarise themselves with the Malvern Hills, as they took the children for walks on the hills and intended going for a weekend sometime without children.

The weekend prior to this Adventure, Mabel and June had taken a group of children to the house and had been invited by the people from St. Gabriel's church to take the children for a picnic on a local farm. Whilst at the farm, June spotted an old Morris Minor saloon abandoned in the farmyard and in conversation with the farmer about her 'Moggy' was invited to take any parts that she might want for her car, provided she removed them herself.

After consulting with Mabel, June arranged to collect the parts the following weekend. Unfortunately the farmer's family were all going to be away at a wedding, but he said that it was okay for them to help themselves. June phoned Irene to ask if she was okay to go that weekend and she was so, since they had not managed to fit in an 'adventure', due to work commitments the previous two years, they decided to make this their third. Mabel said that she would book the Monday off work to give them an extra day.

On returning to Birmingham they cleared it with Ron Arnold, the Trust's founder and chairman of the executive committee, for them to stop at the Highball House, after the group which was in there for the weekend had left.

Saturday
Collecting Mabel and Irene in her car (Mulligatawny Rose) June headed along the A38 to the Waseley Hills to visit friends of hers who used to work at Woodland Camp in Streetly, where she worked as a volunteer. Gordon

3. THE MALVERN HILLS 1984

1984 June and Irene on Chase End Hill, Malvern

1984 June and Irene with Moggy in farmyard

Redford was the country park warden there and with his wife Kate gave them a very warm welcome and a cup of tea. After a pleasant interlude they set off for Hanley Swan and headed to Shepherd House.

When they arrived, there were three leaders in the kitchen preparing food for the children who were out on the hills. After a look around the grounds and a go on the swings they went on a walk near a disused railway line which took them through a field of Friesian cows at the rear of the centre. They found a field nearby with no cows in it and settled down to eat the picnic which they had bought with them.

After lunch they returned to the Highball Centre and having thought that they would be rattling around in this large house they decided to get bed and breakfast accommodation nearer to the Malvern Hills. They informed the leaders in the house of their decision and wished them a safe journey home. Climbing into the car they set off in the direction of Upton to find the farm where there was an old 'Moggy' nestling amongst the weeds in the farmyard. With what tools they could muster from June's car they all set about trying to remove the front passenger seat from the blue saloon car. With a lot of heaving and puffing and WD40 they eventually extracted the seat and stowed it in the back of the traveller.

Since there was no-one in the farm they couldn't get to a tap to wash their hands so Mabel produced a flask of hot water, which was meant for making tea, and they washed their hands in the flask cup on the farmyard floor. This was before the days of wet wipes!

Once cleaned up they set off for Malvern to find some accommodation for the night and headed for the Tourist Information Centre. The assistant was very helpful and phoned to book them bed and breakfast in Ashford Cottage, which was situated near to The Malvern's North Hill.

They drove to the cottage and after introducing themselves to the lady who lived there, deposited their bags before driving back to the main road. They had earlier spotted a Chinese restaurant and decided to have their dinner there. After a pleasant meal they returned to Ashford Cottage and before retiring for the night, chatted to the landlady about her knitting. She showed them a rail of beautifully knitted colourful jumpers which she had made, some to order and some just for general sale, including some Aran sweaters. They looked through them and admired her handiwork thinking that they might place some orders with her, but unfortunately never got around to it, which they later regretted.

3. THE MALVERN HILLS 1984

Sunday

After a lovely breakfast (all the nicer because they hadn't had to prepare it and do the washing-up) they set off to climb parts of the Malvern Hills which they hadn't climbed before. Heading along the A449 towards British Camp they found a small car park by Berington's Quarry near St. Wulstan's church. They parked and climbed up to the disused quarry, which was carpeted with pink cranesbill, mullein and yellow hawkbit, surrounded by grass and silver birch trees. They rested in the quarry and caught their breath after the steep climb before heading towards Wynd's Point near British Camp. They stopped for their picnic lunch and then retraced their steps making their way past Shires Ditch and Berington's Quarry, heading towards Wyche Cutting.

To their delight they emerged into a clearing at Holy Well and were pleasantly surprised to meet a lady who owned the well and was only too pleased to chat to them about it. She told them the history of the well and how it had survived a fire which spread across the tree line immediately above it. Only by the vigilance and hard work of the owners, who ran backwards and forwards with buckets of water, was the well saved, as all of the surrounding trees and shrubs perished.

The lady and her husband were a Canadian couple who had purchased the well with the intention of restoring it to its former glory, as it was in the 18th century when it was the most important spring in the Malvern area. Many remarkable cures were claimed for its waters which at that time were famed for their purity.

In 1823 St. Ann's Well (another well further along the hills and closer to the town) became more popular after the visit of the Princess (later Queen) Victoria who patronised it. Holy Well went out of favour and was allowed to deteriorate. They also learned that Earl and Countess Spencer had been there, on a quest for information on wells for a book which they were compiling.

They were starting to get hungry and so they said farewell to the lady and thanked her for the very interesting chat. They then headed for a nearby pub (reputed to be the highest pub on the hills) where they had chicken in a basket and a very welcome glass of shandy. After dinner they walked back along Pinnacle Hill and collected the car. They needed to look for a Bed and Breakfast in that area so that they were handy to continue their walk the next day on the southern hills.

They came across a 15th century cottage at Holly Bush and to their relief, since it was getting quite late in the day, found that there were vacancies and were welcomed in with a cup of tea by a lovely Scottish couple. Whilst chatting to them and discussing where to go the next day they suggested that they might like to visit Eastnor Castle. They were all quite keen to do this since they had not been there before, and when the landlady offered to telephone the Castle and ask if they could have a private viewing the following day, they gratefully accepted. On that happy note they retired to bed!

Monday

The next morning after breakfast, they set off on their visit to the Castle where they were given a guided tour by Lady Somers herself, after she explained their presence to her husband who was looking out through a bedroom window! They were very impressed with the Castle, especially the suits of armour which Lady Somers said she polished herself. They learned that the Castle had been used on several occasions for filming by television companies, and other events such as steam weekends were often held there. This, they thought, would be a great place to bring the older children on Highball weekends.

Whilst driving back in the direction of the cottage they decided that it was lunchtime, so after parking the car at the foot of the hill, looked for a suitable picnic spot where they ate their sandwiches. They amused themselves by blowing over the top of their empty water bottles to make a whistling sound which they discovered when they held the bottles at an angle and the wind blew across them.

They then climbed up Holly Bush Hill, which was quite hard walking as it was very overgrown and walked along to the trig point at Chase End Hill. Passing a village called Whiteleaved Oak they retraced their steps prior to climbing Midsummer Hill, near a very deep quarry. Each time they got to the top of a hill they paused to take in and appreciate the panoramic views which surrounded them, and try to get their bearings in relation to the Highball House.

After all of that walking and climbing they were feeling the need for some refreshment, so before setting off for home they called in at the hotel by Wynds Point (near British Camp) and had a welcome cup of tea. They chatted about the lovely and interesting places that they had been to during the past three days, and how they had thoroughly enjoyed themselves and each other's company. They resolved to make sure that they found time for another 'adventure' during the following year and at 6.30pm they set out to drive back home tired but happy!

4. Perthy

29th to 31st August 1987

Despite their resolve in 1984 to keep up their annual 'adventures' three years had elapsed before they got around to arranging another one. At this time some friends of June's (Peggy and Stan) offered her the use of their cottage in a quiet part of Shropshire in a village called Lower Perthy. She ran the idea past Irene and Mabel and they said that a quiet weekend in the country sounded very appealing, so they decided to go when the cottage was available. June asked Peggy and Stan if she could take them up on their kind offer and they arranged to go for a long weekend over the August Bank Holiday.

Saturday
They set off in June's old Morris Traveller 'Mulligatawny Rose' along the A5 heading towards Shropshire. Mabel was navigating since they had never been there before and after turning right in Whittington at the church and opposite the castle, they had to keep their eyes open for a left turn to Lower Perthy, just past the petrol station and shop. Having found the road and turned left, they looked out for a row of white houses where they turned right and went down the hill looking out for Bell Cottage on the left. Peggy and Stan's cottage was through a gate at the side of Bell Cottage and along a track to the rear. Without explicit instructions they would never have known it was there, it was really tucked away and wasn't visible from the road.

When they arrived they were delighted to see a mature garden enclosed by a high hedge on two sides and an open view across the fields with the Welsh Mountains on the horizon on the other side. They also spotted a delightful little Bluebird caravan, which they later explored. After retrieving the door key from its hidden place they let themselves into the cottage, stepping over a pile of leaves which had blown in under the gap in the door. They found themselves in what would at one time have been the scullery, which now served as the kitchen, and unloaded and unpacked the food before exploring the rest of the cottage. A dining room with an open fireplace led off the kitchen, which in turn took them up three steps into the sitting room, passing the door to a bathroom. This room also had a fireplace and a staircase leading to the bedrooms, plus a door opening out to the rear of the cottage.

Making their way upstairs and turning right into a corridor the first bedroom, which had two single beds, was on the left and the second bedroom was up two more steps on the right hand side, both had superb views of the surrounding countryside. Mabel and Irene took the room with single beds and let June sprawl out in the large double bed. Sleeping arrangements having been established, they set about sweeping up the leaves from the kitchen floor before making a pot of tea and preparing lunch. They drank their tea from delicate china cups seated at a small table in the dining room, looking out of the window and admiring the view.

As soon as lunch was finished and cleared away, they equipped themselves for a long walk and set off along the A495, this being the main road to Ellesmere. After walking about 3 to 4 miles they arrived at the town centre which they investigated before making their way past The Blessed Virgin Mary church and down the hill to the Mere. This is a huge lake with more water fowl on than they had ever seen and they were amazed at the variety of species of ducks, previously unknown to them. They walked along the edge of the Mere and came to a restaurant which was overlooking the lake, where they thought they might eat the following day.

Returning to the town centre they went to the White Hart public house, where they sat outside and enjoyed a drink. June went off to try to find a church with a Sunday morning service, leaving the other two sitting on a bench chatting and admiring the heart shaped formation of white cobble stones on the path by the pub's doorway.

June returned and reported that she had been unsuccessful in her quest, by which time it was getting dusk. June had spotted a taxi shop near the pub, and suggested to the others that they take the easy way back to the cottage, as they had not yet had their evening meal which they still had to prepare. The other two readily agreed to this suggestion since they didn't fancy the prospect of walking back along the main road in the dark.

They enjoyed the taxi ride back to the cottage, taking the opportunity to have a rest before they all set to making a cottage pie, peeling vegetables, setting the table and lighting fires in the dining and sitting rooms. After consuming the meal and washing up, they retired to the sitting room with a

4. PERTHY 1987

1987 *Irene and Mabel reading a map, Ellesmere*

1987 *June by the cottage in Perthy*

bottle of Malibu and a box of After Eights. Mabel had brought her daughter's board game Trivial Pursuit with her, so they settled down on the rug in front of the fire and played by firelight before making their way up the stairs to their beds.

Sunday

After an early breakfast they set off to Ellesmere once again, but this time in June's car and they found both the Methodist and United Reformed churches. The UR church had a service at a time which suited them, so Mabel and June went in whilst Irene opted to wander around the village. When the service was finished June and Mabel stopped and chatted over a cup of tea to some members of the congregation, who were very friendly and invited them back to their house for Sunday lunch. Unfortunately as Irene had not yet returned from her walk they had to decline and said their farewells before going to look for her, leaving the car in the church car park.

Eventually Irene appeared and they all strolled off in the direction of the Mere, which was formed when the ice receded at the end of the Ice Age. They admired the waterfowl through the large picture windows of the restaurant as they ate. After lunch they went to the RSPB Visitors Centre and into the viewing area with large glass windows overlooking the Mere, where they looked through a telescope and observed swans, ducks, geese, moorhens, coots and also herons which were nesting in the trees on the island in the middle of the Mere.

A warden offered to take a group of them outside to talk about the Mere and its avian inhabitants and they were fascinated by his stories of how the island came about. During the last century the Lord of the Manor wanted to make a garden for the Manor House and he ordered his servants to dig up the soil around the House and take it and dump it on the Mere which was frozen over. When the ice melted the soil still projected above the water and the island had its beginnings which have been added to over the decades, now forming the bird sanctuary covered in a variety of trees and bushes which can be seen today.

The Warden told them that there were black swans on the opposite side of the Mere and they looked for them later on, but didn't spot any. He also explained that there were two types of Willow Herb, the Rosebay and the Great and showed them the more unusual one, the great willow herb which is the hairy variety that grows around the edges of the Mere.

Taking their leave of the group, they espied the ice cream kiosk and after buying three cornets and consulting the map, they set off towards Cole Mere.

4. PERTHY 1987

On the way they came across another little lake called Blake Mere along the side of which runs the Shropshire Union Canal leading to Cole Mere. It was a lovely sunny day and so setting off along the canal they had a very enjoyable walk passing narrow boats, waving to the boaters and at one point battling their way through nettles. Eventually they reached Cole Mere where the canal continues around part of the Mere, then they found the path which went around the east and south of the lake. They followed it until they saw some houses on the edge of the village of Cole Mere. After a short rest they carried on along the path passing the Country Park and finding that they were back at the canal again.

They retraced their steps back along the canal and the main road into Ellesmere and arriving back at the Mere, they went through the gates leading into a park. The park was on the edge of the lake and they looked out for the crack willow trees which the warden had told them about earlier. There were lots of lovely big trees and grassy banks where they sat awhile on June's big square scarf, which had a variety of uses such as a tablecloth, hand towel and for carrying fire wood, before they came to a play area for children. When they got as far as the small jetty where there were rowing boats for hire, they turned around and headed back to the town, having not seen any black swans.

Arriving back at the church, they retrieved June's car and drove back to the cottage where they prepared and ate a light meal. Sitting around the fire they played cards and drank Malibu, discussing the day's events and agreeing that they had discovered yet another lovely part of Britain. Before retiring to their respective beds tired and happy, they decided not to rush out in the morning, but stop in and appreciate the garden for a while, if the weather was fine that is.

Monday

This was also a sunny day so after a full English breakfast, they lounged around in the garden for a while in deck chairs, taking photographs and talking to the dog next door. Eventually they set off for a walk up the lane, and across the fields which brought them out at the rear of a church and onto the main road near a garage and small shop.

Walking along the Ellesmere road towards Whittington they found the canal at Welsh Frankton and a shop which sold supplies to the boaters. It also had a wide selection of buckets, mugs, cups, spoons, and other paraphernalia painted with the traditional canal artwork. Near the shop was a pub called The Narrow Boat Inn where they went next for a drink and lunch before heading back up the hill to the cottage. After tidying up and removing their bedding and belongings, they packed the car and had a cup of tea before returning the door key to its hiding place and setting off for home.

Having enjoyed staying in this lovely little cottage in its idyllic and peaceful setting, they hoped that they would be able to return and explore the area further on another adventure.

5. York

22nd to 25th June 1990

Somehow another two years had slipped by without an 'adventure' so the ladies got together, determined to have one this year. They were looking for affordable accommodation and considering youth hostels, Irene was already a member of the YHA and had previously stayed at the York hostel which was situated by the river. She suggested that they go there as there were so many interesting places to visit in York and the hostel, which was the original home of the Rowntree family, was within walking distance of the city centre. They liked the sound of this, so Irene obtained YHA forms for June and Mabel and once enrolled she booked places for them.

Friday
At 2pm Buz very kindly ran them to New Street Station and, after purchasing their tickets, they boarded the train for York. Mabel and Irene had to help June with her luggage, because she had been given an injection for tennis elbow in her right arm and the needle had hit a nerve, so she was in a lot of pain.

The hostel was quite a long way from the railway station so they took a taxi and arrived at about 6pm.

They were shown to a large dormitory and chose beds near to the window, Mabel had a top bunk and June and Irene chose bottom bunks (they were terrified of falling out!). After making their beds and staking their claims by putting their bags on them, they set out to look for somewhere to eat.

They walked along the riverside path into York city centre, crossing over the Lyndal Bridge and continuing on came to another bridge where, when looking over the parapet, they spotted several restaurants along the side of the river Ouse. Descending the steps at the side of the bridge they strolled along looking at the various eateries and decided to eat at the Lowther Hotel, as they liked the look of the menu. They all tucked into spare ribs followed by Mississippi mud pie with a nice bottle of wine, it was so delicious that they said that they would go again another day.

Making their way from the hotel up to the bridge they walked towards the Minster, familiarising themselves with the city centre and its layout as they were planning to walk around the alleyways the following day. The Minster had scaffolding around it and clearly there was work in progress on the stonework (this seems to be an on-going situation). Retracing their steps back towards the river, they picked up the riverside path and strolled contentedly back to the hostel listening to owls hooting and watching bats flitting to and fro.

At the hostel they made themselves hot drinks and retired to their bunks where they slept soundly.

Saturday

After washing in the wash hand basins in the room, they went down to the kitchen and cooked bacon and eggs which they ate in the refectory before returning to the dormitory to search for Irene's spectacles which she had mislaid. Hunting high and low, and rifling through Irene's bunk to no avail, they were confronted by a very irate young woman, who suddenly appeared from a bed around the corner. She was clearly annoyed and pointed out to Irene where her specs were (they had fallen off the washbasin and were lodged on a pipe underneath) and then rather rudely berated them for making a noise. She said that they had woken her up, which surprised them since it was quite late and all the other hostellers had breakfasted and departed for the day. Duly admonished they collected their rucksacks and beat a hasty retreat making their way along the riverside into York. It was a pleasant day, sometimes sunny and sometimes overcast, but at least it didn't rain, although they had their cagoules handy just in case!

The plan for the day was to follow the snickelways walk from a guidebook which Irene had borrowed from her friend Joan who owned a flat in York. Before setting off to find the snickelways they couldn't resist having a quick look around York Minster where they admired the Rose Window, which had recently been restored and which had been featured on the children's television programme 'Blue Peter', the RAF memorial and the many interesting and decorative tombs and artefacts.

Following the instructions in the guidebook 'A Walk around the Snickelways of York' by Mark W Jones, they started off at Bootham Bar, an

5. YORK 1990

archway known as the 'Hole in the Wall'. This contained the guard house and the 2000 year old entrance, being one of several, into the old city incorporated into the original city walls.

Passing through the archway they looked out for The Hole in the Wall pub, which had a covered passageway running along its side. Turning into the entrance they followed the alleyway and upon turning right they emerged into Precenter's Court where a marvellous view suddenly appeared of the west front of York Minster towering 200 feet above them. This is the only street which offers this awe inspiring view of the Minster's pinnacles shimmering in the sunlight causing them to catch their breath and stop for a while to admire it. Passing out of the court they entered Dean's Park, a small park and pleasant pathway which led to the Minster's yard, the library being all that is left of the 13th century Archbishop's palace.

They then went through a gate and into a yard, leading to a long passageway which brought them out at the Treasurer's House in Chapter House Street where they continued on to Ogleforth emerging at Goodramgate.

Spotting that there was a flower festival at Holy Trinity Church they made their way to the secluded churchyard (previously known as Tonge's Court) where they decided, as it was lunchtime, that they would sit outside and eat the sandwiches which they had prepared at the hostel that morning.

After lunch they went into this intriguing 13th century church with its quote 'higgledy-piggledy box-pews that face in all different directions and a floor which slopes this way and that'. The pews belonged to the wealthier families who would have shut themselves in partly to keep warm and also to separate themselves from the 'commoners'. There was a squint-hole – an angled opening through which the priest down in the chapel altar could keep an eye on the high altar – an early example of closed circuit viewing; this was called a 'Hagioscope'. They admired the magnificent floral arrangements and wandered around taking photos, appreciating the hard work which the Friends of Holy Trinity put in to maintain the church to such a high standard.

Before they emerged once again onto the busy thoroughfare of Goodramgate they stopped to look at York's, and maybe even Europe's, oldest surviving houses circa 1400 on Lady Row, the other side of the houses are now shops on Goodramgate. Making their way back towards the Minster they headed to College Street and entered into the large courtyard of St. Williams College, where there was an antique fair in progress and so they stopped for a look around and some tea and cakes. Wandering past the shops they stopped

THREE HAPPY WANDERERS

1990 *Mabel and June in a poppy field, York*

1990 *Row of gabled houses, York*

now and then to buy gifts for their families, June bought a wooden snake for her son John, which wriggled when its tail was held.

Upon entering King's Square, previously the site of the medieval Christ Church, demolished in 1937, and prior to that the site of a Roman fortress gateway, they spotted some jugglers. Stopping to watch them for a while they also noticed a circle of pennies on the ground, which they were pleased to be able to add to, this was a fund raising event aiming at getting a mile of pennies to be donated to the charity Christian Aid.

At this point they decided to look for the Fosse Bridge on the river at Fosse Bridge Reach, and having lost their bearings they asked a man for directions. Much to their amusement they realised that they had asked a tourist (they thought that maybe he had a German accent) and surprisingly he knew exactly where they needed to go and gave them very helpful directions. Following his instructions they eventually arrived at the river where they could see the bridge but not access it from that point. In the opposite direction upstream they saw the Navigation Warehouse, formerly a flour mill and afterwards used as a storehouse by Rowntree Mackintosh.

Making their way back towards the city centre they passed Clifford's Tower, the first part of York Castle which was built by William the Conqueror, in order to suppress the locals. The Tower was used by the townsfolk to imprison 150 wealthy Jewish businessmen and force them to commit suicide in order to save the lives of their families. This information is recorded on a plaque at the base of the Tower and when they read this it made them feel very sad.

They then headed back again, along the riverside path, to the hostel where they prepared delicious soup with fresh crusty rolls, followed by cream cakes, which they ate in the refectory. After which they cleared away and washed the dishes, then sat in the communal room and played cards before retiring for the night.

Sunday

Again they cooked breakfast in the kitchen and ate it in the refectory room. After clearing away they started out for a walk along the riverbank, in the opposite direction to York centre. It was a beautiful sunny morning and Irene was brave enough to put shorts on and June was wearing a skirt (almost unheard of) but they carried their small rucksacks with cagoules in, as rain was forecast. They strolled along the pathway at the side of the river admiring the abundance of wildflowers and at one point they just had to stop and sit amongst the mass of red poppies interspersed with white daisies. Watching the river slowly drifting along through the haze of bright red poppies they took photos and just enjoyed being in the rural English countryside.

Eventually it began to rain, so they donned their cagoules and went back towards the centre of York along a long lane whose verges were strewn with poppies and daisies as far as the eye could see, heading for sanctuary in the Minster. They went for lunch in the Treasurers House, but only had a snack as they were planning to return to The Lowther Hotel for dinner later on. Irene and June took the opportunity to change into trousers and trainers which they had in their rucksacks.

After lunch they watched people juggling and flame throwing in St. Sampson's Square, visiting the famous Victorian below-ground toilets before making their way across Church Street and into Silver Street. Advancing upon The Little Shambles they prepared themselves to weave in and out of the four snickleways of The Great Shambles, zigzagging backwards and forwards into the market square and ending up in a tiny street called Whip-ma-whop-ma-gate. Irene recalls that it had started to rain quite heavily and she had to put the guide book in her rucksack to prevent it from getting any wetter; in the event she purchased a new one for Joan as she felt guilty about the sorry state of it by the end of the day.

In 1586 the wife of one of the butchers in The Shambles (this means the street of the butchers) who lived at number 10, was found guilty of hiding a Jesuit priest and was executed by being crushed to death under a door heaped with stones. Today there are a great variety of shops in The Shambles with their pretty bow-shaped leaded windows, not just butchers, and it is known worldwide as a famous tourist attraction.

They went back to the Minster where they sat and enjoyed the choir singing the choral Evensong which was spiritually uplifting and always a delight to hear. Soaking up the atmosphere of this magnificent cathedral with its unique medieval stained glass windows and ornate ceilings was a lovely way to round off the afternoon. Making their way along the riverside, they returned to the hostel where they washed and changed before setting out again for the Lowther Hotel, where they dined and relaxed in a convivial atmosphere.

Walking back through the lamp lit streets with the thought in their minds that they had just passed through what is reputed to be the most haunted place in York (they kept passing numerous signs advertising ghost walks, which created an eerie feeling) they were quite glad to get back to the hostel and snuggle down in their bunk beds.

Monday

After cooking and eating breakfast they packed their bags and called a taxi to take them to the railway station. Upon arrival at the station they deposited their bags (except for their small rucksacks, containing their cagoules) in the left luggage lockers, to free themselves up to stroll around unhampered.

They hadn't finished walking around all of the Snickelways so they walked back into the city centre and commenced the walk from Lady Peckitts Yard, a lovely old alleyway from medieval times where, ascending the steps, they passed a cordwainers (shoemakers) which is one of the Conservation Trust's restored properties. Exiting the alleyway they found that they were in Pavement (probably the first street to be paved in York in 1329) and immediately on the right hand side was Clarke's shoe shop, previously the original Rowntree's grocers shop, which backs onto the old cordwainers.

Making their way down Parliament Street they emerged into St. Sampson's Square which they crossed to enter The Roman Bath public house to have lunch. They sat near a window in the floor which revealed the original Roman bath (one hot room and one cold room) which was excavated in 1930/31 and preserved behind the glass for future generations to admire and study.

After lunch they walked back to the massive, majestic, ornate Victorian railway station and after retrieving their luggage, they caught the train back to Birmingham where Buz was patiently waiting at New Street Station to take them home.

They'd had such an interesting few days and realised that they had only covered a fraction of the attractions that York has to offer, so agreed that they would like to return and complete the Snickelways (snicket, ginnel and alleyway) walk another time. They also resolved (again) to make this an annual event, which they managed to do for the following 16 years.

6. Derbyshire Dales

28th August to 1st September 1991

Having joined the YHA the previous year they looked in their handbook and decided to visit some of the hostels in the Derbyshire Dales. Irene booked them in advance and looking at the distances between the hostels they decided to go in June's car rather than try to hike with their rucksacks.

Wednesday

June collected Mabel and Irene at 6pm from Irene's house in her 'Moggy' and they set off for Sheffield where they were going to stop the first night at June's son John's shared student house. They arrived at 8pm and spent a pleasant evening chatting with John and his (then) girlfriend Cath, before making up their beds on the floor with their sleeping bags.

Thursday

After breakfast at John's they prepared sandwiches for lunch before setting out in June's car for their first port of call, Castleton Youth Hostel. When they arrived at Castleton they parked the car and set off, in their shorts, with their rucksacks and walking sticks to walk over Mam Tor (The Shivering Mountain), passing the entrance to the Blue John Mine on the way.

It was a very hot day and they needed to keep stopping for a swig out of their water bottles and a rest because it was quite a steep climb. At the top of the Tor they sat down to watch the hang gliders swishing across the hill when Irene suddenly ducked down thinking that she was about to be landed upon! They ate their picnic whilst being royally entertained by these youthful athletes.

Down below them in the distance they could pick out the cluster of buildings that was Castleton so they decided to follow their noses, hoping to find another route which would take them back to the hostel. The scenery

6. DERBYSHIRE DALES 1991

was glorious, a panorama of patchwork fields, hedges, sheep and wildflowers, so they stopped from time to time to admire the spectacular scene laid out before them. Despite Mabel's doubts that they would ever be able to get to Castleton 'as the crow flies', they managed to bumble their way over and around the undulating terrain and arrived back tired but triumphant at the hostel, where they soaked their hot and weary bodies in much welcomed baths.

After they had spruced themselves up they set out for the local pub for dinner and there met up with John and Cath who were joining them for drinks. A convivial evening was had by all before Cath and John returned to Sheffield and they fell gratefully into their beds.

Friday

Awaking refreshed they prepared and ate breakfast in the communal kitchen before clearing away, packing their bags, putting them into June's car and setting off for a walk to Peveril Castle. Mabel and Irene had got chatting to a young lady from Canada in the dormitories, and she gave them both Canadian hat badges, which they proudly sported on their sunhats.

Fortifying themselves with bottles of water purchased from the little village shop, they noticed a sign advertising Peveril Castle. It was rather expensive to go into the castle so they decided to take a detour, having spotted a pathway which led around it into Cave Dale.

The Dale had steep grassy sides, the right side rising up to the heights where Peveril Castle stands, and at the lowest point in the centre of the dale there meandered a narrow trickling stream. After a bit of sharp climbing Irene chose to find a comfortable spot to have a rest and read her book (her daily dose of Mills & Boon) whilst June and Mabel followed the stream where they were surprised to see a dead sheep which almost certainly had fallen in and perished.

They scrambled up the precipitous slope until they reached the highest point, where looking back they could just about make out Irene as a tiny remote spot on the hillside.

The two friends sat and absorbed the magnificence of the panoramic scene below them, the sweeping hillside, the peaks and valleys, all shimmering in the morning sunlight. Nature being what it is eventually June was obliged to scramble over the top of the hill to find a 'convenient bush' before they set off back the way they had come, whilst Mabel took a photo of her disappearing rear end.

With a feeling of accomplishment, they retraced their steps to Castleton scooping up Irene along the way. Reunited they all made their way back to the youth hostel and set off in the car to find Ravenstor youth hostel, which they eventually reached via a track through woodland. Parking the car on the edge of the woods they took their bags into the hostel and deposited them with the warden.

It was another beautiful sunny (shorts wearing) day so, donning their small rucksacks containing sandwiches, drinks, emergency supplies and other essentials they headed off for their next walk, along the Monsal Trail. This trail was on the site of a disused railway line which has been developed as a cycling and rambling path and is very easy walking since it is flat and contains no stiles! When they consulted the map they discovered that they could access the trail from the grounds of Ravenstor hostel by crossing a small wooden foot bridge over the River Wye. This they did and having reached the trail they turned right, passing two viaducts along the way, eventually arriving at the now disused Millers Dale Station.

The station was set out with picnic tables so they took the opportunity to take a well earned rest, quench their thirsts (it was a very hot day) and eat their packed lunches. The chocolate covered Kit Kat in June's rucksack had melted, so sitting in the sunshine she happily consumed it by licking it from its wrapper – not a pretty sight! It was a good job that there were not many people about.

From this point their walk took them across the former railway track and up through woods where, after a while, they came out onto a main road and travelling a short distance along the road they turned left over a bridge above the river. They were confronted by a flight of very steep steps wending its way through dense undergrowth upwards and onwards. This afforded them some welcome shade as they huffed and puffed their way to the top, stopping frequently to admire the view (and catch their breath).

Eventually they emerged at the top of the ridge and were delighted at the stunning view of the surrounding countryside, they sat down for a rest and to have a refreshing drink before making their way through fields of cows and over stiles until they reached a walled track where they passed several farm buildings including one marked 'New Barn' on their map, where the track curved to the right and later turned sharp right to Brushfield where they passed Top and Middle farms.

They turned left at Lower farm and continued on a path overlooking Taddington Dale and towards Monsal Head leading to the picturesque view

6. DERBYSHIRE DALES 1991

***1991** June and melted Kit Kat, Millers Dale Station*

***1991** Mam Tor, Derbyshire Dales*

of Monsal Viaduct which greeted them, pausing for a while to admire the scenery; they took photos before setting off once again. Their path took them downhill now towards the viaduct which they crossed and continued on until they came to a tunnel where they turned off to the right onto a path which traversed National Trust land and looked down to the river.

On the other side of the river stands Cressbrook Mill, a formidable looking building, which in the 19th century had been home and workplace to young boys brought from London into virtual slavery to work in the cotton mills for the wealthy mill owners. Not for the first time, they stopped to consider how much better life is for working class people today, and how their ancestors must have suffered at the hands of unscrupulous greedy people.

Crossing a bridge they kept to the path alongside the river Wye until they came to Litton Mill. This is situated on the side of the river to provide water for the spinning of wool and the manufacture of woollen products and for ease of transportation. The site was also chosen because of its remote location to cover up the exploitation of its workers and the unacceptable (even for those days) mortality rate. The bodies were buried in several different sites around the area to cover up the high number of deaths, especially in the young apprentices, who were often beaten and abused.

This area was richly covered with deep green foliage alongside the limestone bluff and they marvelled at the hanging creepers and abundance of rose bay willow herb and other wild flowers. Walking on they came to Bellamy's Bank, a grassy knoll covered in wildflowers which was named after the famous TV presenter and botanist David Bellamy who, it seems, first became interested in flora and fauna on that very bank as a small child. They stayed there for a while looking at the plants, most of which had dried heads, and trying to identify them (Irene had brought her wildflower book with her); they thought that it would be interesting to return to the bank in the springtime to see it in full bloom. After taking a few photographs they strolled along the path and through a gate leading to the grounds of Ravenstor Hostel.

Ravenstor is a substantial house originally built for a mill owner, from the entrance hall of which an impressive staircase leads up to a beautiful stained glass window, and turning to the right they faced a large portrait, this was probably of the original owner of the house. Passing the portrait there is another staircase leading up to the dormitories; making their way up the stairs having been reunited with their bags, they set about unpacking and settling into a large pine clad dormitory.

6. DERBYSHIRE DALES 1991

They then joined other hostellers in the dining room where they had a meal which was cooked by the warden and his wife, after dinner they helped with the washing up (every hosteller has to help in some way with the chores in the hostel). They were shown how to use the washing up machine which looked ancient, but which worked very efficiently. During dinner they sat by a window overlooking the lawns and flower beds and reflected upon what an absolutely fantastic day they had been privileged to experience. The weather had been beautifully sunny and the scenery was a delight to the senses, they couldn't have enjoyed it more if they had tried!

Saturday

After cooking and eating breakfast they cleared away, packed their bags and set off for Eyam in the 'Moggy', which they parked at Eyam Youth Hostel where they were spending the night. They then walked down into the village where they looked at the plague cottage where the tailor who brought the disease to the village lodged and where he was the first victim in Eyam to die of the Bubonic Plague, followed by the two sons of his landlady. The travelling tailor, George Vicars, had inadvertently transported the fleas, which carried the disease, in a roll of damp cloth from plague ridden London.

Illness spread quickly through the village, and the local vicars, the rector William Mompasson (the incumbent) and Thomas Stanley his predecessor, who would have had a lot of influence in those days, instructed the villagers to stay within Eyam in order to contain the spread of the disease. The villagers set a stone boundary around the village and the Earl of Devonshire (whose nearby estate was at Chatsworth House) arranged for the people of the outlying villages to bring food and other essentials to the edge of the village to be collected. This was managed by placing items on rocks and payment was made by coins being left in a hollow in the rocks which was filled with vinegar in order to sterilise the money, at some places running water was used to cleanse the coins.

They saw a notice advertising a carnival procession that afternoon, so they found some benches in the middle of the village and ate their sandwiches which they had prepared at Ravenstor Hostel. They were surprised and delighted when float after float, beautifully decorated with flowers (including their wheels) passed by, with several Carnival kings and queens. Later they discovered that the procession consisted of the floats from several of the surrounding villages which had come together for one massive parade on the bank holiday weekend, which is why there was more than one carnival king and queen.

The procession lasted for hours and when the last float disappeared around the corner they took themselves back to the hostel and deposited their bags in a bedroom. They had a bedroom to themselves instead of having to share with other people. The dormitory had two bunk beds and since none of them wanted to sleep on a top bunk they lifted one of the mattresses down and made a bed on the floor. Having settled themselves in they set off to look for the vinegar holes which they had read about earlier.

They walked up the hill to have a look at the vinegar holes, and on to see the Riley Graves where a Mrs Hancock buried her husband and six children in the space of just eight days. It is a small burial ground enclosed (now) in a circular stone wall. Katherine Mompasson, the vicar's wife, died towards the end of the outbreak and is buried by The Saxon Cross in the churchyard.

Returning to the hostel they had their evening meal and mulled over the events of the day and their surprise at unexpectedly seeing such a magnificent procession.

Sunday

After eating and clearing away their breakfast things, they packed up their bags and set off once more in the 'Moggy' for the parish church of St. Lawrence and the morning service. They did a little detour to look at Mompasson's well before heading down to the village to see the Townend well dressings one of which depicted scenes of the plague of 1665. Well Dressing is an ancient Derbyshire tradition where the dressings are made by placing leaves, petals and flowers and sometimes other materials on a wooden frame filled with local river clay. It is a co-operative activity where members of different groups get together to produce dressings to decorate the wells.

Mabel and June attended the church service whilst Irene explored the village further before returning to the church to meet the other two and then taking off in the car to Matlock.

They drove to Matlock and were surprised to encounter, along the main road, a long row of hundreds of bikers and their gleaming motorbikes shimmering in the sunshine. They found a pub where they could sit outside in the sunshine and eat their lunch whilst watching the river meandering by.

After lunch they drove to Thorpe where they walked along the stepping stones in Dovedale and enjoyed watching children playing at jumping from stone to stone across the river. After a very pleasant interlude they set off for home at 5pm via Ashbourne, arriving back at 7pm.

6. DERBYSHIRE DALES 1991

Whilst they were driving home they agreed that it had been a magical time and that they would all like to return again next year especially to see Bellamy's Bank at Ravenstor covered in spring flowers and to visit Tissington, walk the trail and also stay at Ilam youth hostel.

7. Derbyshire Dales & Chatsworth

23rd to 30th May 1992

Because they had enjoyed their few days last year so much, staying at youth hostels in Derbyshire, they decided to return there for this year's adventure, plus they wanted to see Bellamy's Bank covered with spring flowers. Irene once again booked their places at the hostels and this year they decided to stay a little longer as there were so many beautiful places to explore.

Sadly June had to say goodbye to her old Moggy 'Mulligatawny Rose' this year, but it did go to someone who restored them. Her new car was also a Morris Traveller, it was almond green and she called it 'Almond Blossom', it had a very distinctive number plate which caused much amusement wherever she went, it was OAP 721F.

Saturday

At 1.40pm they set off in the 'new' car from June's house and drove up the A38 heading for her daughter Sue's student house in Sheffield, they arrived at 4pm and after a welcome cup of tea they took Sue shopping. She hadn't been able to get to the shops because she had broken her ankle which was in plaster and she was hopping along on crutches. Shopping over, they took Sue with them to John's house to meet up with him before going out for the evening.

The plan was to stop the night at John's house, but first with John and Sue they went to a Chinese restaurant to celebrate June's birthday, which was on the following day. Sue had difficulty getting up the stairs in the restaurant on her crutches. They all enjoyed a delicious meal, then Mabel produced a magnificent birthday cake that she had made and after lighting the candles and singing 'Happy Birthday' it was cut, distributed and greatly enjoyed.

The three of them returned with John to his student house, after dropping Sue off at hers. John had placed mattresses on the floor in his bedroom for them to sleep on and he slept in his friend's room, who was away for the weekend. With much hilarity they settled themselves down on their floor beds surrounded by John's socks covering the radiators and with the walls hung about with his shirts on hangers. As a student, he was certainly efficient at dealing with his laundry – they were very impressed!

Sunday

June was woken on her birthday with a cup of tea from Irene (who you will have gathered by now was an early riser and very good at making tea). After giving June cards and presents and wishing her a happy birthday, Mabel and Irene went for a walk in the park whilst June toddled off to church.

They all returned to John's house where he made them brunch, consisting of bacon, eggs, tomatoes and toast with lots of tea. Sue and her friend Vikki called around and June gave them a large chunk of birthday cake to take and share with their housemates (it was a large cake!) as they didn't think that they could eat it all and of course they left some for John too!

Taking their leave of John, Sue and Vikki, they set off in June's car to Bakewell Youth Hostel and having deposited their belongings there, left the car and walked into Bakewell village where they mooched around the shops and of course bought some Bakewell tarts!

They returned to the hostel where they were served a dinner of ham and cheese salad followed by apple crumble. Later in the evening they strolled into town and found a friendly looking pub, where they sat outside on benches and drank lager and lime. June and Irene were entertained by the barman demonstrating to Mabel how to play golf with a walking stick and they passed a very pleasant evening before ambling back to the hostel. Their bedroom was a dormitory set a little below ground level, so they set about choosing beds and settling down for the night.

Monday (Bank Holiday)

They awoke to a lovely sunny day and after breakfast they set out for one of their exploratory walks. They were following a walk from a book and according to this they were supposed to go through an enclosed path 'likely to be overgrown' it said – and it certainly was! There was no possibility of getting through the brambles, but there was a gate next to the path, so they went through it and into a large field. They came across an outdoor market

1992 Irene's breakfast butty

7. DERBYSHIRE DALES & CHATSWORTH 1992

in full swing where they took the opportunity to look for bargains and settled on buying new shorts. Passing on through the market stalls, they walked alongside a little river and through a field dotted with sheep and lambs and eventually came to a place where they had to turn right over a stile and up a steep hill.

On their left was somewhere which they just could not pass by without a visit – Haddon Hall. A most beautiful old manor house, kept as it was when it was a family home, the kitchen having all of the original old cooking implements. In the sitting room an attendant pointed out to them French windows which opened out into the gardens, through which many years ago the daughter of the house had eloped with her lover. The Hall was in a picturesque setting with terraced gardens which were accessed by elegant stone stairways and balustrades.

Roses in full bloom surrounded the mullioned windows and climbed high up the stone walls of the house. They sat on a bench admiring the lovely old house and the interesting shapes of the topiary, before heading down to the lake where they sat upon the grass, watching the waterfowl as they ate their sandwiches and Bakewell tarts.

Reluctantly they tore themselves away to continue their walk and retracing their steps they picked up the path, clambered over a stile and up a hill which was swathed in buttercups, stopping to look back after a while at the panoramic view. Following the walk in the book, they ended up back at Bakewell youth hostel where they washed and changed before having a hostel meal. This was meatloaf, mixed vegetables, potatoes, ice cream and fruit. After dinner Irene and Mabel sat outside and played a board game called Othello with two young lads who were staying at the hostel. June filed her nails, wrote up the diary and listened to the radio and then they all retired to bed, tired but happy.

Tuesday

After breakfast they set off in the car for Ravenstor hostel where they deposited their bags as they were staying there that night. They then drove to Tideswell (the name of the road in Birmingham in which Irene was brought up) and after parking in the square they visited St. John the Baptist church, a very impressive building which was built in the 14th century and known as 'The Cathedral of the Peak'. It owes its harmonious appearance to the fact that it was built over what was then a very short period of time for such a building, it was completed in sixty years and is a landmark for many miles around.

THREE HAPPY WANDERERS

Tideswell itself dates back before Norman times and was an important market town for wool and lead and was very prosperous which enabled the townsfolk to afford to build such a large and beautiful church.

Toting their rucksacks they set off with the book of walks and passed through Litton Dale which was now very pretty as the spoil heaps from the lead mining had, over time, been covered with grass and wild flowers. Crossing over a stile they headed into Tansley Dale which also has a history of lead mine workings and had now become a very pleasant ramblers' trail. Following on into Cressbrook Dale they were confronted by a massive rock formation dominating the area which stood on a hill overlooking the dale. This imposing dome shaped rock, they later discovered, was called Peter Stone named after St. Peter's Basilica in Rome due to the similar shape. Locally it was called Gibbet Rock because in the 19th century a murderer, Anthony Linguard, was hanged from the rock in chains as an example to the ungodly.

The book that they were following had very poor directions for this walk, but they eventually found their way along with difficulty. It was a lovely hot sunny day and they were sporting their new shorts purchased from the market the day before. As the day grew even hotter they were getting thirsty and peckish so they looked forward to having lunch at an inn mentioned in the guide book, but much to their disappointment the inn was closed. They were greatly relieved to spot a nearby transport café and after their long walk they eagerly scrambled through the door and ordered bacon and eggs and mugs of refreshing tea. One of June's favourite photos of Irene was taken in this café where Irene is pouring brown sauce onto a massive sandwich with a look of delightful anticipation on her face.

After refreshment they continued their walk and also continued losing their way, but it was no great hardship as they delighted at the undulating scenery which was unfolding before them as they meandered up hill and down dale. Eventually they reached Tideswell again and finding a little traditional butchers shop they bought bread and milk and Mabel bought locally cured bacon to take back to her husband Doug. Irene was about to buy oatcakes but was checked by June who pointed out that there was blood dripping onto them from some meat hung up above.

They collected the car from the square then went back to Ravenstor and after settling in they enjoyed another hostel meal. After dinner they walked to the local pub, The Anglers Rest, where they refreshed themselves with pints of shandy before strolling back in the cool evening air along the Wye riverbank to the lower hostel gate. Back at the hostel they found the games room and

Irene and Mabel played scrabble, while June did a crossword puzzle before retiring to their bunk beds and sleeping the sleep of the exhausted!

Wednesday

They awoke to a bright sunny day and after making themselves tea and bacon butties and doing the washing up they set off in the car to Chatsworth House for the day. It is the Elizabethan home of the Duke and Duchess of Devonshire, built in 1555 and set in 1000 acres of parkland with 100 acres of formal gardens. The approach to the house is impressive, set on the banks of the river Derwent and the house can be seen for miles away and is open to the public for most of the year.

Before exploring the extensive gardens, they went on the tour of the house which is richly furnished with silver, sculptures, tapestries, paintings, porcelain and elaborate inlaid furniture and lavishly decorated throughout with painted walls and ceilings. After an hour or so of admiring these beautiful works of art they made their way outside to the splendid gardens and sat eating their lunch near the spectacular fountains and cascade waterfall, watching children paddling and splashing around on the steps.

They wandered through the magnificent yellow laburnum archway, under a stone bridge which was bedecked with creepers, from the top of which afforded a superb view of the lupin gardens and maze. They would have liked to have gone into the maze, but it was not open that day, so they settled for admiring the topiary instead. A wooded area led them along a rhododendron and azalea walk and along the banks of a lake. The more formal gardens around the house had herbaceous borders, rose gardens, a serpentine shaped hedge and ring ponds with semi submerged rocks. Many happy hours were spent drinking in the magnificence of the gardens, before they took their reluctant leave and headed back to Ravenstor hostel.

After a wash and brush up and change of clothes they strolled along the riverbank once again to The Anglers Rest for dinner. They enjoyed the meal and recounting the events of the day, agreeing that Chatsworth House had been admirable and worthy of a visit at another time. Ambling contentedly back to the hostel they settled down for another restful night.

Thursday

Awaking refreshed they prepared and ate breakfast and after washing the dishes and packing their small rucksacks with drinks, sandwiches, first aid items, cameras, a wildflower book and cagoules they set out to walk to the

Monsal Trail. They made their way from the hostel to the river Wye, crossed the small wooden bridge and passed two viaducts before reaching Millers Dale Station.

Armed with their pamphlet of walks about the Monsal Trail they set off towards Chee Dale. Passing some old lime kilns they descended into the dale via a flight of steps and proceeded to walk along the riverbank. When they arrived at a section where the only way through was over stepping stones in the river, they found that their walking sticks really came into their own! After this precarious crossing they rejoined the path and turned sharp left over a bridge then sharp right under a larger bridge, after which a left turn brought them back onto the Monsal Trail.

Ambling along the site of the old railway track they eventually came to a tunnel and passing through saw another tunnel ahead where they stopped to take photos and after a short distance they crossed over the river on another bridge. Quite a way further on they came to a brick built bridge and passing underneath it they turned left over a stile and up a grassy path leading up the side of the dale. Crossing several stiles through buttercup meadows where they stopped to rest, eat their sandwiches, admire the May blossom on the hawthorn trees and take yet more photos of the stunning scenery.

Continuing up the hill, they crossed a stile into a lane which led them down through Blackwell where they left the lane to follow the walk past some farm buildings, and following the map they descended through fields and tracks into the dale once again. They re-joined the river, crossed a bridge and followed the path back to Miller's Dale Station. They took the now familiar route back to Ravenstor looking forward to their evening meal which was prepared for them by the hostel's staff. After this they played board games, chatted to other hostellers and packed their bags ready for departure the next morning as this was their last night in the hostel.

Friday

After the obligatory breakfast and washing up, they finished their packing and clambering into the car with their bags to set out for their next destination which was Ilam Youth Hostel. It was a dull overcast morning, which started out wet and drizzly, but kindly cleared up for them as they walked around. After depositing their bags at Ilam Hall they drove to Tissington 'The Mother Place of Well Dressing' to look at the six famous well dressings. Tissington, known as Derbyshire's most beautiful village, is a private and a most delightful village with a lovely old hall, charming cottages and an invaluable supply of pure water from the wells. It also boasts an excellent walking trail along the defunct railway track which is also greatly appreciated by cyclists for its absence of hills. They walked a short way along the trail and vowed to return to walk the whole of it another time.

After stopping at a convenient bench to eat their lunch, they strolled around the village, going from well to well admiring the talent and skills which had gone into the making of the well dressings where the villagers had used bluebells, hydrangeas, wallflowers, coffee beans, alder cones and other blossoms which were available in the spring; only natural materials are allowed to be used.

It was a very pleasant and interesting day and before returning to the youth hostel they went food shopping and bought large baking potatoes and salad to have for their evening meal. At the youth hostel, a Welsh lady showed Irene how to do baked potatoes in a microwave oven (a fairly new phenomenon then) since they had always cooked them for hours in a conventional oven.

After dinner they walked around the grounds of Ilam Hall and wandered down to the church where they took photographs before strolling along to the village and taking a look around. It was a very pleasant evening and would have been perfect if June hadn't been badly bitten by midges and had to take an anti-histamine tablet before she went to bed.

Saturday

June had problems waking up despite Irene and Mabel encouraging her to come and help to prepare breakfast (it was her turn) and she was itching like mad from the midge bites from the previous night. She decided to take another anti-histamine tablet before getting up and in her befuddled state bashed her head on the bunk bed above. After taking the tablet she got dressed and went to join the others in the kitchen, who couldn't understand why she was acting so strangely and kept nodding off. They went back to the dormitory and packed their bags and put them in the car, ready for departure later on.

Eventually they set off on a walk along the river Manifold but June was struggling to keep up which was most unusual and when she sat down on a stile, leaned on her walking stick and promptly fell asleep, Irene and Mabel realised that there was something wrong. It was clear that June was not going to be able to continue on the walk so they took her back to her car where she lay down on the back seat and fell asleep. By this time they had figured out that the anti-histamine tablets were having a very adverse affect on her; this

1992 Tissington well dressing

was quite worrying as she had to drive them all home later on that day, since neither Mabel nor Irene could drive.

Leaving June to sleep off the effects of the tablets Irene and Mabel set off once more to walk along the riverbank of the Manifold which emerges in the grounds of the hostel near a local spring which feeds the river then disappears underground to Wetton Mill. After a pleasant stroll in the morning sun they returned to Ilam Hall, checked that June was still asleep in the car and went for a walk around the extensive grounds, which are overlooked by the impressive Thorpe Cloud Hill, and admiring the flower beds and the fountain in the formal gardens situated around the Hall.

Having worked up an appetite Mabel and Irene went into the National Trust cafe in the hostel grounds and had some lunch before taking a sandwich and drink back to June who was beginning to rally around by this time. When she was recovered and fed and felt awake enough to drive safely, they set off for home eating Kendal cake to give them energy and stop June from nodding off again!

They had thoroughly enjoyed their second visit to Derbyshire and agreed that Tissington would be well worth further investigation.

8. Torbay
30th August to 5th September 1993

They were trying to think of somewhere for their adventure this year which wasn't too expensive and June expressed a desire to go to the seaside. When Mabel suggested a place where she had stayed with Doug several times in Torquay and offered to contact the couple who owned it, they agreed that it would be a superb place for an adventure. Mabel contacted Sylvia and Ian McDonald at 'Cintra' who said that they would be happy for them to stay in their large Georgian style house, which had been converted into self-catering accommodation.

Buz offered to take them in his car and said that he would incorporate the trip with a visit to see his Dad who was living in Babbacombe at the time.

Monday (Bank Holiday)
At midday Irene and Buz collected Mabel and June and set off on the motorway to Devon, stopping just past Bristol for a picnic at a service station. Arriving at 'Cintra' during the afternoon, they were welcomed by Sylvia and Ian who took them on a tour of their lovely, well tended garden. They said that they were welcome to use the garden and made them feel really at home.

After unloading their bags from Buz's car, they were taken by Sylvia up a sweeping Georgian staircase to their rooms, where they made a pot of tea to share with Buz before waving him off as he departed for his father's house.

Their accommodation consisted of a large bed-sitting room with an en-suite bathroom, a large double bedroom and a kitchen/diner. Mabel and Irene shared the bed-sit (with Irene in a single bed by the door for a quick escape to have an early morning cigarette). June was kindly allowed to luxuriate in the separate bedroom after they had tossed a coin for it. Once they had unpacked, they walked down the hill to the harbour area where they ate fish and chips, sitting on the harbour wall. They were surprised and delighted when a spectacular fireworks display began across the bay from them, what a treat it was whilst they enjoyed their fish suppers and what a wonderful start to their adventure!

By the time the firework display had finished it was getting quite late and was dark, so they decided to get a taxi to take them back up the steep hill to 'Cintra' where, after organising the kitchen for breakfast they watched television whilst drinking tea before happily climbing into their beds.

Tuesday

Waking to a beautiful sunny day, they prepared and ate breakfast (bacon and eggs), washed up, made sandwiches and after packing their small rucksacks with their packed lunches, set off in their shorts to walk to Babbacombe. Going up the hill from Cintra they weaved in and out of the roads and found their way with the aid of an A-Z to Babbacombe. This was a very interesting walk as it took them past a variety of houses from large detached ones to rows of terraces. They went through several alleyways and across a small park before emerging opposite the Babbacombe Theatre. They walked along Babbacombe Downs to St. Marychurch and espying a museum called Bygones strolled over to take a look; once in the shop at the front they decided that it would take too long to go around the museum and made a mental note to return if they had a rainy day.

Retracing their steps they made their way to Oddicombe Cliff Railway where, after looking out over the cliff to the beach they decided to give their knees a break and ride down in the coach. They noted the times of the last coach as they didn't fancy the steep climb back up as well as the walk back to Torquay.

They walked along the beach to the far end and found that they couldn't get past Petit Tor Point as the rocks were too steep, so they found a quiet spot by some flat rocks and agreed to spend the rest of the day on the beach. They played at skimming stones across the sea, did crossword puzzles, sunbathed, swam in the sea and then ate their packed lunches. Mabel engaged in a very interesting conversation with a lady from Canada who was sitting near to them, whilst Irene and June floated, swam and generally messed about in the sea. Lying lazily sunbathing on the beach they appreciated the blue sky and azure sea with little boats, ferries, yachts, and fishing boats passing by across the bay and enjoyed the antics of the children on their surf boards.

As the sun went behind the cliffs and they found themselves in the shade they got dressed, packed up their rucksacks and returned to the Cliff Railway for a ride back up to the downs. Strolling along Babbacombe Downs towards the theatre they looked for Reddenhill Road and crossing into it, found their way back to Cintra.

Back at the house, after a reviving cup of tea sitting on benches in the garden, they prepared and ate their dinner, whilst recounting the events of the day. After dinner June and Mabel started to do a jigsaw puzzle, which was laid out on a table in June's bedroom, while Irene read a book curled up in a cosy armchair by the fire. After a light supper which included hot chocolate with Horlicks and brandy, they retired to bed and slept soundly.

Wednesday

Once again they awoke to blue skies and sunshine so, after a substantial breakfast (they believed in stoking themselves up for these – to them – strenuous hikes!) they packed up their rucksacks and headed down Braddons Hill Road into the harbour area of Torquay. Turning left past where they ate their fish suppers on Monday, they made their way along the harbour side towards Hope's Nose. They were exploring the area and weren't sure where the path would take them and, when confronted with rocks which led around the headland, they decided to see how far they could get.

They started off tentatively stepping from rock to rock across the numerous rock pools, stopping to examine the fascinating contents of them and marvelling at these micro worlds of the marine life. At Thatcher Point they sat down opposite Thatcher rock and watched the sea gently lapping against the rocks and lifting the great swathes of seaweed and depositing them a few feet away, the sun was shining and they were in heaven. There were no other people around and it was so peaceful and picturesque they were reluctant to leave this idyllic spot, but realised that they needed to press on or get caught by the incoming tide. By this time they had gained confidence in scrambling over rocks and were almost nimbly jumping across the smaller crevasses and feeling much younger than their mature years.

It was so quiet and deserted that they were startled to come across a nude recumbent male figure sunbathing on the rocks where, no doubt he thought no-one would see him, he had a hat strategically placed – on his face – which amused them no end as they went chuckling on their way. Rounding the headland and with Hopes Nose in view before them they realised that the tide was coming in fast and covering the rocks ahead and were spurred into action to find a part of the cliff face which they could climb up. Happily for them there was a place within reach which they could just about manage to scramble up, it was very steep and it is true to say that they were more than a bit scared!

8. TORBAY 1993

1993 Irene and a pony

1993 June and Mabel skimming, Babbacombe Beach

It was with much relief that they gained the top of the cliff and collapsed upon the grassy headland. After catching their breath they found a bench and had their picnic, extremely glad of the drinks that they had packed.

After a short rest they looked for a route to take them to Ansteys Cove and found Marine Drive so heading north they struck a path, which would take them along the coastal path called Bishops Walk. Meandering around the headland they came upon a large bed of very prickly looking nettles, Mabel had been saying that her knee was aching (probably due to the rock scrambling) and told Irene and June about a remedy which her father had passed on to her, which involved hitting a painful spot on the body with a bunch of nettles. Much to June and Irene's amazement she collected up a handful of nettles and proceeded to thrash her left knee with them! Whilst the other two fell about laughing she explained that it gave a tingling sensation and seemed to relieve the pain somewhat.

They arrived at Ansteys Cove after taking a path leading down from the cliff walk and were delighted to discover a café overlooking the sea which sold tea and cakes which they were happy to indulge in whilst taking a well earned rest. Picking up the path again they plodded on towards Babbacombe passing Redgate Beach and around Walls Hill began to feel a little weary from the day's exertions. When they arrived in St. Marychurch they agreed that it would be sensible to catch the bus back, bearing in mind that they still had that steep hill to climb at the other end. Entering the bus near the museum they alighted at the other museum in Torquay.

Dragging themselves up Upper Braddons Hill Road and stopping for a rest on a bench conveniently placed about half way up the hill, they arrived at Cintra huffing and puffing and recovered themselves with cups of tea. They took it in turns to sit on the reclining chair in Irene and Mabel's bedroom before setting about the task of preparing dinner. Once dinner was consumed and cleared away they adjourned to June's bedroom and continued to add to the jigsaw puzzle before retiring to bed.

Thursday

After a bacon and egg breakfast they cleared away, packed their bum bags and scooping up their walking sticks from the umbrella stand in the porch and set off down the hill. Finding a short cut by a row of Georgian houses, they crossed a car park and went down some steep steps emerging at the side of a pub near the harbour.

Approaching the kiosks where ferry trips to Brixham were booked, they bought their tickets to go on the Seaways Express Ferryboat and since they

8. TORBAY 1993

had a little time to wait, went into Debenhams where Irene looked at wedding outfits since her daughter Rachel was planning to get married the following May.

Boarding the ferry they enjoyed a bracing trip across Torbay which took about fifteen minutes and afforded them many photo opportunities. Alighting at The Quay in Brixham they admired the quaint shops, the sounds of the halliards rattling against the masts of the boats in the harbour, and the herring gulls screeching and dive bombing the incoming fishing boats. The pastel shades of the multicoloured fishermen's cottages banked around the sides of the harbour blended into a panoramic vista of the bay, and it is an artist's paradise.

It was such a hot day that June resorted to taking off her polo shirt and strolled around in her bikini top and shorts. They took photos and looked at the replica of Sir Francis Drake's 'Golden Hind' promising themselves to go aboard one of the days.

Walking around the harbour they followed the directions to Berry Head Country Park along Berry Head coastal road, passing a swimming pool at Shoalstone Beach which has been built into the rocks where children were playing and they were very tempted to jump in and cool off. The path zig-zagged from coast to streets and this eventually led them to Berry Head headland where they stopped to read a notice about some of the bird and plant life around the cliffs which are home to razorbills, kittiwakes and has a large colony of guillemots.

Following the path they passed through Berry Head Fort which was built on an iron age hill fort site during the Napoleonic wars and they were delighted to find a café and, as is their custom, went in to have a cup of tea after which they paid a visit to the loos which were situated around the back of the building and accessed from the outside. Irene had disappeared around the back to have a sneaky cigarette (she was trying to give up smoking and didn't want the other two to see her) but Mabel sneaked around the opposite way and caught her on her video camera. They all had a good laugh before moving on to the coast guard station and small lighthouse, the beams from which can be seen up to 20 miles away because of its elevated position. Beyond that they found a bench, overlooking a panoramic view of the cliffs and the bay where they sat to eat their picnic and absorb the ambiance of the whirling seabirds and the waves crashing against the rocks.

Irene wandered off to have a cigarette and returned to say that she had found an excellent spot from which to watch the gulls drifting by, so Mabel and June went to where she indicated and lay down on the springy turf right on the very edge of the cliff. It was a very surreal experience with the blue sky merging into the sea, the warm breeze gently wafting past and the guillemots wheeling about below them, it was almost as though they could just take off and fly themselves and they could begin to understand why people do in fact jump off.

Before June could try out her imaginary wings they rejoined Irene who was having a nap on the bench, and scooping her up they all headed off to the other fort area called the Redoubt, where they clamboured around the ruins consisting of a brick built artillery house and ramparts. Retracing their steps back past the car park they commented upon the variety of wildflowers and the brilliant yellow of the gorse bushes all around them.

Heading back towards Brixham they stopped at Shoalstone Beach to watch with fascination a group of children enthusiastically leaping off the rocks into the foaming brine. They were whooping with glee and shouting to one another as they jumped and were clearly having a whale of a time. At first they felt very concerned for the childrens safety but it soon became clear to them that this was a commonplace activity for them and they were clearly in command of the situation.

Pressing on they reached Brixham and walking around the harbour they followed the Overgang (the spot where William III of Orange landed with his Dutch army during the Glorious Revolution of 1688, and meaning 'transition'). Following the Torbay coast footpath they wended their way through Elberry Cove and Broadsands, and then climbing uphill they walked parallel with the Paignton and Dartmouth Heritage Steam Railway, stopping to wave to the passengers and the train driver who blew his whistle for them.

When they arrived at Goodrington Sands they agreed to give their throbbing feet a treat, so divesting themselves of their footwear went for a paddle and wriggled their toes in the cool refreshing sea, then found a stall selling sweets where they bought flapjacks (just to revive their flagging energy!). Irene reminisced about when her children were young and they went there for holidays as the family had a beach hut there, it was an ideal family resort with gardens, boating lake, putting green, and children's play equipment with a large golf links nearby.

It was beginning to get dark by this time so they decided to take the road into Paignton instead of the costal path which was quite a bit longer and they were all getting a bit weary. When they arrived in Paignton they debated whether to get something to eat there or carry on to Torquay; they were all very tired by this time and agreed that they didn't want to walk any further (June's left hip was hurting and she was very glad to sit down).

Having spotted first a taxi rank and then a fish and chip shop, they decided to get fish and chips and take them back to Cintra in a taxi to save them having to walk up the hill, which they would have had to do if they had eaten in the harbour area of Torquay as previously planned. Having bought their supper they wrapped it up in several plastic bags so that the taxi driver wouldn't be able to smell the fish and chips, as they didn't allow takeaway food in the taxis. They were mightily pleased to arrive back at the house and sit down to their supper; they reckoned that they had walked about eleven and a half miles which was a bit more than they were used to, since they consider themselves to be strollers rather than hikers. Their beds were very welcome that night!

Friday
It was a unanimous decision to have a lie in and a lazy day after yesterday's strenuous day so they took their time getting up (except Irene who went into town to fetch a newspaper at some ungodly hour!). Taking their time over a nice cooked breakfast, Irene had brought kippers and croissants and apricot preserve from the shops, they read the papers and listened to the radio before washing the dishes and preparing a shopping list, since their provisions were running out.

Armed with the list they set off for the town centre, turning right at Cintra and going up the hill before negotiating two flights of steps; Irene was playfully complaining about the steps (having already been up and down them once that day) saying that the other two deliberately found steps for her to struggle with. Once down in the shopping centre they looked for a shoe shop so that Irene could replace her sandals one of which had split when clambouring over the rocks on Wednesday. Having made her purchase they then made their way to the market and mooched around the stalls, enjoying the sunshine and the pleasant atmosphere and buying food for the next couple of days including crusty bread, cheeses, salad and a bottle of red wine for lunch. Mabel had bought some scone mix with her so they looked for a shop to buy some clotted cream to go with the scones she promised to make.

Huffing and puffing their way back up the two flights of steps, laden down with shopping they were glad to take advantage of the strategically placed bench to catch their breath, before carrying on to Cintra where they deposited the shopping and immediately put the kettle on for an essential cup of tea! After a short rest they prepared lunch and took it out into the garden and sat at a little white painted wrought iron table, enjoying their well earned 'ploughwoman's' lunch in brilliant sunshine with just enough gentle breeze to keep them from overheating.

After lunch they lay on the grass in the well tended spacious gardens, sunbathing and chatting (and sometimes nodding off!) and when Ian and Sylvia came out to water their numerous plants they showed them their secret walled vegetable garden where they had a nursery of Torquay palm trees which they had grown from seed; some years later Ian gave Mabel some seedlings which her husband Doug planted and both Mabel and June eventually had stately palms growing in their back gardens.

About four o'clock (tea time) Mabel went up to their kitchen and made delicious fruit scones which they consumed on the lawn with lashings of tea, apricot jam and clotted cream, after which they lay in the sun and had a little nap, this truly was an idyllic day!

When the sun went down they went indoors for their evening meal, after which they did the jigsaw puzzle, played cards and scrabble and rounded off a very pleasant relaxing day.

Saturday

Putting their best foot forward, after breakfast, they walked down to the harbour and headed towards the Princess Theatre and gardens en route for the Medieval Village of Cockington. Continuing along the promenade they crossed the road at Abbey Sands beach and walked past a large area of gardens with bowling green, swimming baths, and lying behind them, Tor Abbey gardens and glass house. Passing Corbyn Head they turned into Seaway Lane, a typical Devon lane with high hedges consisting mainly of blackthorn either side, with wild flowers in the hedgerows.

Cockington is an exquisite, picturesque, typically English (or how they like to perceive it) country village with thatched cottages which date back to the Doomsday Book. A 10th century forge (partially re-built in the 14th century) with a workshop at the rear producing miniature horseshoes, sits in the centre of the village. Opposite the forge is a tall wall with an archway leading past two lovely old cottages to a mill stream with a water mill. Further up a grassy slope there sits an old inn, designed by Lutyens, called The Drum Inn (whose cellars are reputed to be haunted). The piece de resistance is the manor house, Cockington Court (the site being home to the Squires of Cockington for almost 700 years) which has a sweeping cricket pitch laid out before it, with a tiny Saxon church to the side of it.

8. TORBAY 1993

Arriving in the village square they were surrounded by thatched cottages with the old forge to one side where they marvelled at the sight of the pretty buildings, and the horse with its yellow painted carriage with holidaymakers happily alighting from it set on enjoying the beautiful sunny day. They looked at the forge which also has a facility for selling the small horseshoes which it produces and noticed that visitors had pushed pieces of paper with their names on onto the thatch. All of the buildings in the village have thatched roofs including the public toilets in the car park!

One of the cottages was a shop and tea rooms with a winding path leading them through ornamental gardens, with masses of multicoloured summer bedding plants, pixies and a clock dial made of various coloured pebbles. The words 'Rose Cottage' were picked out in white pebbles and the whole thing was surrounded by geraniums; Mabel was very pleased to discover that this was the clock from a jigsaw puzzle that she had done many years before. They sat overlooking the gardens and drank their tea before making use of the facilities in the car park and then setting off up the hill to find the Court.

Making their way past the forge, they passed Weavers Cottage tea shop on the right and further up came to a small gate in a wooded area. Passing through the gate they heard the crack of leather on willow and were delighted at the idyllic scene which opened up before them. Surrounded by rolling grass banks was a cricket pitch set in the hollow, where there was a match in progress with the players dressed in whites and colourful supporters sitting on the banks either side and in front of the pretty white painted pavilion.

They walked along the long sweeping driveway which was the approach to the splendidly imposing brick built 17th century Manor House shimmering in the sunlight which was reflecting off the white paintwork. The house is also in a hollow like a jewel set into the surrounding hills and the green foliage of the statuesque trees around it. Because the village had for a long time been owned by The Prudential it was retained in its unspoilt and relatively original state.

To their delight they found that the Court contained a tearoom, craft centre and souvenir shop, so after looking around the craft centre and shop they succumbed to the temptation of Devon cream teas in the café. This consisted of huge fruit scones with masses of strawberry jam and lashings of clotted cream and pots of tea, on tables set with dainty china tea sets and blue gingham tablecloths. The pretty young waitresses, who cheerfully took their order, wore black dresses with white frilly aprons and mop caps, and they felt that they had taken a step back in time to a more tranquil and very different way of life.

As they were settling the bill they saw the horse and carriage arrive outside the church conveying a white lace bedecked bride, so they rushed outside to watch this charming tableau and were just in time to see six bridesmaids and two page boys alighting from another carriage. Family and friends were gathered around in their colourful clothes, completing this pleasing spectacle. After taking a photo of the happy group they watched them make their way into the church, then they returned to the lawn outside the Manor House and settled down to watch the cricket match in the sunshine.

After a while they made their way around the back of the Court to track down the organic garden which was advertised in the shop. On the way they passed a paddock with stables and watched the horses being unsaddled and groomed before being settled into their stalls. Passing by they spotted the path leading to the organic garden at the end of which was a gate in a tall wall which surrounded the garden.

Pushing open the large oaken gate and entering the garden they surveyed the neatly laid out beds which contained herbs, vegetables and fruit bushes, with fruit trees espaliered in the borders against the walls. A lady appeared out of a small wooden building and introduced herself as the person who was restoring the gardens and introducing the organic methods and techniques which would have been used when the garden was originally constructed in the 17th century. She offered to take them around and explain what they were trying to achieve (there was a volunteer working with her, to whom they chatted later) encouraging insects to pollinate the crops, natural pest control and making fertiliser from comfrey. They sat and watched, in the shade of the tree situated in the corner of the garden, the bees buzzing around the bright blue borage flowers and frogs hopping around the wildlife pool. They started chatting to the volunteer who had been made redundant from his job and so offered his services to help with the restoration; June thought that this would be a lovely thing to do when she retired.

Then after a quick look in the greenhouse, noting the French marigolds growing alongside the tomatoes, they set out to ramble around the formal (also walled) rose garden. After this they headed towards the church and had a quick look around, admiring the floral displays left behind after the wedding, then went to find the game keeper's cottage. Following a path through the woods they came first to a small lake, which to their amazement had fish leaping up and breaking the surface, it soon became clear that they were catching the flies and midges. There were lots of fish and some appeared to be lying on the concrete ledge at the side of the lake, almost as if they were sunbathing. Moving on, they passed another lake with water lilies and ducks and they commented upon how peaceful and pleasant it was.

They headed towards the woodland walk and emerged from the woods to be enchanted by the sight of a romantic looking 16th century Game Keeper's Cottage nestling in the shadow of Manscombe Woods which, they discovered, were planted for the purpose of rearing and shooting pheasants. After looking around the outside and peeping through the windows at what was left inside after arsonists had set fire to it in 1990, they started on the long walk back, as it was getting towards dusk and they had missed the last horse and carriage which would have taken them down Cockington Lane to the seafront. In the event they walked down the lane and found a path running parallel to it, which they took in order to get off the road and walk over the wetlands on a boardwalk.

As they were wearily trudging along the wooden walkway in single file, to keep their spirits up they were calling out to one another as if they were the three main characters from 'The Last Of The Summer Wine' TV programme. Irene being Compo who was always lagging behind with Mabel and June vying for the character of Clegg (the one with the dry wit) since neither wanted to be the bossy Foggy.

Their voices must have carried in the still evening air, as they heard a disembodied voice suddenly say 'Can I be Wesley?' (the mechanic from the programme). There was a high hedge in between them and the lane, so they couldn't see who was on the other side, but they burst out laughing anyway. When they got to the end of the walkway and rejoined the road they discovered that it was the volunteer from the organic garden who had called to them, and he said that he had long identified with Wesley and was amused at their nonsense. They walked along with him into Torquay chatting companionably and made him an honorary member of their 'club' and when they got to the seafront they went their separate ways, bidding him farewell and promising to return to the 'secret garden' another year.

Making their way along the front and up Upper Braddons Hill (stopping to rest at the bench by the Olivia Court Hotel, with the large acorn on its gatepost) they eventually arrived back at the house where they prepared the last dinner of this adventure. They finished the jigsaw puzzle and took it in turns to relax in the recliner and admire the pictures on the wall of the sitting room (especially the magical one of the white unicorn rampant) before gladly retiring to bed.

Sunday

They arose early and had breakfast then set about the task of packing their bags and the remains of the depleted food supplies. Whilst waiting for Buz to arrive (at 10.45am) they had a last wander around the garden with Sylvia and Ian and thanked them for their hospitality, asking if they would let them come again since they had enjoyed themselves so much and felt that there was a lot more of the Torbay coast for them to explore. Buz arrived and fetching their bags from the canopied front porch, they packed up the car and set off waving to Sylvia and Ian as they stood in their porch with the sun shining through the glass roof onto the multicoloured and profusely flowering and trailing hanging baskets and tubs.

Buz took them to his Dad, Charles's house where he welcomed them with cups of tea and coffee and his delicious homemade cakes before waving them off on their return journey. Three hours later they arrived at the home of Margaret and Mark, friends of Irene and Buz who lived in Poulton in Somerset, who were expecting them for lunch.

They had a lovely visit with them, Mabel had never met them but June knew Margaret from their teenage years and later when she was also one of Irene's bridesmaids.

At 4.30pm they started out yet again (for the third time) waving goodbye to Margaret and Mark, thanking them for the tasty lunch, and saying how pleasant it was to meet up with old friends again. On the journey home they recounted to Buz all of the interesting places which they had visited and how many more that they had left unseen and would like to go back and explore. He said that he would be happy to take them again the following year if they so wished and as it happened they took him up on his kind offer.

9. Torbay

27th August to 4th September 1994

The previous year they decided that there was a lot more adventuring to be done in Torbay and as Buz had offered to drive them there, they took him up on his kind offer and booked their rooms with Sylvia and Ian who were prepared to have them again! Sadly, Irene's father was ill in hospital at the time and so she decided to just come for the weekend and then return to give support to her family.

Saturday
Irene and Buz picked Mabel and June up and started off on the long journey south to Devon, where they were greeted in Babbacombe by Charles, Buz's father, who had prepared a late lunch for them. He kindly offered to give Mabel and June a lift as far as Goodrington on the Tuesday as they were planning to walk to Brixham which is a fair step. After lunch they went into the garden to see the memorial plaque to his late wife Frances which was on a flowering cherry tree. Taking their leave they headed on to Cintra to be greeted by Ian and Sylvia (who had kindly got some basic provisions in for them) and settled themselves into their rooms, whilst Buz drove back to spend the night with his dad. After a light supper and a game of cards they retired for the night in the same rooms which they had used the previous year.

Sunday
Since Irene only had this one day before returning home, they made the most of it by setting out, straight after breakfast, down the hill to the museum on Babbacombe Road. From there they crossed into Torwood Gardens and made their way along Meadfoot Road which took them to Meadfoot Beach. It was a warm morning so they were wearing their shorts which enabled them to paddle about in the sea, but the weather was mixed and not quite hot enough

for swimming. They enjoyed scrambling amongst the rocks and peering into rock pools at the micro lives of tiny crabs and sea anemones.

They had lunch in The Meadfoot Beach Café before heading back to Cintra (and that long walk up the hill) so that Irene would have time to pack her bag before Buz came to pick her up. Buz duly arrived and they watched them depart feeling very sad that Irene's dad was so ill and that she could not stay with them. Sylvia and Ian came to see them off and then they went around to the spacious back garden and whilst Ian was watering the numerous plants they sat chatting and drinking tea with Sylvia.

Feeling somewhat deflated at Irene's departure they cooked dinner and started doing a jigsaw puzzle of a pretty country cottage before retiring for the night.

Monday (Bank Holiday)

This was a warm but cloudy day and after breakfast they set off with packed lunches in their rucksacks, down the hill and into Torquay heading for Cockington Village. As they passed by Torre Abbey they decided to go in on the way back from Cockington as they passed it last year and thought they might investigate it further.

Strolling along Seaway Lane they were hoping that there would be a cricket match in progress as there was last year (not that they are particularly cricket fans, but the match gave an ambience of rural England which felt like stepping back in time). When they got to the village, their first stop was at the blacksmith's forge where they took some photos and empathised with those old smiths who must have had quite a hard life (as did most of the proletariat) in medieval times. There was no work in progress, but the horseshoes that are made there were still for sale. Carrying on up the hill they retraced their steps of the previous year and arrived at the edge of the cricket field and much to their delight there was in fact a match in play. The scene was tranquil and relaxing, with families scattered around the edges of the pitch, sitting on the grass and watching the men in white, occasionally clapping a well executed stroke of the bat against the red leather ball, or the bowler's well delivered aim sending the bales flying off the wicket. Ambling along towards The Court they were soaking up the atmosphere of peaceful serenity when they heard a clip clopping behind them and turned to see the horse with its carriage approaching along the road carrying some women and children.

When they arrived at The Court they saw the man from the organic garden with whom they had joked the previous year about The Last of the

9. TORBAY 1994

***1994** June on a coastal path walk, Torbay*

***1994** The Giant Rock near Watcombe beach*

Summer Wine characters, who called himself Wesley, disappearing into the tearooms. They were pleased to see him there and thought that it would be nice to catch up with him later in the walled garden, which they planned to visit after sitting on the grass eating their picnic and watching the cricket.

After an enjoyable interlude they wandered around to the rear of The Court and along to the organic garden which they entered and noticed a new feature from last year. Where there had previously been a hut in the corner was now a delightful thatch roofed lean-to shack with wattle and daub walls. They headed towards it and the lady appeared from inside to whom they had spoken last year. After exchanging greetings she explained that the thatched shack was part of the restoration of the garden. They went inside and were amused to see that the thatchers had left the ears on the corn which had been used for the roof, no wonder mice like to live in thatched roofs with a ready made larder to hand! They asked if 'Wesley' would be coming back and were disappointed to hear that he had left for the day, she said that his name was Adrian, which didn't seem right to them as they had come to think of him as 'Wesley'.

They passed through the large oak gate and walked around the outside of the walls until they came to the spot where the thatched shack had been let into the wall, where June took a photo of Mabel sitting by a new door which led into the shack. Returning to the Court they went into the tearooms and ordered and consumed tea in delicate china cups and had their favourite fruit scones served with lashings of clotted cream and jam. They appreciated being able to sit at a table covered with a blue gingham tablecloth and being served by waitresses dressed in black and white with lacy caps and aprons.

Tea time over they walked down the road heading for the Gamekeeper's cottage when suddenly a squirrel surprised them by leaping into a waste bin in front of them; camera poised, June caught it on film on its way out!

The Gamekeeper's Cottage was not open, but looking through the window they could see that some restoration work had taken place since last year and a notice indicated that it was now used as a place for the local schoolchildren to visit to study natural history. After taking a quick look around and a few photos they headed along the winding woodland walk which led them to Cockington Lane and eventually down to the seafront.

They walked back towards Torquay and found the lane leading to Torre Abbey, its grounds and gardens; this was set back quite a distance from the road and since it was late in the afternoon they wondered whether it would be too late for them to look around. When they arrived they found that the

Abbey was closed for the day so they resolved to return another time and consoled themselves by just having a quick look at the gardens.

Rather than return to Torbay Road they thought they would try to find their way back along Belgrave Road which eventually led them to Abbey Road and the flight of steps which brought them out at the top of Upper Braddons Hill Road. Their instincts served them well and they must have been heading in the right direction despite the lack of a compass!

They were glad to be back at Cintra and rest their aching feet, so after a cup of tea they prepared a scratch meal of bacon and eggs, before putting their feet up and having a lazy evening in front of the television – too tired even to do the jigsaw puzzle!

Tuesday

They awoke to a dull and overcast day and after breakfast they packed up their 'pods' and chatting to Sylvia waited for Buz's dad Charles to arrive. On Saturday when they first arrived he offered to give them a lift as far as Goodrington as he heard them discussing a walk to Brixham and thought it would help them to chop off a few miles of hiking.

About 10.30am they saw his car pull into the driveway so picking up their pods and walking sticks they went out to meet him and introduce him to Sylvia, with whom he reminisced about the years that he worked at The Torquay Times which was not far away. On the way to Goodrington, Charles pointed out places of interest that had been a part of his life since moving down there with his wife Frances some 35 years previously. On the outskirts of Goodrington he dropped them off at Cliff Park Road car park where he could turn around and head back to Paignton to go to his Bridge club.

They were at the beginning of the coastal footpath which leads to Brixham and also runs parallel with the Torbay Steam Railway line as far as Broadsands. Putting their best foot forward they set off down the path and took a hasty photo of a steam train which passed by very close and they waved to the children who waved back.

When they got to Broadsands Beach which was quite rocky they followed the path to the headland where they eventually emerged at Elberry Cove. Tentatively stepping across the pebbles they crossed the beach and re-joined the path which led them through a copse and out into open ground with a golf course to their right which stretched on for quite a long way. They walked for about a mile with a clear view of Torbay and all of the marine activities, the delightful sailing boats bobbing along on the waves and the fishing smacks going to and from Brixham harbour. Passing by Churston Cove and Fishcombe Beach they stopped for a while at the Battery Grounds for a comfort break where they took photos before proceeding to Freshwater Quarry, the Overgang and the Quay leading to the harbour area.

It being lunch time they sought out a fish and chip shop which overlooked the harbour so that they could watch the boats bobbing about on their moorings and the fishing smacks and ferry boats coming and going. There was lots of activity yet it seemed quite peaceful and relaxed and they enjoyed watching the fishermen at their various tasks such as mending their nets and setting out their creels to dry on the quayside. After lunch they wandered around the shops where they spotted a notice about a local swimming pool, so thinking that it would be pleasant to have a swim (but not wishing to risk a dip in the sea since it was not sunny enough for their liking) they decided to look for the indoor pool. Proceeding at a leisurely pace they made their way through a maze of streets and finally arrived at Brixham Leisure Centre where, to their disappointment, they found that it was not open. In disgust they sat down on a wall by Astley Park and ate chocolate bars to console themselves.

Making their way back to the harbour they found a little café and had cups of tea, then they decided to catch a bus back as it was coming on to rain. They found the bus stop and it wasn't long before a bus arrived and they boarded with a sigh of relief as it was beginning to rain more heavily although it had eased off by the time they got back to Torquay. They got off the bus at the shopping centre and bought two pork steaks, new potatoes and asparagus tips for their dinner and a tub of clotted cream to go with the scones which Mabel planned to bake. Making their way up the steep flight of steps at the side of the post office, they were glad to get back to base for a cup of tea and a chat to Sylvia, relating their day's activities.

Whilst June cooked the dinner Mabel made a batch of sultana scones, some of which they ate with the clotted cream and strawberry jam, with a glass or two of red wine. The evening was rounded off with a session of doing the jigsaw puzzle which they particularly liked doing as it was a beautiful thatched cottage with a rose garden.

Wednesday

After a bacon and egg breakfast they made sandwiches for lunch and packed their rucksacks, including their Mary Quant capes as it was dull and overcast. They collected their walking sticks from the stand in the hall and headed off up the hill towards Babbacombe.

9. TORBAY 1994

Once there, they walked down the path at the side of the cliff railway and half way down towards Oddicombe beach where they turned left along the cliff path heading for Watcombe via Petit Tor Point. Making their way along the coastal path they crossed Petit Tor Downs and continued along a track through some woods which brought them out above Petit Tor Beach. To their surprise they saw people on the beach and in the sea with no clothes on and realised that this was a nudist's beach. Resisting the temptation to join them they continued on passing Torquay Golf Course on their left, Roundhouse Point, Shag Cliff and Smugglers Hole on their right until they reached the path which led down to Watcombe Beach, where they stopped for a while to eat their picnic lunch and have a paddle in the sea.

Gathering up their strength, in the heat of the mid-day sun, they wended their way back up the hill until they came to a wooded area. Entering this shady wood with its fallen trees and rocks overgrown with plants and shrubs they were quite entranced with the ethereal atmosphere of the deep hollows. A child might have imagined it to be a fairy glen where magical creatures might peep out from behind the huge trees and massive boulders. They lingered for a while and climbed upon one large rock to take photos and soak in the rugged beauty of the area. A fallen tree served as a seat where they sat and rested and refreshed themselves with cartons of yoghurt.

Emerging from the woods, they looked up to see an enormous rocky outcrop near to a black and white gabled house (which they thought might possibly have been the home of Isambard Kingdom Brunel, since they had been told that he had lived in a large house near there). They stopped to take photos before continuing up the road towards a car park in search of a public convenience and after finding it and using the facilities, they saw a notice which they stopped to read. It was about The Giant Rock, and they realised that this was the enormous rocky outcrop which they had noticed as they left the woods.

Apparently in Victorian times it was a famous beauty spot where the wealthy would arrive in their carriages to visit for the day. In 1853 the local choral society held a 'Spectacular' and over 7,000 people came, many of whom had come by train from as far away as Bristol and Birmingham. The 'Spectacular' was held in front of The Giant Rock and included The Highland Games and a choir of 1,000 voices, there was also a Highland Regiment beating the retreat on the top of the floodlit Rock. After the demise of the china clay industry the area deteriorated and became overgrown with scrub and trees and in 1992 it was cleared to make a picnic area and reveal The Giant

Rock once more. At the same time the turning circle for the carriages was restored as a part of the picnic area.

From the car park they walked to the turning circle and saw how tight it would still have been to turn the larger carriages around; they thought that the drivers must have been very skilful. They sat at the picnic tables there for a while after walking around the circle and trying to imagine what it would have been like in Victorian times.

Continuing along Beach Road they came to the main Teignmouth Road where they stopped to chat to a man who was walking his dog, as they wanted to find out where Brunel had lived, since they knew that it was somewhere in the area. He very kindly directed them to Brunel Manor and asked them if they knew about the wood carvings of Brunel in the woods near to the house. He urged them to go and look at them saying that they were very interesting and celebrated Brunel's life and works. They thanked him and followed his directions, crossing the main road and making their way through a small housing estate before reaching the woods (known locally as Brunel Woods) where they searched for the statues, coming upon them unexpectedly in a clearing.

They later discovered that the four sculptures were known as 'Brunel's Dance' and that the artist Keith Barrett was commissioned by Torbay Council in 1993 as part of the regeneration of Watcombe Woods and a memorial to the great man. Several trees were blown down during The Great Storm of 1990 when many specimen trees were destroyed throughout the United Kingdom. One of these trees was a Sequoia redwood tree which had been planted at Brunel's request when the woods were a part of his Watcombe Park Estate, at the time when the Manor House which he designed was in the process of being built.

One of the sculptures was a tall totem pole depicting Brunel's many and varied engineering achievements which was carved from the fallen Sequoia tree. Brunel, complete with top hat (who appears to be dancing) and the fire figure were carved from Douglas firs and the Water figure from Cedar; the fire and water carvings represent steam power used in the works for which he is famous such as bridges, boats and trains. They spent some time admiring these, so didn't get around to looking for The Manor House as it was getting quite late in the afternoon and they didn't fancy being lost in the woods in the dark! They agreed that they would have to return with Irene one day as she was particularly interested in Brunel and his achievements, so they were quite happy to leave the hunt for the Manor House until then.

They made their way back to the main road and looked for a bus stop, since they had already walked a long way and it was getting late, and waited hopefully for a bus. Happily for them, one arrived before too long and they were glad to have a ride to Babbacombe, where they went to a fish and chip café so that they could sit and enjoy their dinner with a welcome cup of tea.

It was a lovely evening, so they decided to walk back to Cintra along the well lit roads, and marvel at the spectacular sky after the sunset. They spent a quiet evening doing the jigsaw and making plans for the following day, before soaking in the bath and retiring to their beds.

Thursday

They were late waking up and found that it was a bright sunny day, so they decided to spend the day on the beach. After their customary bacon and eggs they packed up their bags with swimming costumes, towels and a picnic and set off for Oddicome Beach. Heading up the hill from Cintra they walked towards Babbacombe through the housing estate and made their way to Babbacombe Downs where they descended via a path which zig zagged its way down to the beach.

Finding a smooth spot on the pebbly beach they donned their swimming costumes by wriggling around under their towels before laying them down to sunbathe upon. Since the sun goes off that beach in the middle of the afternoon they made the most of the morning and lay prone with occasional rolls over to toast the other side! They had of course plastered themselves liberally with sun tan lotion beforehand and took regular dips in the sea to cool off to prevent getting sunburnt.

June was happy to listen to a talking book on her Walkman and Mabel read a Cadfael book, now and then they would get together to do a crossword puzzle and stopped for lunch when they got hungry.

When the sun sank behind the cliffs they dressed, packed up their bags and headed back along the beach towards the cliff railway and followed the steep path up to Babbacombe Downs. They made their way from there to Walls Hill, an open grassy area and followed the path to Anstey's Cove Road and turning right along a track they came to Babbacombe Road, which led them down to Torquay harbour. Since it was such a lovely sunny evening they decided to have fish and chips sitting on the harbour wall enjoying the last of the sun, whilst watching the colourful boats bobbing up and down in the bay. Eventually they trudged their weary way back up the steep hill to Cintra where they did some more of the jigsaw puzzle before retiring.

Friday

Having had a fairly lazy day yesterday they opted for a big walk today, so after the usual cooked breakfast they packed their bags, picked up their sticks and put their best feet forward en route to Goodrington. Walking up the road from Cintra and turning left they descended the steps into Grafton Terrace at the end of which were another set of steps which lead down to Fleet Street by the post office. From there they proceeded to the Strand and into Torbay Road, where walking along the coast road they passed Torre Abbey Meadows where they reminded themselves that they had planned to return to visit the Abbey. They agreed to get back in time to go around the Abbey since the last time they went there it had closed for the day.

Arriving at Paignton they stopped for lunch and a well earned drink at the harbour, where they sat and admired the boats before continuing on around Roundham Head and into The Cliff Gardens. This brought them out onto Goodrington Sands where they were glad to change into their swimwear and go for a dip in the sea. They relaxed on the beach for an hour or so, sunbathing and swimming and reading their books. Then reluctantly they tore themselves away from the beach and made their way back to Torquay the same way as they had come, in time to visit Torre Abbey.

The Abbey lies back from the road behind Torre Abbey Meadows and is Torquay's oldest building dating back to 1196, being an offshoot of Welbeck Abbey. It was built by six White Canons (named for their distinctive white habits) of the order of St. Augustine. The purpose of The Abbey was to pray for the souls of King Richard Coeur de Lion and his father Henry II. In Medieval times part of the gardens were used as a cemetery whilst an orchard and herb gardens provided medicinal plants to benefit both the resident monks and the wider population of the (then) tiny fishing hamlet.

Entering the Abbey through the imposing stone-built archway they made their way around the rooms studying the artefacts and wandering into the chapel and the dining room looking at the art collection, including the Thrupp sculptures. It was getting late in the afternoon so they didn't have long to linger, and ran out of time to visit the nearby Spanish Barn. This was a tithe barn which was originally built to store the huge amounts of grain and other produce grown in the Abbey's vast lands. It became known as the Spanish Barn when it was used to hold prisoners captured by Sir Frances Drake from the flag ship Rosario of the Spanish Armada and is the only surviving Armada prison. It was used during World War II as a gymnasium by The Royal Airforce when it was based at the Abbey.

After an interesting visit they wended their way back along the front and up the hill home. They had worked up quite an appetite, so whilst Mabel peeled the potatoes for bangers and mash, June prepared the mixture for pancakes. These were eaten wrapped around ice cream with chocolate sauce poured over the top. Any hope of losing weight through all of their walking was dashed at this point! Replete and contented they did the jigsaw puzzle until bedtime, after washing the dishes of course.

Saturday

They decided to go to Brixham again since the weather had not been very good on Tuesday and also they fancied a boat ride, so after breakfast walking sticks at the ready they set off for the harbour to catch the ferry. It was a lovely sunny day and the sea breeze was very pleasant as the ferry chugged its way to Brixham Harbour. Once there they strolled around the harbour enjoying the sights and sounds of the little boats fluttering their flags on the masts and rattling their halyards.

Their destination was Berry Head so they took the road leading uphill from the harbour and stopped when they arrived at the gun emplacement which relates to the Napoleonic wars. They paused for a while to have a rest and a drink from the bottles in their bum-bags, whilst admiring the view across Torbay. Pressing on to the top of Berry Head they reminisced about the time when Irene was with them and she fell asleep on the bench in the sun. Making their way towards the Fort they decided that they would have their lunch in the café there, so stopped for jacket potatoes and cups of tea followed by ice cream.

They then walked to the lighthouse and sat watching the seagulls wheeling and gliding around the cliffs calling to one another, before making their way around the headland to The Old Redoubt which is the remains of the defence system from the Napoleonic wars. Mabel noticed that there were a lot of blackberries growing in the hedgerow so they set about picking some to take home with them the following day. They habitually carried some polythene bags in their bum-bags, so these came in very handy for putting the blackberries in. Retracing their steps back to the Fort café they had a cup of tea before making their descent to Brixham harbour where they spent a pleasant hour browsing around the little gift shops and buying presents for their families.

Returning to the fish and chip shop in which they had eaten on Tuesday, they went upstairs into the café to enjoy their repast whilst watching the tourists milling around The Golden Hind, and the hustle and bustle of the harbour.

They then made their way to the bus station where they caught the 7.14pm bus back to Torquay, where they slowly wended their way back up the hill to Cintra in the dark, their way illuminated by the soft glow of the old lampposts.

Sunday

After breakfast they tidied away and washed the dishes before June packed her bags in readiness for her departure in the afternoon. Mabel was remaining behind as Doug was joining her there for a further week.

Whilst June stripped her bed and tidied up her room to minimise the cleaning for Sylvia, Mabel made a batch of fruit scones for them to enjoy before departing for home.

At 1pm Irene and Buz arrived and took them to Charles' for lunch at his flat in Babbacombe. After a delicious meal Charles gave them the recipe for his tart called 'bits and pieces' with fruit, breadcrumbs and syrup which they had all enjoyed.

When they returned to Cintra to collect June's luggage and drop Mabel off, Charles came with them and they all spent the rest of the afternoon chatting with Ian and Sylvia whilst strolling around their garden. They had a welcome cup of tea sitting outside in the sunshine, accompanied by Mabel's scones with clotted cream (which they had stopped to buy en route).

After a very pleasant afternoon Irene, June, Buz and his dad bade goodbye to Mabel, Sylvia and Ian and set off for home about six o'clock. They dropped Charles off at his flat and had an uneventful journey home arriving about nine o'clock. On the way June related to Irene the events of the week, particularly the discovery of the Isambard Kingdom Brunel carvings, which Irene said that she would like to see on a future Adventure.

10. Torbay

27th August to 3rd September 1995

Since Irene was not able to stop for the week last year as her father was ill and sadly never recovered, they decided to return to Torquay again this year and pick up from where they left off. Buz was happy to chauffeur them again and spend some time with his dad who lived nearby.

Sunday

Irene and Buz collected Mabel and went on to June's house for an 8.30am start. After a three hour journey they were glad to arrive at Buz's dad's flat and have a cup of tea and a wander around his (shared) garden admiring his tomato plants. He made them very welcome and it was a lovely start to their adventure on a nice sunny day.

Once rested they all went to a pub for lunch in Charles' car since Buz's car was full of their luggage and provisions. After lunch they returned to the flat and swapping over to Buz's car continued on their journey to 'Cintra' bidding farewell to his dad.

Sylvia and Ian greeted them as they arrived and helped them with their luggage up the stairs to their now familiar rooms. Sylvia had kindly fetched milk and bread to save them the task of hauling them up the steep hill. They unpacked their food boxes and made mugs of tea which they took down to the garden to drink whilst Sylvia and Ian were showing them the latest additions to their garden. Buz admired the new paving that Ian had laid and Ian explained how he had made the paving stones from concrete and gravel, adding a special ingredient (to their surprise) washing-up liquid for a nice smooth finish!

After a while Buz went back to his dad's where he was stopping the night before returning to Birmingham and work. They waved him off and went back upstairs to unpack their bags and put away their provisions, then prepared a light tea before digging out the jigsaw puzzle in order to make a start on it. They always aimed to complete the jigsaw puzzle whilst they were away, but didn't always succeed.

They stuck to the same sleeping arrangements as previously and all had a good night's sleep.

Monday (Bank Holiday)

It was a lovely sunny day so after breakfast they packed their bum-bags, picked up their walking sticks and set off down the hill to Torquay Harbour. They thought that this would be a good day for a ferry ride to Brixham, so sorted out a ferry and booked their tickets. They had a little time to kill before the ferry left so they had a wander around the little shops and the park, admiring the profusion of flowers in the beds and the Torbay palm trees. Returning to the departure point they picked up the ferry and set sail for Brixham, enjoying the sea breeze in their hair and the gentle swell of the waves.

On arrival in Brixham Harbour they were pleased to discover that there was an open day at the wholesale fish market. They decided that this would be an interesting way to spend an hour, so following the signs set off to New Fish Quay and The Fish Market. It was indeed an interesting experience watching the fish merchants sorting out the fish for home consumption and exporting. One of the men explained to them that some of the more unusual fish were rescued and sent to the Brixham Aquarium. There was a three foot long shark which drew the attention of several small children who prodded and poked it shrieking with mock fear. They had never seen such a variety of fish and such large crabs and lobsters. It amused them to watch the fish merchants constantly retrieving the crabs as they wandered off along the counter.

As they strolled back along the quay they reflected upon the history of Brixham and how it had originally developed because of the harvest of the sea and is now also a thriving holiday resort, with colourful yachts as well as fishing boats bobbing about in the harbour. Looking at the fish reminded them that it was lunch time, and they strolled down to the fish and chip café near The Golden Hind and sat outside eating their lunch, whilst watching the holidaymakers enjoying the various activities in the harbour on a lovely sunny day.

After lunch they went to look at the statue of William of Orange which, they understood, was upon the spot where he was rumoured to have landed before ascending to the English throne. From there they walked around the

10. TORBAY 1995

__1995__ Fishmongers, Brixham Harbour Torbay

__1995__ Irene and Mabel on the ferry boat to Brixham

Quay and along the coastal footpath to Broadsands, passing Freshwater Quarry, Fishcombe Beach, Churston Cove and Elberry Cove.

Arriving at Broadsands they found a mobile shop selling cups of tea, which they had eagerly anticipated, and where they stopped to refresh themselves and use the facilities. Finding a nice grassy bank they spread their Mary Quant capes out and lay down to have a sunbathe and watch the seagulls whirl around, screeching as they followed the fishing boats diving for rejected fish. Time was getting on, so they decided to catch the bus back to Torquay and made their way along Broadsands Park Road (passing under the viaduct) arriving at Dartmouth Road where they looked for a bus stop. After a short wait they hopped on the bus back to Torquay Harbour where they wandered up the hill back to Cintra and a welcoming cuppa.

Having prepared and eaten their dinner they settled down to the serious business of adding to the jigsaw puzzle before going to bed.

Tuesday

It was a bright sunny morning so after breakfast they set off to Babbacombe to spend the day on the beach. Packing up their trusty bum-bags with waterproofs (just in case) and picking up their walking sticks, they set off up the hill to walk through the Victorian housing estate. They always found this walk very interesting, looking at the gardens and variety of house types and noting the changes since last they were there.

In Babbacombe they mooched around the shops and then headed towards Marychurch where they caught the cliff railway down to Oddicombe beach. Once there they looked around for a deck chair for Irene as she preferred sitting up to read her book. They then established themselves on a quiet spot near the rocks at the far end of the beach, with Irene putting up her deckchair (shades of Mr. Bean) to June and Mabel's amusement, whilst the other two spread out their Mary Quant Capes and covered them with large colourful towels.

As soon as they had changed into their swimming costumes they ventured forth and dipped their toes into the sea to see whether it would be warm enough to swim in later on. After a short paddle they went back and lay down (or sat in Irene's case) for some serious sunbathing (being careful not to burn). They really enjoyed relaxing, reading and doing crossword puzzles in between sunbathing and having dips in the sea.

Lunch was sandwiches (which had been prepared earlier) for Mabel and June and a pasty for Irene, which she fetched from the beach café, bringing

10. TORBAY 1995

back cups of tea for the other two. Later on June and Irene went snorkelling around the rocks where they found many varieties of seaweed, sea anemones and a few fish. June has always been fascinated by the underwater world and had 'persuaded' Irene to join her – Mabel declined the offer! The afternoon was spent in this pleasant manner before they packed up their belongings and set off back along the beach to the cliff railway. When they got there they found that there was a very long queue so decided to walk up the path at the side, stopping to 'admire the view' now and then.

They retraced their steps back through the streets to home where they unpacked their wet swimwear and towels and draped them over a lovely free-standing mahogany towel rail to dry. Dinner was prepared and consumed and after clearing away they settled down to an evening of playing cards. Irene and June used to play a game called Bezique when they had lots of time to spare in their youth. Since having their children they rarely had the luxury of the amount of time it takes to play the game, so took advantage of the opportunity to play. Mabel had never played this game, so they elected to teach her and the entire evening was spent in this fashion.

They then took it in turns to have a bath and wash off the sun tan lotion and sand acquired on the beach during the day, before retiring.

Wednesday

As usual Irene woke the other two with a cheery "good morning" and mugs of tea. It was a lovely sunny day so after a substantial cooked breakfast they set off down the hill in their shorts with their pod bags and walking sticks. They walked along the sea front, past the harbour and the Pavilion, where they came upon gardens with some very interesting topiary-looking shrubs which were in fact wire frames with damp moss inside into which something resembling ice plants were inserted. The whole scene represented a horse and cart with four figures of people, three about to climb into the cart and one leading the horse.

They took photos and continued along the front heading towards Cockington where they intended to spend the day. After a pleasant stroll up Seaway Lane they arrived at The Forge which had been renovated since the previous year and looked as though it had been re-thatched. The interior of the forge had been made into a shop which sold horse brasses as well as the traditional miniature horse shoes.

After looking at these they wandered around the other little shops in the square where Irene and Mabel bought large colourful glass marbles for family members who collected them. They all bought walking stick badges, ferrules and bags of sweets, then went into Rose Cottage where they walked around the gardens counting the gnomes and admiring the bright red geraniums before having cups of tea in a covered area overlooking the garden.

Once refreshed they made their way to the car park where the public conveniences were and then continued on up the lane towards The Drum Inn. Mabel wanted to show the other two where she had an enjoyable holiday with Doug and her son David in a farm house in Stantor Barton in 1957. As they walked past The Drum Inn they saw a notice advertising a ghost walk on the coming Saturday evening and thought that it would be a fun way to round off their week, so made a note to book tickets later in the day, having already decided to return to the pub for lunch.

Carrying on up the lane they turned up a bridleway which led steeply upwards through woods and open fields which afforded them a magnificent view of Paignton and the surrounding area and the farm house where Mabel had stayed. Mabel described how David had played amongst the hay stacks and that they all had to walk through the fields of curious cows in the dark, dodging the 'country pancakes' after attending a firework display in Paignton.

After Mabel's trip down memory lane they returned to The Drum Inn where they were served with enormous, delicious, mouth watering, hot beef sandwiches, with lovely cool shandys by the Landlord. They chatted to him about the ghost walk and he told them that the inn had its own resident ghost in the cellar which he said he would show to them later on if he had time. He said that it was the ghost of a young man who was going to the inn to attend a meeting and on the way was killed in a motorbike accident. They found out some time later that Irene's sister-in-law Judy was at that meeting when she was about seventeen. They were sitting in an inglenook fireplace and it was a very spooky atmosphere, so whereas June and Irene were keen to go down into the cellar, Mabel declined the offer! Before leaving they bought tickets for the Saturday night ghost walk.

Lunch over; they made their way up the lane to the cricket field and Cockington Court. They were disappointed to find that nothing much was happening in the area compared with last year (no cricket match and spectators and no wedding) and it was quiet and deserted. As they approached the Court they saw that the café and shop were closed and that there was some exhibition being organised, so it was clear that they were not going to get their afternoon cream tea there.

10. TORBAY 1995

Wandering around the side of the Court they made their way to the organic garden, Mabel and June were keen to show Irene the new thatched roofed building within the walled garden. Once again they were disappointed not to find either the lady who managed the gardens or the volunteer Adrian (or Wesley from 'The Last of the Summer Wine' TV programme). They looked around the gardens, examining the borage, comfrey, nettles, different varieties of mint, the wildlife pond, the compost heap and the tomatoes in the greenhouse.

The previous year Mabel and June had noticed that an area at the rear of the gardens was being developed, so they all went around to the back of the walled garden and found raised wooden beds. This new project looked like a picnic area with flower beds and seating facing a round pond in the centre. They speculated upon how the finished garden would look before leaving to make their way back down, past the Court, cricket pitch and the church. Along the pathway they stopped to watch the antics of the squirrels and saw a man walking past with a young lady and they were convinced that he was the famous photographer Lord Lichfield; it would indeed be a perfect place to take photographs.

Heading down Cockington Lane they noticed a tea shop by a hotel and since they had been deprived of their cream tea in the morning agreed to try out the Cockington Court tearoom's opposition. Upon entering the tearooms they found that they could sit at tables outside and enjoy the view and the passing traffic (the horse and carriage). On the opposite side of the road there was an old barn and other farm outhouses which had been converted into several separate dwellings of thatched roofed cottages with gardens. It was very sympathetically done and blended in well with the surrounding buildings. They fantasized about selling their houses and living in this idyllic courtyard habitation with all of their families and friends.

Their cream teas were delicious with jumbo sized scones and considerable quantities of strawberry jam and clotted cream, accompanied by copious cups of tea from the large crock teapot. Some time later they trudged slowly down the lane and along to the seafront where they found it necessary to sit and look at the waves crashing against the breakwater! Having caught their breath they continued along the way to Cintra and up that steep, steep hill only stopping half way up to have a rest on the strategically placed bench.

Since none of them could face a large meal they abandoned cooking dinner, had a light supper and after a further attempt at the jigsaw puzzle, retired to bed.

Thursday

They awoke this morning and wondered where they should go today so they looked at the map and decided to go a bit further to the north to Shaldon. Both Irene and Mabel had been there in the past and were anxious to show the area to June who had never been there. So after breakfast they set out to catch the bus at the stop by the museum since they felt that it was a bit too far to walk to Shaldon.

It wasn't long before a bus arrived and bundling their sticks and bum-bags aboard they settled down for the fifteen minute ride. When they arrived they made their way towards the shops and found one which sold Cornish Pasties; they bought three for their proposed picnic lunch, and then wandered onto the beach where some men were fishing with large nets from the shore. They watched as they hauled in their nets and unloaded the squirming fish from the nets into trays on the beach. This is a traditional form of fishing still carried on by the local fishermen. Irene recalled how years ago she had seen them catching huge salmon and was amazed at the size of them, sometimes requiring two men to pick up one fish, and sometimes they were so strong that they wrenched themselves from the fishermen's grasp and leapt back into the water.

Across the estuary of the River Teign lies the town of Teignmouth, one of the most popular holiday resorts in the area. It was such a picturesque view with the sun shining on the white houses, the deep blue water and the boats bobbing about in the estuary that June stopped to take three photographs which she could later join together to make a panoramic picture.

Mabel remembered that there was another beach on the other side of a huge hill called The Ness, reached by a narrow tunnel which has been cut into the headland. They found their way to the tunnel and walked through it in single file, emerging onto a soft sandy beach where they found a suitable spot to lay out their capes in order to sunbathe and eat their picnic. Several hours and crossword puzzles later they reluctantly dragged themselves away from this idyllic spot as they had decided to go to the cinema and needed time to get back to Torquay and have dinner first.

Making their way back through the tunnel they caught the bus, discussing where they might go to eat before going to the Odeon cinema in Torquay to see the film 'Waterworld'. Arriving at the museum bus stop they walked back up the hill to Cintra where they showered and changed before strolling down to the town. They found a little pub where they had dinner before setting off to the cinema. They enjoyed this fantasy film starring Kevin Costner, who also produced it, and which is now recognised as one of the classics.

10. TORBAY 1995

It was dark by the time they came out and they climbed the steps by lamplight chatting happily about the film and the probability of the world ever getting into that state. When they got back they had a drink of Horlicks, accompanied by chocolate biscuits, before retiring contentedly to their beds.

Friday

Once again the sun was shining when they awoke so after breakfast they made up packed lunches, picked up their trusty walking sticks and set off to walk along the coast to Paignton. Their route took them through Torquay, past Abbey sands, Corbyn Head (a headland where they paused to look back at the view of the bay and take photos) and Livermead Beach, where Mabel realised she had left her walking stick at Corbyn Head. June and Irene sat on a bench while Mabel walked back to retrieve her stick before pressing on to Hollicombe Park, where they went through an iron gate to be met by pretty flower beds and a wooded area. The path from the park leads down under the railway bridge to Hollicombe Beach. Irene recalled that she had always known it as gasworks beach when she took her young children to visit their grandparents, who then lived in Paignton.

On the beach they played at skimming stones across the waves for a while, and then followed the path at the far end of the beach to Marine Parade. Carrying on along the Parade they came to Preston Sands where they stopped to eat their sandwiches sitting on a wall on the seafront. After a short break they walked along The Esplanade and passing the pier they stopped to look at the seafood stalls crammed with whelks, cockles, mussels, prawns, jellied eels, crabs and oysters. When they arrived at the harbour they stopped at a café for a cream tea, sitting and enjoying the spectacle of the colourful boats jiggling for space by the jetty.

They continued on their way along the cliff road to Roundham Head, when they stopped to admire the view all around the bay from Torquay to Brixham. As they were strolling around The Head, June became aware of a young man walking behind them as they walked around Cliff Gardens. He stopped each time that they did and kept quite close behind them. His manner made June feel uncomfortable so she asked Mabel to secure her rucksack which was loosely dangling from her shoulder and appeared to be the centre of the man's attention. It seemed very odd to June that he would be strolling around alone, wearing motorbike gloves and carrying a helmet. She asked the other two to stop suddenly and appear to be looking at the view, she then swung around and looked straight at the man who promptly turned on his heels and walked swiftly off in the direction from which they had just come.

Recovering from this disturbing episode (all the more so because they had only ever encountered very nice friendly people before, and it shook their faith in the local people for a while) they descended to Goodrington Beach. Spreading out their capes they lay down on the beach to catch the last of the afternoon sun and top up their tans. After a while Irene went off to find a kiosk and brought back cups of tea which they drank whilst watching the water-skiers skimming the waves (and sometimes falling in!).

They decided that it was getting too late to walk back, so they headed for the bus stop (near to the Torbay Pottery shop) on the main road and caught the bus back to Torquay. Getting off the bus by The Princess Theatre they walked into the town centre and headed up the steps by the post office to home.

Once there they prepared and ate dinner accompanied by the usual glass or two of wine, then carried on with the jigsaw puzzle before hitting the hay.

Saturday

Another warm sunny day greeted them, so once breakfast was out of the way, and their bags packed for swimming they ambled down into the town on the way to the beach. Since they were passing Debenhams and Irene was looking out for a suit for her daughter Becky's wedding, they popped in to have a look at their range of outfits. She found a Berketex suit which she liked, and the shop assistant was very helpful in providing details so that Irene could buy it when she returned home.

Strolling along the promenade they headed for Abbey Sands, where they spread out their capes (these were particularly useful since the sands were often quite damp before the sun had chance to warm them). The remainder of the day was spent swimming, sunbathing and generally relaxing. For lunch they ate the fruit and cakes which were left in their larder, as they wanted to use up the odds and ends since they were leaving for home the following day.

At around about six o'clock they packed up their bags and left the beach to go to Cockington Village where they had booked tickets to go on a ghost walk. Ambling along Cockington Lane they looked forward to dinner in The Drum Inn. Last time they had eaten there they had enjoyed the meal so were anticipating a tasty repast. They were not disappointed as the cottage pie was delicious, but they never did go down in the cellar to look for the ghost.

10. TORBAY 1995

Once replete, they walked to the car park for the eight o'clock Ghost Walk. There were a lot of people gathered for the walk and eventually a small group of actors in medieval costumes arrived to lead them up the hill to the grounds of The Court. Their first stop was on the edge of the cricket field where the assembled company were asked to sit on the grass to listen to the players' performance. They then enacted some grizzly stories, punctuated by ballads which were accompanied by a guitar. Then they all walked up to the lovely little church, where once again they sat upon a large tarpaulin listening to more scary stories and medieval songs. It was quite dark by this time and the moon was shining above the church, lighting up the spire and creating a spooky atmosphere. By this time their limbs were getting numb and they were happy to start walking back along Seaway Lane. On arrival back at Cintra and after a warming cup of tea, June and Irene packed their bags for departure the next day. Mabel was once again stopping and Doug was joining her there for a week.

Sunday

It was an early start to the day as Buz was to collect Irene and June and set out for 9.15am, so after breakfast they put their bags downstairs and went in search of Sylvia and Ian to say 'goodbye'. When Buz arrived the friends said their farewells, and leaving Mabel to finish tidying up, June and Irene settled into the car and set off for Combe Abbey.

Buz was keen to go to a Veteran Car Rally in the grounds of Combe Abbey, since he was the proud owner of a Mark 9 1959 Jaguar, which he was in the process of restoring. When they arrived, there were cars of all shapes and sizes and they spent an interesting day wandering amongst them and paying particular attention to the Jaguars.

After an uneventful drive whilst relating to Buz the events of the week, they eventually arrived home at 6.30pm, having come to the conclusion that there was still more adventuring to be done in Torbay.

11. York

25th August to 31st August 1996

Mabel was unable to go on this year's adventure, so Irene and June took advantage of the offer to use their friend Joan's flat in York. Irene had been there before and thought that June would enjoy exploring the places which they hadn't managed to visit on their previous adventure there with Mabel in 1990.

June's daughter Sue had arrived back from a holiday in Australia and was returning to work in Sheffield after a flying visit to see her Mother and collect her car, so she took June to Sheffield with her and Irene arranged to get a lift with Buz the following day, as she wasn't due back from holiday until then. It meant that June could spend some time with her children and that Irene had time to unpack and repack as June's son John had offered to take the friends to York on the Tuesday.

Sunday

At 9pm Irene and Buz arrived at John's flat where June had been busy during the day, whilst John was out playing tennis, re-arranging the furniture in the lounge in order to make space for a futon to be laid out on the floor for Irene and Buz to sleep on. John came back from tennis and Sue arrived at the flat to join them all in a Chinese take-away. They had a very pleasant evening catching up with news of their families and friends and Sue returned to her flat whilst the rest of them settled down to sleep at John's.

Monday

At 8am John went off to work and June took Irene and Buz mugs of tea and enquired how they had managed on the floor! After breakfast they waved goodbye to Buz who returned to Birmingham.

Sue arrived in her car and took them to collect John and his car from The Children's Hospital where he was working, so that they could all visit the

11. YORK 1996

Industrial Museum and craft centre in Sheffield together. After a very interesting morning looking at Sheffield's industrial past they had lunch together before Sue left, arranging to pick them up later.

John took them to the big new shopping precinct Meadowhall where they wandered around looking at the shops before he left them to return to the hospital. They decided to while away the next couple of hours watching Tom Cruise in 'Mission Impossible' at Warner Cinemas. Sue and her friend collected them in her car and took them to meet John at the Children's Hospital for tea, after which they spent a very pleasant hour walking around two nearby parks before Sue and her friend took their leave of them and they returned to John's flat for the evening. Unfortunately John was called back to the hospital around 11.30pm so June and Irene retired for the night. He arrived back about 1am.

Tuesday

At 8am John went back to the hospital whilst Irene and June had breakfast before he returned at 10.30am and performed a (very) minor operation on June's arm. At 12.30 he drove them to Leeds where they visited a park with a tropical house and aviaries with exotic birds and enjoyed walking around the colourful walled garden before having lunch. They stretched their legs again after lunch before continuing on their journey to York where they arrived at 5pm having been delayed in the rush hour traffic.

Relieved to have at last arrived at Joan's flat they set about making cups of tea and omelettes from the provisions which they had purchased along the way. After a rest their resident surgeon performed yet another minor operation, this time on Irene's right foot, giving her a hydrocortisone injection as she had a very painful foot following an accident a few months previously when she had twisted it. Much to Irene's delight the pain disappeared instantly (she was somewhat nervous about having this procedure as she hates needles) and afterwards she was able to explore York pain free.

After re-assuring himself that his two patients were alright, John left to return to Sheffield around 8pm. They then set about sorting out their sleeping arrangements and unpacking before having a light supper, after which Irene phoned Buz to let him know that they had arrived safely. They then listened to a play on the radio called 'Magic Cottage' before retiring.

Wednesday

Irene (who usually gets up hours before most people) went to the shops to buy bacon for breakfast (they did the full English in those days!). They decided to

1996 *Clifford's Tower, The Mount in York*

1996 *York Minster*

11. YORK 1996

just relax for the rest of the morning around the flat before making up a picnic to take and eat along the riverbank.

About 1pm they set off to test Irene's newly injected foot and finding the River Ouse, they sauntered along the banks unsure whether the lovely sunny weather was going to desert them since there were a few clouds hovering about. Happily for them it remained dry and hot and after eating their picnic lunch they lay and dozed in the sunshine on the riverbank. Re-covering their wits they resumed their ramble and came upon a long field full of corn on the cob (maize) which grew to a height of about 6 to 7 feet, where they stopped to take photos as they hadn't seen corn so high before.

On the way back they happened upon a pub called Tom Cobleigh's and as it was now 6 o'clock and they were in need of some refreshment they went in for a drink and ended up having dinner there, followed by a couple of Barley Wines. By 8 o'clock they thought that it was time to make a move as they still had quite a long way to go and after the Barley Wines they found it hard going for the next hour.

They were very pleased when the flat hove into view and exhausted from their efforts decided upon an early night. June fell into her bed and was asleep as soon as her head hit the pillow, whilst Irene opted for a soak in the bath before retiring.

Thursday

They were disappointed to wake to a cold and overcast day and were later getting up than they had planned, since they wanted to beat the crowds to the Jorvik museum. Dragging themselves into consciousness at 8 o'clock they had a quick breakfast and caught the number 32 bus at 9 o'clock into the centre of York where they joined the queue (not too long) at the museum. They had a short wait and were soon wandering along the replicated streets of old York in Viking times, accompanied by a 'Viking' guide dressed as a fur trader.

York was built in AD71 by the Roman 9th legion and grew into an important trading city where the rivers Ouse (which was then tidal and gave access to the North Sea) and Foss met. It was named Eboracum and Constantine the Great was made Roman Emperor there in AD306. In AD867 Viking warriors came storming up the Ouse on the high tide and invaded with their 350 long boats, thus it was re-named York which was derived from Jorvik or Yorwik.

As they meandered through the reconstructed narrow cobbled streets they were privy to the smells, sights and sounds which would have pervaded the streets in the Viking era. Actors and artisans were re-enacting scenes from this time which made it come very much to life for them, since replicas have been faithfully copied from skulls and clothing remains found on the site by The York Archaeological Trust which was founded in 1972. The Coppergate Dig of 1979 on the site of an old sweet factory revealed the remains of 10th century Viking-age buildings, in all 40,000 well preserved everyday objects were discovered.

At about 12 o'clock they left the museum and made their way to the Elim Pentecostal church where they refreshed themselves with cups of tea. They noticed that they sold home-made soup and made a mental note to return there for lunch.

They then went on a guided tour of Barley Hall, which was originally built in 1360 as a town house for Nostell Priory. It was extended in 1430 and later was owned by William Snawsell, Lord Mayor of York and local goldsmith. By the 17th century the house had been divided into several dwellings and an internal corridor became a public short cut and is still a public right of way to the present day. The Hall was purchased by The York Archaeological Trust in 1987 and was restored to its former glory and opened to the public in 1993. They wandered through the rooms, particularly admiring The Great Hall with its stunning high ceiling, beautiful timber frames and the famously rare window made from deer horn.

After the tour they returned to the Elim Pentecostal church where they enjoyed delicious home-made soup with fresh crusty rolls and rested for a while. From there they made their way to the Castle Museum, which started out as two prisons in the 18th century, its most famous prisoner being Dick Turpin who was hanged there for horse stealing in 1739. It contains room settings from different periods, displays of historical objects such as toys, armour, weapons, industrial machinery, farming equipment and household paraphernalia. It is best known for its re-created Victorian Street Kirkgate with its rows of shops with lighting and sounds to evoke the sights and sounds of the era. The contents of the shops were collected by a Doctor John L Kirk who founded the museum and wanted to keep these objects safe for future generations. They spent a very interesting couple of hours perusing the exhibits before heading to the museum coffee bar for their usual cup of tea and cakes!

They needed some carrots to accompany their evening meal of mince, so they looked around and found the outdoor market near to the Shambles and made their purchases before catching the number 32 bus back to the flat.

Having eaten their simple but delicious meal they listened to story tapes before retiring to their beds.

Friday

When they had prepared, cooked and eaten breakfast, June wrote up the diary whilst Irene did the washing up. Chores completed they set off to catch the bus into York city centre where they looked for the post office to buy stamps for their postcards which they intended to send to their families (and Mabel of course).

They thought that it would be a good idea to have an overview of York, so they caught the open top bus which took them on a tour of the city which cost £4 each. They were able to get on and off the bus if they came to a place that they wanted to stop and see. They toured all the way around the city listening to the fascinating commentary from the guide and taking photographs of the stunning buildings.

The bus dropped them off near Bootham Bar gate in order to do the traditional walk around the Wall. The Romans and the Anglo-Danish raised the earth ramparts and they were strengthened by the Normans. These formed the foundations of the existing wall which was built in medieval times. The Romans built the original wall and substantial parts still remain amongst the carefully restored and maintained medieval wall, which is open to all to walk around during the day, but which is closed to the public at dusk. The wall which encircles the old city is 3 miles long and since they had lots more to fit into the day they only walked part of it and as it was lunch time, they descended the steps at Micklegate Bar. Traditionally this was the monarch's entrance to the city and was where traitors' heads were displayed as a deterrent to aspiring traitors!

They found a cosy café and had a light lunch since they planned to have tea and cakes before going on a ghost walk, the advert for which they had spotted previously. After lunch they again caught the tour bus and alighted near to the river Foss where they walked along the snickelways and the riverbank. It was a cool day so they didn't linger by the river for too long, but returned to the Shambles area where they went to a tea shop overlooking the market and had tea and cakes (just to keep them going!). They then wandered along to the shopping centre to buy some souvenirs before making the obligatory visit to the majestic York Minster.

This cathedral is the fourth one to be built on this site, the first being in the 7th century and the present one having been built between 1220AD and

1472AD. This magnificent building is to the west of the city, close to the city walls and positively shimmers with a golden glow when the sun shines upon it. The stained glass windows (of which there are 128) date from the 12th to the present century and are the Minster's most striking feature. It is the largest medieval structure in the United Kingdom and was the brain child of Archbishop de Grey. Before leaving they once more admired the opulent ceilings via the large mirrors on trolleys (to save them from having neckache!) and the stunning rose window.

Leaving the Minster they headed for the pick-up point at Minster Gate for the ghost walk. The guide gathered the walkers together, and after setting the scene with gruesome tales of marauding Romans and Vikings, set off around the streets, stopping at places reputed to have ghostly visitors and strange happenings through the centuries. They felt that the violent history of York warranted a few spine chilling mysteries.

Afterwards, tentatively making their way back to the flat in the dark along the river bank, they looked nervously over their shoulders from time to time and were very relieved when they reached it.

Upon arriving back at the flat and after a reviving cup of tea, they prepared and ate dinner before packing their bags for departure the following day. They fell into their beds tired but happy (and maybe a little apprehensive after the ghost walk) and were soon asleep.

Saturday

After breakfast they finished packing their bags, tidied up the flat and at 10.40am hired a taxi to the National Express coach station where they caught the 11.30am coach to Birmingham. The coach stopped for a 'comfort break' in Leeds, so as there was an outdoor market nearby they got out and had a good mooch around.

They arrived at Digbeth coach station at 4.20pm where Buz collected them and took them to the Scouts Open Day before getting back home about 6pm. They thoroughly enjoyed their York Adventure, but agreed that they would have enjoyed it even more had Mabel been with them.

12. South Woodchester

2nd to 5th May 1997

They decided that they would like to return to the Cotswolds again (the area in which they had their first 'Adventure' in 1980) and since Mabel's son David was working near Stroud at the time, they thought that they would ask him for a lift on his way to work. He agreed to take them on the Friday and collect them the following Monday as this would fit in with his shifts. Irene looked for some accommodation in South Woodchester because it was a convenient place for David to drop them off and she booked rooms in Home Farm for them.

Friday
At 11.30am David collected them and set out for Home Farm, arriving at 12.50pm, where he helped them to unload their bags and take them into the house, before going on to work.

They were greeted by Elizabeth Ewart-James who showed them to their rooms, Irene and Mabel were sharing a twin room and June was in a single room. After unpacking their bags they went out into the garden and sitting in the shade of the trees, ate the picnic which they had brought with them and Elizabeth came out with cups of tea for them. It was very hot and after sunbathing for a while June started to burn, so they all covered themselves with sun cream and changing into shorts and sandals set out for a walk to Nailsworth.

Walking down Frogsmore Lane at the side of Home Farm it wasn't long before they stopped for a mug of tea from a refreshment van, in a lay-by, just before they reached an entrance to the cycle and walking track, which until the 1980s was an old railway line. It was a pleasant cool walk along the track which was shaded by tall trees, and approaching Nailsworth they rested on a bench in a memorial garden underneath a clock. Pressing on they found the

Tourist Information Office and armed themselves with leaflets about the area before looking for a Boots shop, where June bought a pair of sunglasses.

They set out to find the famous local ice cream and were told in the Traidcraft shop that it was sold on the top of Selsey Common! They found a café selling Sidoli's ice cream and settled for that, sitting outside in the sun and enjoying it. June mooched around and found a Health Centre where they could avail themselves of an aromatherapy massage for £25! They passed that offer up and settled for a wander around the shops and a look at the Egypt Mill restaurant and Bistro bar – very atmospheric, but a touch pricey for them.

After a leisurely stroll back along the old railway line, June soaked in the bath whilst Irene and Mabel read their books, then they all got changed and ambled amiably down the road to The Ram Inn for dinner, which Elizabeth had recommended. June had lamb lasagne, white chocolate fudge cake and barley wine, whilst Irene tucked into a 16oz steak with chips (helped by June) a pint of lager and half a lemon syllabub. Mabel devoured a beef and mushroom pie and chips, half a pint of lager and the other half of the lemon syllabub. Irene and June finished off with coffee and whiskey and they all staggered back to Home Farm and fell into their respective beds, where Irene and June slept like logs, whilst Mabel tossed about for a while and read her book.

Saturday

They awoke to the aromatic smell of bacon cooking and after a cup of tea (made by Irene in the bedroom) trotted down to breakfasts of fruit juice, cereals, bacon, eggs, mushrooms, sausages and tomatoes, followed by toast and marmalade, tea and coffee. Breakfast over, Mabel and Irene went to the post office (the front wall of which was covered in a profusion of purple wisteria flowers) to purchase provisions to sustain them on their jaunts for the following three days, as the local shops were closed on the Sunday and Monday (the latter being a bank holiday). Back at the house they all set about preparing a picnic for later on and packing their rucksacks. Since it was a gloriously sunny day they changed into shorts and sandals and set off to walk to Stroud via Selsey Common.

Along the way they saw a great variety of wildflowers and thoroughly appreciated the scenic views, over the rolling hills and dales, marvelling at the beauty of this typical English countryside. There was an abundance of bluebells, daisies, buttercups and wild orchids, and with the skylarks calling overhead; it was the perfect spot for their picnic, sitting on the brow of the hill overlooking the valley below.

12. SOUTH WOODCHESTER 1997

***1997** June and Irene and wild garlic near Selsey Common in May*

***1997** The famous Mary Quant capes, Slad Valley*

As they continued along the way they were astounded at the carpets of wild garlic spreading across the floor of the woodland, with their bank of white flowers resembling a snow drift, stretching right down to the river banks. There was an amazing mixture of smells: garlic, wildflowers and the mayflower with its nutty aroma from the hawthorn trees which shaded the path along the side of the canal. They saw moorhens and mallards, all male, they wondered where the females were – sitting on nests perhaps?

Sainsbury's island brought them back to the concrete jungle and after another short walk along the canal, and obtaining directions from passers-by, they arrived in Stroud town centre, where they were hailed by their landlady and her son Robin! They looked around a charity shop where June purchased a ferrule for her walking stick and both Irene and June bought sunhats.

After a very pleasant interchange with the young lady in the Tourist Information Office, who convinced them that it would be a doddle to walk to Painswick, they planned to go there the following day but realised that they would have to walk there as there were no buses running either Sunday or Monday. A well earned cup of tea was called for, so they found a little café and refreshed themselves, discussing their plans for the next day.

Whilst strolling back via the canal bank and disused railway track, they took a diversion (just to see where it led) and were pleasantly surprised to find themselves at the site of an old church. There was very little left of the building, just an archway and part of a wall with a window in it, this was covered in ivy, but the avenue of yew trees leading up to the church were still very much alive and in evidence. There were many large and unusual looking gravestones and tombs and a large square patch of grass which looked as though it may have had a building on the site at one time. They speculated upon this and commented upon its unusual position within the site. They later discovered its origins.

They found themselves to be in North Woodchester and walking along the road passed the war memorial and The Ram public house before arriving back at their lodgings. There they had a quick wash (especially their feet!) and a change of clothes before setting out for their evening meal at The Ram. Mabel chose lamb lasagne, chips and lager; Irene opted for stew and dumplings with lager, but June came unstuck when choosing pheasant, as it was bitter and tough. Happily the landlord refunded her money and she filled up on garlic bread and two barley wines, which was no great hardship! They all shared a chocolate roulade between them and left early with the intention of making a start on the jigsaw puzzle which Irene had brought with her.

12. SOUTH WOODCHESTER 1997

They strolled back along the road admiring once more the beautiful wisteria outside the post office, this time lit by the moon and street lamps. Arriving back at the house they divested themselves of their jackets and settled down to do the jigsaw puzzle. They duly started upon this, with Irene reading out the mystery which they were meant to solve upon completion of the puzzle. However the table was too small to accommodate the 750 piece puzzle, so they just completed the sides and went to bed!

Sunday

They awoke to a dull and overcast day, although quite warm, so after another tasty cooked breakfast and donning their boots (except the intrepid Irene, who didn't mind cold wet feet) and carrying their Mary Quant capes in their rucksacks they set out for Painswick. Once again they walked along the railway track and canal towpath heading towards Stroud, however as they approached Stroud it started to rain, so they ducked into a little pub and asked for tea and coffee! (not normally sold in pubs in those days). Well there were no cafes open, so what else could they do?

The landlady was very obliging and took pity on these three bedraggled old ladies, providing them with hot drinks and allowing them to dry off. The other customers in the pub were very friendly and they soon got into conversation with them. Apparently they were planning a 'Bad Taste' evening and asked them for some suggestions and since June had done one some years ago there was quite an interchange of ideas. The more they thought about it, the more they liked the idea of having a 'Bad Taste' party for the Home-Start Volunteers in the summer – maybe a barbeque at Irene's house? They joked that Mabel would almost certainly be off on one of her many holidays and not be able to be there.

Once the rain had stopped they set off again, but didn't get very far as it was by now lunch time, so after finding a little park, with a bench just the right size for a three person picnic, they ate the sandwiches that they had prepared earlier.

After lunch they explored the grounds of the nearby church, and June (who was well ahead on the points game – a game where points are allotted to the person who spots anything unusual or of particular interest), gained LOADS of points by spotting the place where John Wesley had preached, standing on a butcher's box, in The Shambles. Photos were taken before they headed up the Slad Road and into Slad Valley which is 'Cider with Rosie' country and where its author Laurie Lee was still living.

Not long after this 'Adventure' they heard that Laurie Lee had sadly died.

June raced away on points by spotting a fox at close quarters, sitting in some long grass. Since it had started to rain again they stopped to put on their Mary Quant capes. It must be said that they looked quite a sight, the three of them in identical multi-coloured capes straggling about the countryside in the pouring rain, 'The Last of the Summer Wine' TV show didn't compare! They must have raised many a smile, and indeed one cheeky woman admitted, as they passed a group of people, that they had been having a good laugh at them!

As it was raining quite steadily they took cover in a bus shelter, next to The Woolpack pub which was closed (shame!) and a red public telephone box. After a while, when they had shaken off the excess water from their capes, they became aware that they were being observed by the family which lived in the house opposite.

Now this was no ordinary house, but an old schoolhouse and the school master's house which had been extended to adjoin it. Consequently it was a very long house with about ten windows facing them. Members of the family kept appearing and re-appearing at the various windows to have a look at them and the two teenagers, a boy and a girl, were not able to conceal their delight and amusement at such a strange sight with dad peering over the top of his glasses in disbelief! Mum was more discreet and sneaked a look by peeping around the curtains.

By this time, **they** were in hysterics, laughing at **their** antics, then – the phone rang in the telephone box next to them, and they just **knew** that it was the family in the house opposite. After egging each other on to answer it, they all bottled out and then speculated as to whether the family was going to invite them into their house, out of the rain, for a much needed cup of tea. For years to come, they rued the day that they missed an opportunity like that on an adventure!

Because the rain was pretty relentless and the road in front of them looked grey and bleak, they decided to call it a day, despite having not quite reached Painswick (they were somewhere in Slad). They set off walking fairly briskly back to Stroud, where Mabel's leg started to hurt, so they took the easy option and got a taxi back to base, deciding that it was a good £6 worth!

Back at the house June was delegated to get a jug of milk from Elizabeth, so that they could have a cup of tea, and while Elizabeth was pouring the milk, she noticed the badge on June's sweat shirt and asked what it signified. June explained that it represented the national voluntary organisation and charity

12. SOUTH WOODCHESTER 1997

'Home-Start' and that she was employed as a manager for one of the schemes in Birmingham. When she described the ethos of the scheme, supporting families with young children, Elizabeth, who told her that she was a social worker, expressed an interest in having a similar scheme in the Stroud area, to support the families that she worked with. June promised to send her details of whom to contact in the national organisation in order to set up a scheme, and some years later was informed that indeed more than one scheme had been set up as a result of this chance conversation.

They eventually got their cups of tea, and after washing and changing, they trod the now familiar path to The Ram. Mabel had lamb lasagne (again – must have been good!) and lager, Irene chose Irish scampi and chips with lager, and June had half a pint of peel-on prawns with barley wine. They all shared garlic bread, chocolate fudge cake, Mississippi mud pie, and rum and raisin cheesecake with cream and ice cream.

After stuffing their faces they took part in the pub quiz, well – suffice it to say that they didn't win, in fact they came last; apparently the team which comes last normally comes in for a fair amount of ragging (which Irene discovered after chatting up one of the locals) but in deference to their age, they were spared the humiliation. The majority of The Ram's clientele were the local students, so they didn't feel too disgraced in losing to them, it amused them no end when they later found out that the quiz questions had been 'cleaned up' out of respect for the three old gals.

They had a very pleasant evening with friendly people and staggered back tired but happy, where June nearly fell asleep in the bath and went to sleep with her wet hair wrapped up in a towel, and Mabel read her book in bed with her eyes closed! No-one heard Irene snore that night!!

Monday

Once again Elizabeth did them proud with a delicious cooked breakfast and when they had eaten they packed their bags ready to go home (shame!). They set out for a shortish walk, in very mixed weather, a bit cooler than the previous day with some sunshine and light showers. Mabel and June opted to wear shoes, but the indomitable Irene ploughed through the wet fields in her sandals.

They walked towards North Woodchester through a field of buttercups, passing through a squeeze stile (which was *indeed* a squeeze after all of their visits to The Ram) where they encountered a man with his greyhound at the top of the hill. He told them that the sunken square of grass which they had noticed at the ruined church was a Roman mosaic pavement, which 'the powers that be' have chosen to keep covered up (for protection perhaps?). As they headed towards the ruins to have another look at it, they came across the Parish Church and Mabel recalled that her friend's daughter was married there and that *her* daughter Marion was a bridesmaid at the wedding. After looking around the church they continued on their way to the ruins once again.

By the time they had arrived at the old graveyard, Mabel's knee was becoming very painful and she had to sit and rest it while June and Irene explored the area further and took some photos. Very carefully, June 'excavated' an inch of the area which the man said was a Roman pavement with a plastic teaspoon (which she just happened to have in her bag) and after scraping down a little way she encountered a hard surface. Irene and June examined a piece of what *could* have been the Roman pavement then very carefully replaced and restored the patch, after taking a few more photos.

Mabel's knee was still very sore so June offered her the use of her walking stick and along with her own stick she managed to hobble very slowly to The Ram trying to avoid bending her knee. June went on ahead to reserve a table and order lunch as they were a bit behind in their schedule and had to be back at the house for when David arrived to collect them.

Irene and June had the roast beef dinner and Mabel had cheese on a granary roll, they all chose strawberry cheesecake for dessert, this was all consumed with the usual lagers and barley wine. The food and company were excellent and they determined to return to this friendly pub sometime. Lunch over, Mabel and June walked slowly back to Home Farm, whilst Irene finished off her pint and got a lift back in David's car, as he had arrived at the farmhouse and gone off to look for them at the pub.

They said their 'goodbyes' to Elizabeth, who had looked after them very well and set off with David at 2.30pm. After spending the journey recounting and recording the three days events (in between Irene's little sleeps) they arrived at June's house at 3.45pm. They all thanked David for making this break possible and after she had done her unpacking, June typed up the notes from the Adventure, noting that it took longer to do the typing than it had taken to travel to Stroud and back! A good time was had by one and all and they hoped that Mabel's knee would mend quickly and not put her off going on future 'Adventures'.

13. Torbay

29th August to 2nd September 1997

Mabel was suffering from asthma so was not able to go on this Adventure and since the house in Torquay had already been booked, Irene and June decided to invite a friend of June's, Pauline, to take Mabel's place. Pauline was used to going on walks with June and wasn't all that surprised to be invited to join the friends on an adventure and was thrilled to be included since she didn't have a holiday planned. As she was not relaxed travelling by car, they decided to go on the train.

Friday

Since Pauline lived not far from June, at 8.20am June collected her and returned to her house, where at 8.45am Rachel, Irene's eldest daughter, picked them up. All three then went to Irene's house to collect her before setting off to New Street Station in Birmingham. Waving Rachel off and thanking her for the lift they caught the 10.28am train arriving in Torquay at 1.45pm. They had taken a packed lunch which they ate on the train so were raring to go when they arrived at Torquay Station, where they caught a taxi to 'Cintra'.

As it was Pauline's first time at the lovely big house, she was quite blown away by the house and gardens which she described as 'magnificent'. They were pleased that her first impression was more than favourable and added to that was the warm welcome which they received from Sylvia, the landlady, who was waiting to greet them as they drew up. Each of them had brought some food items with them, but they were very glad that Sylvia had offered to get them milk and bread since it was less for them to carry. Removing their luggage from the taxi they followed Sylvia up the stairs to their apartment where they sorted out their sleeping arrangements, Irene having the big bedroom and June and Pauline sharing the bed-sitting room.

After unpacking and putting the food items in the kitchen, they re-joined Sylvia downstairs, as she had invited them to have a cup of tea with her in the garden. She explained that her husband Ian had injured his back and was staying in bed for a few days, hoping that this would help with his recovery. Normally Ian would have come and greeted them and shown them around the gardens, talking about his latest project and offering them cuttings from his shrubs and plants. This pleasant task fell to Sylvia and they had a very enjoyable afternoon sitting in the sun drinking tea, inspecting the gardens, explaining Mabel's situation and catching up with family news.

The evening was taken up with unpacking and strolling down the hill to Torquay Harbour where they bought fish and chips from their favourite chippy. They sat eating them on the harbour wall whilst watching the boats bobbing about on the sea and the lights coming on around the bay, illuminating the town and reflecting in the water. After watching the sun setting on the horizon they introduced Pauline to the long haul back up the hill to Cintra huffing and puffing as they were out of practise with hill walking. A well deserved cup of tea was enjoyed before retiring for the night.

Saturday

They awoke to a lovely sunny day so decided to go for a long walk along the beach near Babbacombe. After a delicious bacon and egg breakfast they donned their shorts and sunhats, picked up their walking sticks and with the waterproof map holder slung around Irene's neck set off to walk to Babbacombe. Going up Braddons Hill Road they found their way through the housing estate which leads to Babbacombe Theatre. When they got there they looked to see what was showing in the following few days. There was a variety show on called 'Alive with Laughter and Music' and as they all like comedy and music they went in and booked tickets for the Monday evening. Making their way to the steps past the theatre, they descended them to join the cliff path leading to Oddicombe Beach. Once on the beach they looked for a quiet spot to lie and sunbathe, spreading out Irene and June's Mary Quant capes to sit on.

After sunbathing for a while they played at skimming flat stones across the top of the waves to see who could get the most bounces. This energetic pastime over they went for a paddle in the sea to cool off their feet before having lunch. Clearing away the picnic things and gathering up their belongings they continued along the coastal path to Petit Tor Point. They scrambled up the narrow pathway to the top of the cliff with the aid of their trusty walking sticks

13. TORBAY 1997

1997 Irene and Pauline playing poo-sticks in Torbay

1997 Pauline and June on Babbacombe Beach

and collapsed on the Point near a golf club where they admired the panoramic view of two beaches and the sparkling blue of the sea.

For some unknown reason, which is lost in the mists of time, they played a game of throwing their walking sticks across the grass to see whose stick would fly the furthest. The starting point was a bench which they stood upon, then hurled their sticks towards the golf course. For some reason this activity seemed highly amusing to them and they fell about giggling and being generally ridiculous when a group of walkers appeared over the edge of the cliff and were no doubt taken aback at the sight of three women slinging their walking sticks about and collapsing with laughter. They all muttered 'good afternoon' and they scurried off leaving them to their midsummer madness.

After a discreet visit to the bushes (they contemplated asking to use the facilities in the golf club but chickened out) they walked passed the golf course and onto Petit Tor Road following through to St. Marychurch Road. They continued on through Ellacombe by a series of small roads, alleyways and Brewery Park where they happily discovered some large pinecones. Having just walked through a golf course and seen the golfers playing, they decided to try their hand at golf, but in the event they played a sort of hockey, passing the pinecone to one another with upside down walking sticks. This seemed a jolly good idea to them and despite the curious glances of passers-by they made their way in this fashion along the streets until they came to the top of Braddons Hill Road.

They noticed a lady watching them from her garden who swiftly disappeared and re-appeared in her bedroom window. They found out later from Sylvia that her neighbour had gone to fetch her husband to show him the amusing sight of three ladies walking down the middle of the road passing a large pinecone to one another with their walking sticks. Still playing 'hockey' Pauline whacked the pinecone under a parked car, so June and Irene tried their best to retrieve it but to no avail. After several attempts to fish it out from under the car they abandoned it, deciding that it was 'game over'.

Worn out from their efforts they had to fortify themselves with cups of tea before setting about the task of getting dinner ready. Baked potatoes were popped into the oven and eaten when cooked with grated cheese and salad followed by apple pie and custard. Several glasses of wine and a few crossword puzzles later they climbed into their beds and slept the sleep of the exhausted.

Sunday
Irene was outside in the garden smoking a cigarette, whilst June and Pauline were dragging themselves into consciousness when they heard Sylvia calling them from

13. TORBAY 1997

downstairs. She sounded quite distressed, so Pauline hurried down the stairs to see what the matter was, calling to June to follow. She told them that Princess Diana and Dodi El Fayed had been in a car accident in Paris and that it sounded very serious. They were a bit stunned by the news and sat on the bottom of the stairs while Sylvia went back into her sitting room to check whether there was any more news. At this point Irene came in from the garden at the same time as Sylvia returned from her room and announced that Princess Diana had died. They were all very shocked by the news and found it hard to believe that Diana, who was such an icon and a part of their British way of life, was no longer there to be loved and admired by the nation, as she undoubtedly had been.

Not wishing to believe this awful news they sat on the stairs and speculated as to whether she might still be alive and desperately wished that it was so. As more news of the crash came through, it was clear that there was no hope that either her or Dodi were still alive, but miraculously Diana's bodyguard was alive although unconscious, the driver having died instantly. For about an hour they sat on the stairs talking to Sylvia, each of them recalling their own impressions of the princess and what she meant to them personally. With heavy hearts they tore themselves away, went back upstairs and prepared and ate breakfast (for which they had little appetite).

The original plan for the day was to go to Brixham on the ferry and although they felt dispirited and very sad, they decided to carry on with the planned visit and make the best of the day. So, after breakfast they walked down Braddons Hill Road to the ferry and sailed off to the lovely old fishing village of Brixham. As they approached the sun was shining on the old pastel coloured houses lining the harbour, the fishing boats and the yachts were bobbing about in the quay and this helped to lift their spirits a little, but they were left with a feeling of profound sadness all day.

They decided to have a look around The Golden Hind which was very small but incredibly interesting. The carvings were very skilfully done especially the figurehead of the leaping golden hind. The cramped conditions left a lot to be desired particularly when they realised the vast distances that the ship would have travelled. The tour over, they sat on the harbour wall eating fish and chips and occasionally throwing a few scraps to the screeching seagulls which were wheeling around overhead.

After a while they set off to walk the mile and a half to Berry Head, passing Freshwater and Shoalstone Beaches, rejoining the Berry Head Road for the short walk to Berry Head Hotel. There was a pavement café nearby so they sat down and had a cup of tea before they re-joined the coastal path which climbs up to the Berry Head Country Park. There they explored the Northern Fort which was built in 1803 and whose ruins consist of an armoury, a jailhouse, the remains of a barracks and fortification walls. Pauline was impressed by the big replica cannons facing out to sea on the ramparts on the left hand side.

They wandered over to the lighthouse area and sat looking at the splendid panoramic view around the headland. Whilst Irene had a little nap on a bench June and Pauline crept very close to the edge of the cliff and lay down peering over the top at the guillemots wheeling about below. This was a very surreal experience and June had a strong urge to jump off and fly with them, fortunately she resisted the urge!

Once she had woken up from her little nap, Irene went over to the other two and held on to their ankles in case they fell off. They were looking at the nests to see whether they contained any young birds, but the breeding season being March to July they were bound to be disappointed. The guillemots were known locally as the Brixham penguins because of their black and white colouring and ability to dive down into the water 160 feet to catch fish.

After a while they retraced their steps and made their way back to Brixham harbour, where they bought ice creams before catching the bus back to Torquay and began the walk up the hill to Cintra. After a short rest on the bench half way up Braddons Hill Road they finally made it back and were glad to sit in the garden for a while relating the day's events to Sylvia and discussing the death of Princess Diana over a pot of tea. They prepared and ate steak and salad for dinner followed by strawberries and clotted cream which they had bought in Torquay on the way back. The evening was spent in heavy hearted silence reading books, doing jigsaw and crossword puzzles before retiring for the night.

Monday

The day was very dull and overcast, so after the usual bacon and egg breakfast they gathered up their wet weather gear and set off to walk to Cockington Village via Torquay's front, passing the Princess Theatre and Tor Abbey grounds. It rained on and off as they walked along Seaway Lane to Cockington, but not enough to deter the intrepid trio who dived into Rose Cottage Tea Gardens for a sustaining cup of tea. Then they visited the Forge where Pauline spotted some small chrome covered horseshoes and they all bought some to give to various friends and family. June and Irene were happy to show Pauline their favourite places which included the magnificent cricket pitch which sweeps across the front of the traditional manor house where they found a bench and sat down to eat their picnic lunch.

13. TORBAY 1997

Pauline was delighted with the scenery as they enjoyed their sandwiches and looked around at the splendid old manor house, the lovely little church and the statuesque trees which surround the whole area. The peace and quiet was only disturbed by the blackbirds, thrushes and numerous song birds calling to each other from the branches. Lunch over they wandered around to the rear of The Court and entered through the huge oak gate into the Organic Garden. Pauline was very knowledgeable about wildflowers and they spent a very happy and informative hour pottering around inside the walled garden, inspecting the pond for fish, newts and frogs and smelling the herbs. Again it was very peaceful and relaxing as there was no-one there but them and they enjoyed having it to themselves. Leaving the walled garden they made their way past the stables and admired the horses in the yard before moving on to the formal rose gardens at the rear of the manor house.

Strolling around the rose beds and inhaling the heady perfume of the flowers, they felt that it was time for another cup of tea. Upon entering The Court tea shop they discovered that it was under new management and were disappointed to find that there was no longer clotted cream to go with their scones. The new regime only provided whipped cream, which is not the same thing at all! The waitresses were not (as previously) dressed in black and white, with frilly aprons and the blue and white checked table cloths had disappeared. They were a bit fed up with these unwelcome changes as they had been telling Pauline what a lovely Olde English atmosphere they had enjoyed there previously.

Nevertheless they managed to eat and enjoy their scones and looking on the bright side, it was after all better for their expanding waistlines! Tearing themselves away from the village which they have come to love over the years they walked back down Seaway Lane and into Torquay. Once more they tackled the climb up the hill to Cintra where they made a quick snack of beans on toast as they were going out for the evening.

After a wash and brush up and change of clothes they walked through Ellacombe to Babbacombe to go to the Theatre. The performance started at 8.15pm and before taking their seats in the stalls they ordered three glasses of wine to drink during the interval. There was a variety show on called 'Alive with Laughter and Music' which, looking back, seems very ironic considering the previous day's tragic news. The show was excellent and despite their underlying sadness they managed to enjoy it, joining in with the sing-a-longs, laughing at the comedian and marvelling at the skill of the magician. Tired and weary they caught the bus home where, after a nightcap, they retired to their beds, deciding to leave their packing until the morning.

Tuesday

Breakfast over they cleared away and set about packing their bags and tidying up the rooms prior to their departure for home. They strolled around the garden with Sylvia and Ian who had come out to say goodbye. He had been lying flat on his back all week and this was the only time that they saw him on that visit. Princess Diana was of course the main topic of conversation and they all still felt very sad at her passing.

They went back into the house for a snack lunch before the arrival of Charles (Irene's father-in-law) at 1.30pm to take them to Torquay station. Whilst they gathered up their belongings Charles chatted to Sylvia under the clematis draped pergola, where he told her about the time that he worked at The Torquay Times newspaper office when the family first moved from Birmingham. After hugging Sylvia and bidding her farewell, they promised to return the following year with Mabel and set off for the station where they caught the 2.38pm train, waving goodbye to Charles through the window.

Once safely ensconced on the train, June phoned Buz on her mobile phone to let him know that they would be arriving at 5.54pm at New Street Station. After an uneventful journey, reading books and doing crossword puzzles they were met by Buz (who can always be relied upon) and taken to their respective homes, where they bade one another farewell.

Irene and June agreed that despite not having their friend Mabel with them (which always made them feel as though they had a limb missing) Pauline had been excellent company and they had enjoyed having her along. The adventure was undoubtedly marred by the tragic news of the Paris car crash (they would always remember where they were when they heard the awful news) but they managed to enjoy most of their time in that beautiful and scenic part of England.

14. Torbay

30th August to 6th September 1998

The previous year Mabel was unable to go to Torquay, but this year the three friends were pleased to be back together again and they decided to return to Torbay since Sylvia and Ian were happy to accommodate them again.

They opted to travel by train as Buz's dad had moved back to Birmingham. It seemed unfair to expect Buz to drive all that way and not have a break before driving back, since his father was no longer living down there. Also Doug was coming by train to join Mabel for a week when Irene and June left.

Sunday
Early in the morning Buz picked them all up and took them to New Street Station to catch the train to Torquay. Whilst on the train they talked about where they should go during the week, so getting out the Torbay map they set about making a plan. One of the places they were determined to return to was the woods with Brunel's statue in it, which Irene had not seen. On arrival at Torquay Station they hailed a taxi which took them to Cintra, where Sylvia and Ian were waiting to greet them. Sylvia had very kindly done some shopping for them, since they hadn't come in a car and couldn't carry all of their provisions for the week. They sorted out what they would have for dinner and packed the rest away.

Once their bags were unpacked and cups of tea consumed, they took a stroll around the gardens and inspected the trees in the 'secret garden'. It all seemed so familiar to them, having been there on four adventures previously, and of course Mabel had been going there with Doug for many years before that.

After dinner they relaxed over a few glasses of wine and made a start on a jigsaw puzzle.

Monday (Bank Holiday)

After their early morning cup of tea they remembered that it was the first anniversary of the death of Princess Diana. This made them feel very sad and they talked about her and the way in which she died whilst they ate breakfast and June and Irene recalled how last year Sylvia had told them about Diana's accident. After breakfast they realised that although Sylvia had bought them quite a few staple items and they had taken some food with them, there were still a few things that they needed for dinner.

They headed off up the hill and made their way down the steps which brought them out by the post office in Torquay where they went to the indoor market to look for a butchers and greengrocers. Having chosen some steaks and vegetables they looked for a bakery to buy some naughty cakes and Cornish pasties. Shopping completed they climbed up the steps and headed back home, having shared out the shopping to spread the weight between them.

When they arrived at Cintra, Sylvia was in the garden, so they stopped to say 'hello' and said that they would put their shopping away, make a cup of tea and come and join her in the garden. This done they all settled down around a white wrought iron table and shared a pot of tea and chocolate biscuits. The main topic for discussion was Princess Diana and the circumstances surrounding her death; they still found it difficult even after a year to believe that she was dead and felt very sad. They weren't really in the mood to go out walking and all just wanted to sit around quietly so they got out the pack of cards and played Patience and Rummy, appreciating the sunshine.

After an al fresco lunch they lay in the garden, swung on the swing, wandered in the secret garden and read books. Despite the sad topic of conversation, they enjoyed spending time with Sylvia (and occasionally Ian who was watering the numerous flower beds). When supper-time arrived they went indoors and cooked the steaks, eating them whilst watching the memorial programme to Princess Diana on television, then had an early night.

Tuesday

Having had a lazy day yesterday they decided to walk to Paignton, since the sun was bright and welcoming and they felt like a dip in the sea. Passing through Torquay they enjoyed the scenery along the way, the moored yachts, dredgers, pleasure boats and water-skiers, there always seemed to be something to stop and look at.

14. TORBAY 1998

When they reached Paignton they walked along the front and stopped at Preston Sands. Laying out their Mary Quant capes having changed into their swimming costumes, they settled down to have a sun bathe before tentatively dipping their toes into the sea to test the temperature of the water. When they decided that it was warm enough to go in, June and Irene went in for a swim whilst Mabel settled for a paddle.

Once dried off, Irene fell asleep in a deck chair which she had hired earlier, while Mabel and June went to the beach café and bought hot cheese pasties and tea for lunch. Making the most of the day, they stayed on the beach until quite late then caught the bus back to Torquay.

Once back at Cintra they cooked and ate dinner, then watched television for a while before retiring.

Wednesday

Despite the fact that it was a bit dull and overcast they decided to go to Cockington and hoped that the weather would improve later in the day. Packing up their rucksacks, after breakfast they picked up their sticks and headed off to Cockington. Passing through Torquay they made their way up Cockington Lane, stopping when they got to the forge. They went into a small thatched roofed shop and bought some postcards to send to their families.

It had started to rain so they went to The Drum Inn for lunch, which consisted of lovely crusty baguettes and shandy; they lingered there for a while chatting to the locals and waiting for the rain to stop. After lunch they emerged from the pub and turning left continued on up Cockington Lane to walk across the fields which they hoped would eventually bring them out at the back of The Court. When they reached Nut Bush Lane they turned left and cut across the fields, heading in what they thought was the right direction. They had crossed a field with several horses in when a young woman led a horse through the gateway and stopped to talk to them when they admired it. She told them that the horse that she was leading had been hers since she was a young girl. When she went to college she said that she had sold the horse, but after finishing her course discovered that the horse was not being looked after properly, so she bought him back. It took several months of nurturing to restore the horse to its former healthy condition.

Pushing on towards The Court they came upon a small copse with apple trees in and thought that no-one would mind if they scrumped a few to eat. Following the footpath across the fields and along the edge of the woods they emerged near to the rear of the organic walled garden. Walking past the newly developed area they entered the walled garden and were disappointed that neither the lady who ran it nor 'Wesley' the volunteer were there. The garden looked a bit neglected and they wondered whether the same people were still tending it, so after a quick stroll around went back through the heavy oak door and made their way past the stables and headed for the rose garden.

They lingered longer in the rose garden inhaling the heady fragrant scent of the last few roses of summer, then carried on to the lovely little church and spent a while absorbing the peaceful atmosphere and admiring the stained glass windows.

Wandering back down to the forge area they looked for the Garden Tea House which they had spotted on a previous visit and where they had agreed to have a cream tea. They really indulged themselves as the scones were huge and there was an abundance of clotted cream and strawberry jam. They helped themselves to steaming cups of tea from a lovely old crock tea pot with a thatched cottage design, which matched the milk jug and sugar bowl. To their dismay the rain had started again, so they lingered over their tea, and discussed what to do next. They recalled that earlier on they had noticed a horse and carriage waiting for passengers to be ferried down to the sea front. Looking at one another they realised that they had all had the same thought, they often said that one day they would have a ride in one, and this apparently was that day!

Once the rain stopped and the sun came out they left the tea shop and walked back towards the forge area, where after taking a photo of Irene and Mabel by a carriage they climbed up into it and settled down to a pleasant ride down to the end of Cockington Lane. They all developed ideas of grandeur, with Mabel waving in a genteel manner to nobody in particular, and Irene fantasising that she was riding down The Mall nodding to the cheering crowds. They all had a good view over the hedge tops and felt that it was a good £2's worth.

Alighting from their lofty perch they walked across the road and descended to Livermead Beach where they sat on the rocks and watched the 'white horses' roll up and down the sands. After a while they commenced on their way along Tor Bay Road, stopping at the Tourist Information Centre to pick up leaflets and bus time-tables. They also popped into the theatre to see what was playing during the week that might appeal to them.

Making their way up the hill, they were quite glad to be back at the house where they spent the evening playing cards and Scrabble after preparing and

14. TORBAY 1998

eating dinner. Before retiring they agreed that it had been a very pleasant day, despite the lack of sunshine.

Thursday

In sharp contrast to the previous day, they awoke to a lovely sunny morning, so they thought that a walk to see the woods with Brunel's statue in might be a good idea. Before setting out, and after a lovely cooked breakfast, they wrote out the postcards which they had bought in Cockington the previous day, with a view to posting them somewhere along the way.

Putting their best feet forward they set off down the hill to the museum to catch the bus to Babbacombe. Once there they took the cliff path to Watcombe beach where they shrugged off their packs and lay down to sunbathe for a while before eating their picnics. After lunch they made their way up the footpath leading to the woods with the rocky outcrop which includes the Giant Rock. Irene, who had not seen these woods before, was quite delighted with them as the other two had been when they first saw them.

After a wander through the glades they returned to the path and made their way up the road towards the car park where they found the Victorian turning circle, used for turning around the horses and carriages. They looked around the circle which had become very overgrown and neglected and June and Mabel were sad that Irene hadn't seen it in 1994 when it had not long been preserved.

Continuing on towards the main road they headed towards Brunel Manor, crossing the road and entering the small housing estate. It wasn't long before they came to the gateway to the woods, and entering into its dark interior looked for the clearing where Brunel's statue stands along with the other three which are tributes to his achievements. Irene was very impressed with the statues and spent some time working out the different aspects of his works on the totem pole. She felt that it was a fitting memorial to the great man since they were carved out of a 65 foot, 13 ton Sequoia red wood tree which he had planted and was blown down in the infamous gales of 1990.

Brunel imported and planted many exotic trees and plants from around the world, such as Monkey Puzzle trees, and the Monterey Cypresses. Whilst admiring the carvings Mabel and June were disturbed to notice that they had deteriorated since they last saw them and felt that perhaps they should be protected for future generations to enjoy. They all took photographs of the statues and one another posing by them, before setting off around the perimeter of the woods to look for Brunel Manor.

THREE HAPPY WANDERERS

1998 Mabel and June by Brunel Manor

1998 Irene and Mabel, Cockington Village

14. TORBAY 1998

The Manor could be seen from the edge of the woods, so they stopped to peer over its wall and discovered that it was an hotel. Brunel purchased the land which included the woods and the (now) nearby housing estate with a view to building his retirement house. He discovered the area when he was surveying for the G.W.R. and was so impressed with the wonderful views across Torbay that he purchased the 26 acre plot of land. He designed the Manor House, grounds and gardens, but sadly didn't live to see the completion of the house which he was building. There didn't seem any way for them to get closer, so they skirted around it and eventually came to the main road which they crossed over to catch the bus back to Torquay harbour.

Since it was dusk by the time they got there they decided to go to a quaint little pub overlooking the harbour for dinner, where Mabel and June had steak and kidney pies and Irene had chilli con carne, which she didn't enjoy as it was very salty. The view compensated for the indifferent food, as they could see the strings of multi-coloured lights framing the bay, the illuminated rocks, gardens and tankers with the little boats bobbing about by the harbour wall. Too tired to walk back up the hill they strolled along and hailed a taxi to take them back to their welcoming beds.

Friday

They awoke to a wet miserable day, so after breakfast they agreed that a quick trip to the shops would be as much outdoor stuff as they would want. So donning their cagoules, they walked swiftly up the hill to gain the steps descending to the post office. With shopping list at the ready they dashed around the shops buying food for the next few days and some for Mabel and Doug for the following week. Irene had broken her small wheeled suitcase when she was in Thailand the previous year and saw one on special offer in a shoe repair shop. She decided to buy it, so they put the food which they had bought into it, and took turns in pulling it along and carrying it up the many steps back to Cintra. June bought a handbag which also went into the suitcase (to keep it dry). Heads down against the rain they trudged back up the hill trying to keep it from driving into their faces.

Once back at the house they dried out and, with mugs of tea to revive them, they occupied themselves by June and Mabel continuing the jigsaw puzzle whilst Irene read a Sci-Fi book curled up by the fire. When they were rested and refreshed they set about preparing dinner, with Irene making the mixture for the cottage pie, Mabel peeling the vegetables and June making an apple crumble.

They had only been out shopping and were getting itchy feet and since it had stopped raining, decided to go up the hill to a little pub for a drink. Donning their cagoules (just in case) they set off, discussing what to drink bearing in mind that they hadn't yet had dinner and didn't want to be staggering back! They were pleased to see that the pool table was free and decided to have a game. Mabel had never played, so the other two showed her what to do and passed a pleasant hour potting the balls and drinking shandy.

Having worked up an appetite they hurried back down the hill anticipating the lovely aromas of cottage pie combined with apple crumble. Once back at Cintra they consumed their dinner with great relish and made short shift of the crumble and a few glasses of red wine! Having cleared away and washed the dishes they finished doing the jigsaw puzzle before retiring to their beds.

Saturday

This was in effect their last day since June and Irene were returning home the following day and Mabel was staying for an extra week with Doug who was due to arrive by train today. After breakfast Irene and June made a start on packing up their bags whilst Mabel washed the dishes and peeled some potatoes, then they wandered down the hill into the harbour area and had a last look around at the boats.

Strolling along the sea front they came across a shopping mall called The Pavilion near to the area where the boat leaves for Brixham. This used to be an ice skating rink in the days when Irene went to Torquay with her young children, but has since become a café where they popped in for a cup of tea. On the ground floor there was a small shop where you can have your photograph taken in fancy dress and June fancied trying on the Victorian outfits, but chickened out!

Walking back to the shops by the marina they decided to indulge themselves in their last packet of fish and chips (this adventure) and sat on the harbour wall in the sunshine enjoying the busy nautical scene before them.

Reluctantly they dragged themselves away from people and boat watching to make their way back up the hill to see whether Doug had arrived. When they got back they found him sitting in the garden with Sylvia and Ian drinking tea, so after greeting him they joined him in a cup of tea and they all sat chatting until dinner time. Mabel had peeled the potatoes earlier, so it took no time at all to make bangers and mash (which is one of Doug's favourite meals) and warm up the last of the apple crumble. After doing the washing

14. TORBAY 1998

up they all settled down to a lazy evening watching the television and turned in early as they had to get up to catch the train in the morning.

Sunday

They awoke to an overcast and rather dull looking day so Irene and June were not as sad as usual to leave Torquay, but sorry that the weather was not so good for Mabel and Doug. After their (now traditional) bacon and egg breakfasts, the bags were taken down to the porch in readiness for the taxi, but before it arrived Irene and June said their goodbyes to Sylvia and Ian. Mabel and Doug had decided to accompany Irene and June as far as Newton Abbot where they had to change trains on a very tight time schedule. They had to cross a bridge to change platforms for the Birmingham train, and Doug very kindly carried the two suitcases whilst the three friends dashed across the bridge to try to secure two seats on the train.

After an uneventful journey back home Buz met Irene and June at New Street Station and took them to Irene's house for tea where they were met by June's son John and his girlfriend Neena, and Irene's daughter Becky with her husband Karl and their daughter Alice.

It was a lovely way to finish off the Adventure relating their stories to their families who have always been happy for them to abandon them for one week a year.

15. Isle of Wight

29th August to 5th September 1999

At this time June's son John was living in Southampton and going over to the Isle of Wight paragliding. June had often thought that she would like to go to the Isle of Wight when her son had talked about it at different times over the years, so she suggested this to Irene and Mabel as a possible place to go for this year's Adventure.

Since neither of them had been there before, they were also keen to go, so Irene set about finding a place to stay in Shanklin, as it was accessible by train from the ferry terminus at Yarmouth. She booked in at the Appley Private Hotel, Queens Road, Shanklin and June contacted John to see if they could stay at his house en route. He said that it would be alright to spend the night at his house, and that he would take them in his car on the ferry and drop them off at the hotel the following day. He was planning to go paragliding around that time anyway, so it would coincide with their trip. They arranged to go down to Southampton by train, where John would collect them at the station, work permitting.

Sunday
At 10.30am Irene and Buz collected June after picking up Mabel, to take them all to New Street Station to catch the 12.06pm Virgin train to Southampton. It was essential to catch this train; since they had special tickets which Mabel had purchased a month before for the bargain price of £15 each.

They arrived at Southampton Central Station, after missing the stop at Parkway Airport Station, following an interesting journey where they incorporated the help of all and sundry to complete a crossword puzzle. It certainly got people in the carriage chatting and they even waylaid a man passing through who was able to assist with the corporate task.

15. ISLE OF WIGHT 1999

1999 The Crab in Shanklin Old Town

1999 The Victory at Portsmouth

Hailing a taxi to get to John's house, they clambered in and set off, but it became apparent after a while that the taxi driver didn't know the way, as the street Havendale was split in two and there was no way through to John's end. After much searching around and with June's prior knowledge of the area, he finally found the entrance to the road and, apologising profusely, he only charged them £10 after they made it clear that the clock fee was not realistic – he certainly made a loss on that fare!

Retrieving the key from under the plant pot, they let themselves in as John was at work. They made themselves at home relaxing in the garden with cups of tea after unpacking and donning their shorts as it was lovely and sunny. When John came home he took them for a tour around Portsmouth which included the Queen Alexandra Hospital where he was working as an orthopaedic surgeon. Afterwards they went to an Italian restaurant at the Marina where they sat outside admiring the boats and eating pasta followed by ice cream.

On returning to John's house they relaxed by line-dancing, reading, and surfing the internet on his laptop for places of interest on the Isle of Wight, before retiring to bed. Mabel and Irene slept in John's bed, June had a bed in the spare room, and John was assigned to the living room floor!

Monday

After cups of tea in bed (courtesy of Irene) and breakfast, John took them to catch the 9.45am Isle of Wight car ferry out of Lymington landing at Yarmouth. When they arrived, John drove to the High Adventure Paragliding School at Freshwater and met the people at the club with whom he was going to paraglide. After driving to a hill to assess the weather, it was decided that it was not windy enough in the morning, so he was told to come back again in the afternoon.

They drove to the Needles where they took the chair lift to Alum Bay and walked along a very pebbly beach before eating their sandwiches, followed by ice cream. Feeling brave, John went for a swim in the sea while they sunbathed and admired the boats. About 3pm they returned to the gliding school at the Bowl, an area above Freshwater Bay ideal for paragliding. They watched John gliding for a couple of hours and then went for a walk over the hill admiring the view of Southampton.

At the end of a very pleasant and relaxing afternoon, John took them through Sandown to Shanklin along the coast road to their hotel, where he saw them into their rooms before setting out to catch the ferry home. They

15. ISLE OF WIGHT 1999

waved him off and after a quick change of clothes they walked to the Chine Inn for a superb dinner consisting of garlic mushroom starters, roast dinners and mandarin meringues washed down with dandelion wine and melon breezers. John phoned to say that he had arrived home, then they walked back to the hotel at ten thirty and retired tired but happy!

Tuesday

They had a full English breakfast before walking to Olde Shanklin Village where they wandered about amongst the very picturesque houses, shops and pubs taking photographs. They strolled through Rylstone Gardens onto Appley Beach where they ate their sandwiches on the seafront by Shanklin lift. The beach there was nice soft sand so they sunbathed until 3 o'clock when they walked along to Hope beach and had a cup of tea in the golf centre. They walked back to the hotel, reminiscing about previous 'Adventures', singing old songs and quoting poetry.

After a brief visit to the hotel (as it was 8 o'clock by this time) they changed their clothes and walked along to the Chine Inn to have dinner, only to discover that they didn't serve food on Tuesdays, so they walked into Olde Shanklin Village and ended up in a very popular fish and chip shop aptly named 'June's'. Returning to the hotel they tried to get a drink in the bar, but there was no-one about. Then a lady rang the door bell and the hotel manager appeared and let her in, then served them to drinks in the bar, where they sat and wrote postcards and started to write up the diary before they retired for the night.

Wednesday

They had kippers and grapefruit for breakfast served by the manager, who was the only member of staff they saw the whole time that they were there. June's room had a tiny toilet and shower, and Mabel's and Irene's room had single beds and an adjoining shower and toilet.

In glorious sunshine they walked through Olde Shanklin village and down to the beach via the Shanklin Chine where they lay and sunbathed all day, dipping in and out of the sea to cool off. They had crab sandwiches for lunch which they bought from a little café just off the beach.

In the evening they went into Shanklin Chine which was beautifully illuminated and wandered along a little stream which led to a forty foot waterfall, fern banks, rare plants and mossy boulders along twisty paths. There was a lovely pool with goldfish in it and they stopped to look at the pipeline

(PLUTO – Pipe Line Under The Ocean). This went under the ocean emerging in Cherbourg, and which during the Second World War provided fuel for the Allied fighting forces in France.

After a delightful visit to the Chine which they all agreed was a magical and surreal experience, they went for dinner at the Chine Inn where they all had prawn cocktails. June had a crab salad and Irene and Mabel had steak and kidney pie with dandelion and mead wine. The food was delicious and they were very contented as they made their way back to the hotel, and their beds, after such a lovely day.

Thursday

Again they had the full English breakfast before setting out to walk the coastal path to Bonchurch where along the path through the Landslip they spotted a plant, which they had never seen before, about eight foot tall with a long spike, in bright blue. Nearby there was a café where they stopped to have a cup of tea and they asked the lady in the café the name of the plant, and since she had been asked about it so often she had written the name on a piece of paper and placed it on the till, it was an Echium Pininana.

Whilst they were enjoying their cups of tea, the café lady's husband appeared with his dog and after some banter with his wife, he joined them where they were sitting on a terraced area in the sun. He was very entertaining (quoting the character from 'The Rise and Fall of Reginald Perrin' – 'I didn't get where I am today…') as well as being very knowledgeable about the local area. He suggested that they might like to look at St. Boniface church, an Anglo Saxon church re-built in 1070, the renowned toilets at Bonchurch and Ventnor (which are half in one county and half in another) and Swinburne House where Charles Dickens wrote 'Great Expectations'. After they had finished their tea they continued on to Bonchurch, a quaint picturesque village with thatched cottages, and where June sat on a stone wishing-seat and wouldn't reveal what she had wished for to the other two!

The Landslip had (previous to the slip) been a nursery, so all along the way they passed many beautiful hydrangea bushes and other plants and flowers covered in butterflies which they kept stopping to admire (and Irene to video with her new 'toy').

They came upon St. Boniface church, a pretty little stone-built church which they were able to enter, since this was in the days when churches were left open. They wandered around admiring the carvings, windows and furnishings.

15. ISLE OF WIGHT 1999

Carrying on towards Ventnor they found a pebble beach where they whiled away the sunny afternoon, sunbathing and swimming in the sea, after having lunch in the café by the beach. They then walked along the road towards Ventnor passing Swinburne House by, as it was time to eat. Spotting a likely looking pub which had a very varied menu, they stepped inside and ordered butterfly prawns which they enjoyed very much accompanied by barley wine and lager. There was a bus stop opposite the pub so they asked the landlord about the running times and since it was quite dark by this time, they decided to catch the bus back to the hotel.

Friday

Once more they had breakfast before setting off on a very long walk on Sandown Beach, where they had a sandwich in a bar by a car park, before walking to the end of the beach. Here they found a quiet spot to lie in the sun for the rest of the afternoon taking dips in the sea which was surprisingly warm. They started to walk back along the road, but since it was getting late, when they came upon a bus stop, they decided to get the bus back to the hotel where they showered and changed for dinner.

Strolling along to the Old Village they found a restaurant called Henry's Kitchen and liked the look of it, so they entered and found it to be a charming place with the story of Henry VIII's life and wives adorning the walls in pictures. It had a cosy atmosphere and they felt very relaxed there, especially after consuming a delicious dinner consisting of rack of lamb (June and Irene), chicken maryland (Mabel), toffee apple and chocolate fudge sweets, followed by a selection of cheeses and liqueur coffees (it has been noted by others that this Adventure was a very gastronomic one and they would not disagree!).

During the meal they phoned John on June's mobile to confirm arrangements for him to pick them up the following day. Afterwards they sat in the bar chatting to the barmaid about King Henry and his many wives, and she told them that the main course dishes were all named after them. Replete and contented they strolled back to the hotel where they packed their bags for departure the next day and went to bed very happy.

Saturday

Breakfast over they gathered up their bags and made their way to Shanklin Railway Station to catch the train for the ferry at Yarmouth. They had contemplated going to Queen Victoria's favourite home Osborne House, but decided instead to get an earlier ferry than they had planned and head back to Portsmouth to look around the Maritime Museum.

Boarding the ferry they found comfortable seats and settled down to watch the approach to the mainland through large picture windows. Alighting at Portsmouth they enquired about leaving their bags in the left luggage facility, but the Station Master said that this no longer existed due to terrorist activities and let them leave them in his office. He must have thought they had honest faces!

Uncluttered they proceeded towards the Maritime Museum, stopping on the way to have lunch in a pub. Then, making their way to the dockyard, they went aboard The Victory, Nelson's flagship, where they marvelled at the appallingly cramped conditions in which the sailors lived, ate and slept. The Officers enjoyed somewhat better conditions and Nelson had his own cabin and bunk bed, but not grand by today's standards. They saw the spot on which Nelson was reputed to have died at the Battle of Trafalgar and where he was put into a barrel of rum to preserve his body until the return to England.

They then made their way across to HMS Warrior which is the oldest commissioned naval vessel in the world, where preparations for a wedding were taking place in the old captain's dining room. It amused them to discover that the ratings slept in the same area as the sheep and, if somewhat smelly, at least they would have been nice and warm! The remains of the Mary Rose (Henry VIII's flagship) was next on their tour, this was raised from the sea bed and has been continually sprayed with oil and water since, to preserve it. Time was running out and they weren't able to visit the other exhibits, as they had to make their way back to the station to collect their bags and meet up with John, which had been previously arranged. He then took them back to his house where Mabel picked a bag full of apples from his tree to take home and make into an apple crumble for the next Highball weekend. They then waited in anticipation as John fetched them all a Chinese takeaway, which was a delicious ending to a fascinating and absorbing day.

They stopped the night at John's again, but this time Mabel and Irene insisted that John slept in his own bed as he had been working late and was very tired, while they slept on the settee and blow up bed in the lounge, with June in the spare room.

Sunday

After a quick breakfast John took them into Winchester, where they wandered around this picturesque and historic city, looking at the cathedral which had

15. ISLE OF WIGHT 1999

a service in progress so they weren't able to go in. They walked around the city centre admiring the lovely old buildings and strolled along the side of the river, before going to the Queen Alexandra Hospital for Sunday lunch. In the hospital's restaurant they had a splendid view through the large picture windows whilst consuming a delicious meal. Lunch over, John drove them to his house to collect their bags, where they thanked him for his hospitality and chauffeuring and helping to make this such an interesting adventure. He then drove them to Southampton Parkway Railway Station, where he waved them off on their journey home.

On the train they chatted about this lovely adventure and the interesting places that they had visited on the Isle of Wight, in Portsmouth, Southampton and Winchester. Once more they all agreed that they would like to go back again, as is often the case after one of their Adventures.

Buz, whose help they always appreciated, collected them from New Street Station in Birmingham and took them to their respective homes; he was getting used to their wanderings by now!

16. Twynings, Tewkesbury

27th August to 3rd September 2000

For this adventure Irene found a farm which did bed and breakfast called Abbots Court in Twynings Fleet near Tewkesbury. Mr Williams ran the farm and kept a prize herd of Hereford cattle, whilst Mrs Williams (Bernie) looked after the guests, and indeed her delicious breakfasts were famous throughout the area for their ampleness (they sadly lost their prize herd during the foot and mouth crisis).

Sunday
Irene and Buz picked Mabel and June up and they departed from Aldridge at 10.30am, arriving at Abbots Court at 11.45am. On the door they found a note from Mrs Williams (Bernie) which explained that she had to go out and where their bedrooms were, inviting them to go in and make themselves at home, whereupon they found their bedrooms, unpacked and had a game of bowls, which they found in the shed in the garden.

Buz drove them around the village to do a 'reccy' and get their bearings and seeing that The Fleet Inn, where they planned to have lunch was packed out, they opted for steak and kidney pudding at The Village Inn.

At 1.30pm Buz took them back to the farm where they met and chatted to Bernie before he departed for home.

After receiving directions from Bernie they set out across the fields, via cowpats and fishing pools and made their way back to The Fleet Inn, where they sat by the riverside enjoying ice creams and watching the boats and doves from the Fleet's dovecote. They strolled back across the meadows and made their way to the farm past fields of towering maize crops, cows, sheep and horses, admiring the flora and fauna.

Back at the farm they had salmon rolls, cakes and grapes for tea (they had brought these with them) and watched TV for a while. Once they had

16. TWYNINGS, TEWKESBURY 2000

discovered the cellar, they were down there playing pool and table tennis and before turning in for the night, they did a crossword puzzle, lying on the three beds in Mabel and Irene's room.

Monday (Bank Holiday)
After one of Bernie's massive full English breakfasts, they played bowls in the garden and then rambled through the farmland and meadows towards the river where herds of cows were drinking. They followed its course until they reached Tewkesbury, whereupon they sought out the Tourist Information Centre. Arming themselves with leaflets of the local places of interest they repaired (of course) to the Butterfly Café for tea and scones.

Full of local knowledge (and scones) they caught the ferry back to Twynings, and strolling up to the village green via Damson Alleyway, discovered the Bank Holiday fete and car boot sale in full swing. After a good old mooch amongst the stalls, they all bought mugs and maps of Twynings and watched Irene play skittles, then walked back to Abbots Court passing through a field of very big, scary horses.

Back at the farm they washed and changed and set out along the dark narrow lanes to The Crown pub at Shuthonger (recommended by Bernie) where the chef from The Fleet had moved. As they were wending their way along the lanes, it started to rain with a vengeance, so they decide to shelter under a large oak tree which was overhanging the road. June had learnt a new line dance that week, so to pass the time while they waited for the rain to stop, she taught Irene and Mabel the dance 'Walkin' After Midnight' in the road.

They laughed so much that they didn't at first notice that the rain had stopped! Continuing along the lane they eventually reached the main road and spotted The Crown on the opposite side. Entering the pub they divested themselves of their soaking wet cagoules and finding a spare table ordered their dinners. They had worked up a jolly good appetite and June and Irene tucked into half a shoulder of lamb each, with lyonnaise potatoes whilst Mabel had lemon sole, all followed by treacle sponge pudding, scrummy!

The walk home was quite an adventure in itself, as it was very dark, and they had to find their way home by torchlight in an unfamiliar area. They nearly jumped out of their skins when a large dog suddenly started to bark as they passed his gateway. It's fair to say that they were all very glad to climb into the bath and their beds!

Tuesday

After breakfast, armed with Bernie's substantial packed lunches, they walked to the post office and couldn't resist buying cakes to take with them (including the famous custard slice!). Walking up through the village and passing the old School House and many pretty cottages, they noticed that there was an open day in aid of the Lifeboats, at Apricot Cottage, on the following Saturday.

Continuing on their way they hit the A38 and turned left towards Puckrup, passing a craft centre and café, where they stopped for a cup of tea and bought some souvenirs. They browsed around admiring the chimineas and garden plants and accessories before continuing on along the A38. After passing the golf course and Manor House to Ripple they eventually came to a bridge which spanned the M50 motorway.

At this point June's son John phoned on her newly acquired mobile phone, checking to see if they were all ok. After crossing the bridge, they followed a disused railway line until they came to The Railway pub which was situated in a very pretty little village. Just before closing the landlord served them shandys and said they were welcome to eat their packed lunches outside on his picnic tables, an innocent enough pastime you might surmise, if you didn't account for Mabel's wicked sense of humour and quick wit.

Their lunchtime repast began soberly enough, sitting outside the quaint old pub bedecked with colourful hanging baskets, feet up on chairs and appreciating their shandies. Delving into their rucksacks they produced their sandwiches and proceeded to eat, with Irene reading her Mills & Boon and Mabel scanning through the local newspaper which she had found discarded in the bar.

The atmosphere was calm, peaceful and serene, the sun was shining and all was well with the world. Further rummaging in rucksacks revealed the cakes which they had purchased earlier in the day, just the thing to round off lunch! June had chosen her favourite cake, a custard slice, and this was a particularly gooey and delicious one, so she tucked into it with gusto making appreciative noises and extolling the virtues of custard slices to her long suffering companions. In a state of near ecstasy, with her eyes closed and custard oozing out of the pastry, she murmured 'this is better than sex'! Quick as a flash from behind the newspaper Mabel (who is perceived to be sweet and innocent by those who do not know her intimately) commented dryly 'you must have had rubbish sex then'!

So unexpected was this comment from Mabel that it reduced Irene and June to tears of hysteria, laughing and spluttering cake everywhere, Mabel

16. TWYNINGS, TEWKESBURY 2000

2000 *Irene and June by the Fleet Ferry, Twynings*

2000 *The Railway Inn, Breedon, of Custard Slice fame!*

joined in and they laughed and laughed until they collapsed across the wrought iron tables.

After recovering their wits they strolled along the lane and came to a village where they found some stocks outside an old house and, with more hilarity, duly administered punishment to Mabel by putting her in them, for reducing lunch to a shambles. They stopped to admire some lovely old maple trees before setting off to walk from Ripple to Brockeridge Common where they passed through a deserted old apple orchard observing that the trees were bedecked with mistletoe and they all felt sad that it had been so neglected. Going back and passing under the motorway at the A38, they returned to Abbots Farm via a field where some kind of experiment was taking place (as the field was laid out in small strips and labelled) and through a field with lots of mushrooms. The next field had a large pond where they stopped to speak to a fisherman and his young son and enquired about their catch.

Arriving back at the farm they showered and lay on the three beds in Irene and Mabel's room watching TV, doing crosswords, writing cards and bringing the diary (a small scrap of paper) up to date. After a light snack they retired for the night.

Wednesday

At 10.30am after Bernie's full English breakfast, they walked through the farm, down to the river Avon by the Fleet Inn and hailed the ferryman to take them across to the opposite bank (this cost them the princely sum of £1 for the three of them!).

A long, straight, rough path with fields either side, containing bullocks and a sign saying 'Beware of the Bull', lead them to a road where they turned left and headed towards Bredon. Walking through the village they passed a beautiful old thatched pub The Fox & Hounds which was bedecked with hanging baskets, cascading with flowers of every hue. On the far side of the village was a country park, where they made use of the conveniences and chatted to a man who told them how to get to Bredon Beacon, passing by a miniature railway in a garden running alongside a very long alleyway.

After ambling their way across the park and fields they eventually came across the alleyway with the miniature railway and were amused to discover signs like 'Frog Furlong Spa' and adverts for Hudson's soap, they managed to take a few photos through the hedge. They emerged from the alleyway onto a large field where they could see Bredon Beacon, and so headed towards it

16. TWYNINGS, TEWKESBURY 2000

singing, to the tune of 'Lass of Richmond Hill' their own version of 'Lasses of Bredon Hill'. It was a gloriously sunny day and they were in very high spirits as they climbed the hill and found a shady glade in which to have their picnic and crash out after the strenuous climb.

Once refreshed, they headed further up the hill and stopped to admire the spectacular view across the valley. They spotted bales of hay in fields which had recently been harvested and made their usual comments about melorolls (ice cream with a similar shape to the bales). This is a long standing joke from when Irene and June worked at Midland Counties Dairy and endlessly typed invoices containing the word 'melorolls'.

After the obligatory photo opportunity they set off back down the hill where they encountered a little old man with a beard and wearing a panama hat, who appeared to be lost. They offered to show him where the miniature railway was and said that if he wished he could join them walking back to the village. He was delighted to be accompanied by quote 'three lovely young ladies' and used June's mobile phone to let his daughter know that he would be back a bit later than expected, as she worried about him when he was out, since he had recently suffered a heart attack. They parted company with him in the village where they purchased drinks at the Spa shop and used their toilets, since neither of the pubs in the village were open, it being before 6.30pm.

Retracing their steps back to the ferry, Irene summoned the ferryman by ringing a bell. He duly came and took them across to the Fleet Inn, where they sat outside (with long refreshing drinks) watching the boats and ferries on the river and the doves flitting in and out of the dovecote.

As it was 6.50pm by this time, they decided to stay there for dinner and were very surprised by the low standard of the meals, considering the high reputation for food that the Fleet Inn enjoyed. Mabel and Irene's mashed potatoes contained hard uncooked lumps floating in a sea of glutinous looking goo, which they sent back and exchanged for chips to eat with the nice Cumberland sausages. June was also disappointed with her bland chicken sauce, but consumed it nonetheless! Earlier in the week they had discovered that the chef had recently left and had gone to The Crown at Shuthonger.

They walked back along the riverbank and uphill through the farmer's fields, arriving back at 9.15pm, and since they were all tired as it had been a very long walk, just did a few crossword puzzles lying on the beds and took their weary sunburnt bodies off to bed.

Thursday

They decided to stay in the village, since yesterday's marathon had left them feeling a little drained, so after another of Bernie's breakfasts, they headed towards a part of the village that they had not previously explored, the new housing estate. After observing the more modern lifestyle of the families in this area, they retraced their steps to the main street where they proceeded to take photos of the interesting old buildings scattered around the village. One of these was Apricot Cottage where they were reminded about the open day on the coming Saturday and made a mental note to support it.

They needed provisions for lunch, so went to the Post Office, bought sandwiches and then returned across the field with mushrooms in it, avoiding the field with the scary horses who took an unhealthy interest in them (more probably their sandwiches). They played bowls on a large uneven lawn; Mabel won the first game and the second game was adjourned when rain stopped play, whereupon they went indoors and consumed their sandwiches, after which, because it was still raining, they adjourned to the farmhouse's games room in the cellar.

With their youth worker backgrounds this was home from home for June and Irene who, in their wisdom, offered to teach Mabel to play pool, who then proceeded to beat them hollow 2 games to nil! June went in search of Bernie and borrowed a cassette player from her and returning to the cellar did a spot of line dancing, encouraging Irene and Mabel to join in.

They spent a very interesting and amusing afternoon thus, before sprucing themselves up to go out to dinner. They paddled up the lane in the wind and rain to the Crown pub once again and indulged themselves by having several starters instead of a main meal; June particularly enjoyed the delicious prawn cocktail. Tired and replete they splashed along the lane back to their nice dry warm beds and retired early at 11pm.

Friday

Having filled them up with her wonderful breakfasts, Bernie ran them to the post office in her car, so that they would be in time to catch the 9.30am bus to Tewkesbury. The first thing they did when they got there was to explore the Abbey and grounds where they took lots of photos including one of a particularly striking sculpture of a group of children sitting in a circle.

By this time they had worked up an appetite and coming across a lovely little refectory on the side of the Abbey they partook of tea and cakes before setting out on the 'Tewkesbury's Alleyways' walk. This trail follows the most

16. TWYNINGS, TEWKESBURY 2000

interesting alleys and courts including the Old Baptist Chapel Court and gardens which contain the gravestones of the Shakespeare family. Proceeding on they came to Lilley's Alley which contained many fine examples of half timbered buildings, where they stopped to photograph a partially exposed wattle and daub wall. They were amused to note the sign in Eagles Alley stating 'Commit No Nuisance' just beneath the arch (as if they would!!).

This led them to the Merchants museum and the Methodist church, both of which they entered and looked around before retiring to The Baker's Oven where they lunched upon baked potatoes and Cornish pasties. They completed the Alleyway's walk and decided that a swim at the Cascades swimming pool would be welcome to relieve their footpath weary feet, whereupon they did a few handstands, swam a few lengths underwater and generally messed about.

Having worked up a healthy appetite, they found a café and consumed vast quantities of fish and chips and apple pie with cups of tea. Deciding that they had exerted themselves enough for one day, they took a taxi back to Abbott's Court where they took it in turns to read aloud from John Betjeman's 'Collected Poems' which June had bought from Alison's bookshop earlier in the day.

Saturday

After the usual hearty breakfast they made a start on packing up their belongings ready for departing in the afternoon when Buz was coming to collect them. This onerous task completed they gathered up their cameras and bags and sallied forth to support the RNLI Open Day.

They walked to the village and headed straight for Apricot Cottage where the Open Day was in full swing. Taking advantage of the lovely weather they strolled around the gardens admiring the plants and getting ideas for their own gardens. They chatted to the stall holders and made a few purchases before heading off to The Village Inn to meet up with Buz for lunch.

In the pub there was a small group of friendly locals to whom they chatted, and June asked the landlord if he knew that there was a poem called 'The Village Inn'? When he replied that he didn't know of such a poem, June (who was feeling particularly brave after a few barley wines on an empty stomach) offered to read it out loud to the assembled company. This caused a few laughs and much amusement amongst the locals. June then offered to type out the poem and send it to the landlord for him to display in the pub, which she duly did on returning home.

THREE HAPPY WANDERERS

After Buz had joined them and they had eaten their steak and kidney pies, they went back to the farm, collected their bags, said farewell to Bernie and thanked her for looking after them so well before departing for home.

Armed with maps of the village, they were all determined to return and adventure further in the area and take advantage of Bernie's excellent hospitality once again.

17. Day Trips (from home)

27th August to 2nd September 2001

This was the year in which Irene and June became eligible for their free bus passes, and since Mabel did not feel up to going away for a week, it was decided that they would stay at June's house and go out for day trips using their bus passes whenever possible.

Monday

At 9.30am, Irene and Mabel arrived at June's house by Buzmobile. It was a lovely sunny morning, so they sat in June's back garden with mugs of tea and finalised their plans for the week, after waving goodbye to Buz.

Day 1 was to be a local walk along the canal in Aldridge. They set off across Aldridge Airport (known locally as 'Greenacres') which in the 1930s operated as an aerodrome. Work began on the aerodrome site in 1932 and it became operational in 1934. During World War II Spitfires and Hawards were repaired at Helliwell's Factory there. Some famous flyers who visited the aerodrome were Jim Mollison, Alan Cobham, Gustav Hamel and Amy Johnson (who pranged a glider that she was trying out). Aeroplanes continued to land there until 1953.

Today it is a playing field, nature reserve and is used to fly kites and model aircraft. After a pleasant stroll across the large open field they entered into a wooded area and walked along the side of a small brook, noticing as they went some fortifications from World War II, which they assumed were used for housing anti-aircraft guns.

This led them to Longwood Lane, which they crossed over to get to the canal and following the towpath towards Walsall, they veered off to walk around the Park Lime Pits lakes and woods. Irene and Mabel had never been to this local beauty spot, but June had spent many happy hours with her children over the years, gathering elderberries and rose hips for wine making, and blackberries for pies and crumbles, as well as enjoying the stunning sunsets over the lake.

After exploring the various paths, pools and wooded areas they resumed their walk along the canal where they met a man with a beautiful Dalmatian dog, so they chatted for a while, and then headed towards The Manor Arms. This is a pub, situated on the side of the canal, with lots of character – no bar – just optics and a real coal fire on cold days. Since it was lunch time and they made home-cooked meals, they decided to eat there, sitting outside in the sunshine while they waited. The meals were delicious and although they had a long wait, it was well worth it. Whilst they were sitting in the gardens they met Tom, an old boyfriend of Irene's daughter Rachel, and his family including a five month old baby boy, so they passed the time very pleasantly talking to them.

Lunch over they continued on their way, resuming their walk along the towpath towards Walsall, passing fishermen and admiring the waterfowl and the reflections of the trees and plants in the water. They veered off when they came to the golf course and walked across a field which led them through to Walsall Arboretum Park where they found a kiosk which sold refreshments, near some bench seats, so stopped for a cup of tea.

The Walsall Illumination lights were being set up so there was lots of activity, with workmen on high cherry pickers erecting lights and excited children running around in the sunshine. After walking around the lake and admiring the swans and geese, they left the park by the main entrance, pausing to look at the beautiful formal flower beds.

Walsall is famous for its leather goods, particularly saddles and other horse riding accessories and Mabel recalled Princess Anne visiting Birmingham and being presented with a riding whip which was made in Walsall. They decided to visit the Walsall Leather Museum, but discovered that it was nearly closing by the time they had made their way across the town, so they had exactly eight minutes to dash around and see as many exhibits as they could. Their intention was to catch the bus back to June's house, but whilst chatting to the museum receptionist, who recognised June from line dancing, they were offered a lift back to Aldridge in her car, which they gratefully accepted. She dropped them off at the White House pub and they ambled along the last quarter of a mile feeling quite hot and tired and were very glad that they had accepted the lift.

It was about 6 o'clock so June cooked delicious rib eye steaks for supper and when they were replete; they lay outside in the sun and fell asleep! Later

17. DAY TRIPS (FROM HOME) 2001

on June ran Mabel home whilst Irene washed the dishes and prepared for bed, since she was staying at June's house for the week.

Tuesday

Using their newly acquired bus passes June and Irene caught the 9.38am bus to Birmingham and were joined en route by Mabel, at the bus stop near her home. From Birmingham New Street Railway Station, they travelled to Kidderminster, where they caught the Severn Valley steam train which terminates at Bridgnorth. They bought day return tickets as they planned to get on and off the train as the fancy took them.

Their first stop-off was Arley, where they had a beautiful walk along the riverbank towards Highley, listening to fish leaping and splashing in the Severn. Irene fantasised about alien wolves stalking them, as the fish were making such a strange noise. After an hour and a half they reached Highley and were disappointed to discover that the pub by the station no longer did lunches and was about to close. They managed to get shandies and packets of crisps before it closed and sat outside eating sandwiches which luckily they had had the foresight to take with them. As it was a lovely sunny day they were happy to sit and eat their lunch overlooking the river whilst deciding on their next step.

They caught the train to Bridgnorth where they looked for the track railway which goes to Upper Bridgnorth overlooking the Severn Valley. Alighting at the end of the track, they were pleasantly surprised to find an area where The Castle used to be, which has been made into a lovely park, with gardens, a bandstand draped with beautiful multicoloured hanging baskets, commemoration statues from the First World War and a large piece of the old castle wall leaning over at a very precarious angle which they pretended to be propping up for dramatic effect on their photographs. They spent a very pleasant hour in this peaceful oasis before making their way back down to the town, where they enjoyed an interesting interlude in St. Anne's church, which was designed by Thomas Telford and contained numerous details about his life and achievements.

At the end of the day they caught the steam train back to Kidderminster and from there the diesel train to Birmingham New Street. Mabel's husband Doug and his friend, also called Doug, were travelling along this route and they bumped into them both at the beginning and the end of the day.

Upon their arrival in Birmingham, they found out why people complain about British Rail, their train to Walsall was cancelled and the next due train

THREE HAPPY WANDERERS

2001 Arley Station

2001 June and Irene by the River Severn at Arley

didn't have a driver! All in all it was an hour and a half before they finally left New Street Station for Walsall, about a quarter of an hour's journey! From Walsall they gave up on public transport and hailed a taxi which took them back to June's house, where she phoned and ordered pizzas for supper as the chip shop had closed. She knew that she had to produce some food for her friends or be eaten alive!! At this late hour, Mabel was too tired to go home, so she phoned Doug to let him know that she would stay the night at June's house.

They all agreed that it had been a great day despite the long wait for the train.

Wednesday

A leisurely alfresco breakfast was enjoyed at the bottom of June's garden, after which Irene and June took Mabel home in June's car to have a rest after the very tiring end to the previous day. They then went on to Aldridge to take June's vacuum cleaner to be repaired, just missing the man by a few minutes! Irene bought a jacket from the indoor market and both found a few bargains before returning to June's house for a spot of sunbathing and R and R.

The afternoon passed pleasantly relaxing in the garden and Buz arrived early evening for a haircut. After June had cut Buz's hair he bought a Chinese meal before going home, which Irene and June consumed with great relish at nine o'clock before retiring for the night.

Thursday

Letting Mabel have another day off Irene and June caught the 9.38am bus into Birmingham and found their way to the Museum and Art Gallery, heading for the Egyptian Exhibition in the Gas Hall. They were both fascinated by the mummies and the process of embalming and wandered around for another hour or so until lunch time, when they partook of Lancashire hotpot in the museum's splendid Victorian Restaurant. Whilst eating they listened to a pianist playing classical music on the elevated grand piano and at the same time admiring the sumptuous décor, especially the balcony which runs around the top of the auditorium.

After lunch they made their way into the Art gallery, which they had often visited in their youth and searched for a favourite painting of theirs. It was of a Victorian man looking longingly at a lady who was wearing a velvet cape and standing by a tree whose trunk was covered in ivy. It was no longer hanging in the gallery, but June spotted some paintings which could have been by the same artist, and upon enquiring discovered that the missing painting was called 'The Long Engagement' painted in 1859 by one of the Pre-Raphaelite artists Arthur Hughes. This art gallery is well known for its collection of Pre-Raphaelite paintings and they were pleased to be able to buy postcards of the painting in the souvenir shop, before returning to the Victorian Restaurant for tea and naughty cakes.

Then they caught the 4.15pm bus back to June's house, rushing home to jump into June's car and race to Aldridge market with the vacuum cleaner, only to find that they had missed the repair man again!

Too tired to go line dancing as she had planned June stopped in with Irene and both had an early night.

Friday

After an early breakfast they bundled the vacuum cleaner into the car for the third time and arrived at the market for opening time, managing to catch the repair man at last! Staying in the Moggy they headed to Mabel's house, where they left the car and collected Mabel before catching the 9.30am bus into Birmingham, then went on to Shrewsbury by train from New Street Station.

When they arrived in Shrewsbury it was overcast and damp and they kept their brollies handy as they headed for the Tourist Information Office, where they learned that there was a conducted tour of the town starting at 2.30pm. They booked their places on the two hour tour and went shopping, looking for black lace gloves for June, who wanted them for a fancy dress party. After this they found a lovely little pub and had a delicious lunch, before returning to the Tourist Information Office for the guided tour. This was a walking tour of the town taking in many historical buildings including the church.

They were so interested in the locality that they said they would like to return again to spend longer in the area, perhaps on a future Adventure. Happening upon an olde worlde café, they climbed the narrow uneven stairs to the Victorian tea rooms and had pots of tea and home-made apple pie with cream.

Later on they caught the train back to New Street Station and the bus to Mabel's house, where June and Irene said 'goodbye' to her and Doug and collected the Moggy to go back to Aldridge. They set off with a parcel of Doug's home grown beans, which they had for their supper with bacon and baked potatoes. Very tasty!

17. DAY TRIPS (FROM HOME) 2001

Saturday

After a hearty breakfast June and Irene toddled off to Aldridge market and collected the repaired vacuum cleaner, and after dropping it off at June's house went on to Brownhills to search the market for bargains. After a good old rummage, and since it was lunch time, they ate hot pork and stuffing rolls to sustain themselves!

June was holding a fancy dress party for the people in her street at her house that night, so they went back to June's house to sort out their fancy dress costumes and have a rest before the party started. June chose a red satin gown with matching nail varnish and earrings and a pair of black lace up boots, whilst Irene dressed as a sheriff, complete with two guns in holsters. June's loft is quite well known locally for its rails of dressing up clothes, boxes of hats, baskets of shoes and boots and suitcases full of accessories and handbags, which she acquired when she put on shows with youngsters during her time as a youth worker.

The party began at 9pm and finished at 2.45am, and was generally proclaimed a huge success, the men dressing up as women or emperors, and the ladies in dance dresses or western outfits. The children brought their own fancy dress, but changed into their outfits in June's loft.

Sunday

This was a very wet and miserable day, so after a full English breakfast June and Irene went into Walsall to Bescott market in June's car. Irene said that it was the biggest market she had ever been to and looked for bargains, dodging the raindrops. Deciding that it wasn't very pleasant getting so wet they thought that they would buy some nice meat and go back and cook a roast lunch. They bought half a lamb for £15 which was cut into joints, steaks and chops and which was shared between them. Returning to June's house they dried off before cooking some of the steak and chops with roast potatoes and runner beans. Relaxing after lunch they played cards in front of a cosy fire before June took Irene home at 6pm.

They all agreed that it had been a very different 'Adventure' from their others, but that they had made good use of their bus passes as planned, and it hadn't cost them much. It had been a very interesting and varied week and they had all enjoyed each others company.

18. Cromer

25th to 30th August 2002

Some of their friends had been to Cromer on holiday and extolled the virtues of that part of England and, since it was an area that they hadn't been to on their adventures, they decided to take a look at it for themselves. Irene sent off for the tourist guide of Cromer and found them a guest house which seemed to be central to the area which they were planning to explore, so she booked two rooms for herself and June as Mabel wasn't able to go with them.

Fred (June's new partner) offered to take them and after all these years Buz was happy to have someone with whom to share the chauffeuring. He would collect Irene at the end of the week as June was going on by train to meet up with Fred at his daughter Debbie's house in Colchester.

Sunday
At 10.30am June and Fred picked Irene up and they set off for Norfolk, it was a long journey broken only by stopping for lunch at a pub along the way and arriving late afternoon. After depositing their bags at the guest house, Chellow Dene, and being shown where Fred could park his car in an alleyway at the rear of the house, they walked to the beach. Spotting the pier, they strolled towards it through formal flower beds which decorated the length of the promenade.

When they arrived at the pier they saw lots of people sitting and standing along the sides who, they discovered upon closer inspection, were fishing with baited lines for the famous Cromer crabs. The children were having a whale of a time transferring their catches into buckets of sea water, some of the crabs were taken home for their tea and some were returned to the sea. They were fascinated watching the comings and goings of the crabbers and also spent quite a long time gazing out at the spacious seascape appreciating the fresh

18. CROMER 2002

air and the gentle breeze after being cooped up in the car in the heat for most of the day.

Making their way back up past the flower beds they came upon the Cottage Café and decided that they would have their tea there as it overlooked the beach and seemed a very pleasant way to spend their first evening.

After their meal they made their way through the winding picturesque streets, stopping now and then to peer into shop windows, many of which displayed shell art. As dusk descended they headed back to the guest house whilst making plans for the following day, Fred was stopping the night and taking them to Sandringham House as it was quite a long way for them to get to without a car and it was somewhere that they all wanted to visit.

Monday (Bank Holiday)

After a sound night's sleep and a full English breakfast they were fit and ready for a very active day ahead.

They headed off in Fred's car and taking the coast road to West Runton they stopped off on the way to Sandringham to visit the Norfolk Shire Horse Centre (Fred particularly likes horses). They spent a very pleasant hour or so looking at the magnificent shire horses, the goats, sheep, pigs, cows and other farm animals, as well as watching a demonstration of ploughing with heavy working horses. There was a large variety of ponies and horses and there were lots of children around enjoying stroking and feeding them and riding on the horse and cart. Before they left they went into the agricultural machinery museum and the huge barn filled with equine tack from days gone by, consisting of saddles, harnesses and the spectacular brasses from the days when horses were used to pull the breweries' drays.

Setting off along the A148 they drove to Sandringham House and having parked the car in a wooded area, they went for lunch in the café before embarking upon the tour of the house and its immediate grounds. The original building was an Elizabethan country house which was purchased by Queen Victoria for her son and was demolished in 1865 as it proved to be too small for The Prince of Wales (the future Edward VII) and his new bride Princess Alexandra.

It was re-built in red brick and stone in a mixture of styles, which was later added to with an extra wing including a magnificent ballroom. Queen Alexandra was fond of animals and her contribution to the estate was to develop a menagerie of horses, dogs, cats, turkeys and other animals including a ram which she rescued from a butcher.

THREE HAPPY WANDERERS

2002 *Buz on beach, Cromer*

2002 *Fred at the Shire Horse Centre near Sandringham*

18. CROMER 2002

The interior was well ahead of its time and included gas lighting, flushing water closets and a shower. It was primarily a family home and despite the large splendid reception rooms has small intimate bedrooms and has been the private home for four generations of sovereigns since 1860. It remains the residence of choice even today for the Queen and her family at Christmas. In 1977 it was opened to the public by Queen Elizabeth II from April to November each year as part of her Silver Jubilee celebrations.

The Duke of Edinburgh accepted responsibility for the management of the vast estate of 8,000 acres when the Queen ascended the throne in 1952 after her father had died in the house the previous year. Conservation has been an important part of his role, planting several miles of hedges and over 5,000 trees every year to maintain the estate for future generations.

They ran out of time to look around the extensive grounds and gardens, which were opened to the public by King Edward VII in 1908, but agreed that they would like to return to do that another time.

Having arrived back in Cromer they returned to The Cottage Café for tea, then back to the guest house where they did crossword puzzles before retiring for the night (Fred decided to stay for another night as it was getting late and he had done a lot of driving already that day).

Tuesday

They awoke to a misty and overcast morning and after the full English breakfast, Fred dropped them at Cromer's North Norfolk Steam Railway station and departed for his daughter's house in Colchester while they caught the steam train to Holt. The railway was built in 1887 by William Marriott and it is a ten and a half mile round trip by steam train from Sheringham Station where the museum and head quarters are housed. This route is know nationally as The Poppy Line since it passes through an area abundant in its fields of poppies and woodland which at other times of the year sports primroses, bluebells and yellow gorse and was indeed a delightful trip in countryside of outstanding natural beauty.

To their delight when they alighted at Holt Station there was the Holt Flyer, a horse drawn bus waiting to give passengers a ride into the centre of Holt which was about a mile away, so they took advantage of this unexpected treat and arrived in style in the market place by a fine memorial cross made of Clipsham stone.

They walked around the attractive small market town, looking at the antiques shops, art and pottery galleries, cafes, tea rooms, pubs and eventually made their way through a jumble of streets and alleyways into the lovely and well kept St. Andrew's parish church where they stopped to rest and have a cup of tea and a bite to eat.

After a short respite they walked to the one hundred acre Country Park where they enjoyed the majesty of the Scots Pine, Oak and Silver Birch trees and the tranquillity of the lake, commenting that Mabel would have loved this spot, and realising how much they were missing her. Due to their reverie they also missed the last train of the day and had to resort to finding a bus that went to Cromer, panicking (just a bit) as they weren't sure whether there was a direct bus route there (Mabel – where are you when they needed you?).

Before finding the bus stop in the town they had walked to the station and after realising that they had missed the last train were just in time to see the dray horses being uncoupled from the carts and stabled for the night.

On arriving back at their guest house they had a wash and brush up and went for dinner at a bistro in the town centre. Irene recalls having pasta and June remembers enjoying a Hungarian goulash, both of them consumed a few glasses of red wine and there was much merriment on the walk home!

Wednesday

Much to their delight when they awoke (after the previous day which was cool and misty) it was a warm and sunny morning and they thought that a day on the beach was in order. So after their usual hearty breakfast they set forth with their trusty walking sticks and an ordnance survey map of the area to have a ramble along the beach and the cliff tops, known locally as Overstrand.

What a delightful walk! They passed people playing golf, enthusiastic hang gliders, ramblers, dog walkers and small children flying kites, stopping to chat to a group of ramblers, to admire the seascape and generally pass the time of day with locals and holiday makers alike.

They stopped to have lunch in the Cliff Top Café before walking back along the cliff and down to the beach where they spent a lazy afternoon sunbathing and swimming in the sea. Making their way back along the pebbly beach and stepping over the wooden groynes they were saddened to sea a large dead grey seal on the beach, and further on they saw another one. A dog owner stopped to explain to them that she had seen yet another one and was trying to keep her dog away from them as they had a disease which was also potentially fatal to dogs. Apparently there was an epidemic and many seals had died, she said that she had phoned the relevant number to report these sightings.

18. CROMER 2002

Continuing along the beach they worked up an appetite for their tea which they had in the Cottage Café. After a pleasant stroll down to the pier to watch the crabbers they returned to the guest house, had a lovely soak in the bath and did a few crosswords before they went to their respective beds and a sound night's sleep.

Thursday

Over breakfast they discussed what they would do with their day and since June had two presents that she wanted to buy, one for her friend Nicola's birthday, and one for her daughter Susan's 'Bon Voyage' (she was taking a four year career break and going to live in New Zealand). They wandered amiably around the town, pausing here and there to admire the craftwork so attractively displayed in the shop windows and making their purchases, stopping of course, for refreshments as and when. After a successful shopping trip they went back to the guest house and washed and changed for dinner which they had in the Cottage Café on the seafront, followed by a stroll down to the pier. Back at the guest house they did a few crossword puzzles before retiring for the night.

Friday

They enjoyed their last breakfast together (on this adventure) then June packed her bags and they set off for Cromer Railway Station. June was going to meet up with Fred who was in Colchester, so that they could drive to Heathrow Airport and wave her daughter off as she departed for New Zealand. Irene saw June safely onto the train and went into the town for a mooch around as she awaited the arrival of her husband Buz, who was spending a day there with her before returning home.

Getting together later on they decided that it had been a very different adventure without Mabel, but that they had greatly enjoyed this part of the country and would like to return with Mabel, particularly to re-visit Sandringham.

19. Ironbridge

24th to 30th August 2003

This year they decided to go to Ironbridge and visit the various museums, whilst at the same time walking in some fascinating countryside with its unique chimneys and relics of the days when iron reigned supreme. They were also drawn to the area by the river Severn and its bridges built by the very talented engineer Thomas Telford.

Irene set about looking for some accommodation for them and found an interesting and friendly sounding guest house with Chris and Elloise at Woodlands Farm Guest House. The old farmhouse contained a small flat with an adjoining bedroom, which suited them perfectly.

Sunday
Buz picked up Mabel and June and with Irene set off for Ironbridge, stopping for lunch at the Meadow Inn beside the river Severn, after which they went to the museum of Iron & Enginuity. There was lots to see and marvel at, particularly the skills of the men and women who worked so hard in difficult and sometimes dangerous conditions in Victorian England.

They then drove to another site, where they watched a squirrel eating a bagel in the car park and where they wandered around a museum with giant furnaces and machinery, which was of particular interest to Buz. After mooching around and examining the exhibits, Buz drove them to Woodlands Farm where they met Elloise and Chris, who were on their way out to church. They unpacked their bags and gave Buz some food to take back home as there was a fridge and kettle, but no cooking facilities as they had expected.

Irene and Buz strolled around the fishing pool, woods and fields, which they discovered later was the site of the original brick making factory, there was still part of the building left which served as a stable for the current farmer's horse. They waved farewell to Buz and sorted out who was sleeping where, June and Mabel in the small bedroom, in twin beds, and Irene on the bed settee in the lounge cum kitchen, before setting off along the lane to The White Horse where they had sandwiches for their tea. When they returned to the farmhouse the bed settee was made up so they scrambled onto it and did crossword puzzles before retiring to their respective beds.

Monday

They enjoyed a very substantial breakfast which was served by Elloise in the dining room overlooking the ornamental gardens, with ponds and flower beds framed in the backdrop of the woods and fields. Much to their delight they saw squirrels scampering around the trees and a female mallard with her brood of ducklings waddling along behind her. After he had cooked their breakfast they watched Chris feed the ducks who were waiting expectantly at the French windows.

It was a lovely sunny day, so with their packs upon their backs, they set off to walk down to Ironbridge, after Chris had shown them the way (it was much further than they had thought when they booked it!).

Emerging into the town via the steps by the church, having stopped along the way to take photos of chimneys, they looked in a charity shop and June asked for a willow pattern plate to be set by to collect on the way back, as she didn't fancy carrying it around all day and Irene took a photo of the toy shop next door. Wandering along the road they saw a beautiful display of hanging baskets outside the Tea Emporium and, after the obligatory photographs they went into the tea rooms for their mid morning refreshments.

Crossing the road they ambled over the Iron Bridge taking photos and admiring the splendid views along the river Severn. Going back across the bridge they walked along the road and followed a path leading to the riverside and eventually they happened upon a group of enthusiastic adults and children coracle racing. It was fascinating to watch, and lots of fun for the participants who often ended up in the water amidst much laughter and high spirits. They had seen the advertisement for this earlier on, but thought that they had missed the event, so they were absolutely delighted to have happened upon it, a truly serendipitous moment! This was quite an unusual event, so they stayed and watched for a few hours, by which time it was lunch time, and since the coracle people had a stall selling food, they availed themselves of hot pork and stuffing baps!

After lunch they walked further along the river towards the power station, taking photos of the three huge cooling towers along the way. Eventually they

2003 Coracle racing at Ironbridge

19. IRONBRIDGE 2003

decided that it was time to make their way back to town, so they took a different route, along the roads, passing The Meadow Inn and noting the opening times!

It was too early for dinner, so they wandered further on and crossed a railway line, before coming to Dale End Park, where there was a magnificent bed of flowers, which was an environmental experiment by Sheffield University where hardy annuals had been sown directly into the ground. They stopped for quite a while to rest and to admire the flowers (and take photos of course).

Heading back to The Meadow Inn, where they were stopping for dinner, they passed Merry Thoughts toy shop and factory and Irene took a photo of Mabel and June by the big Policeman teddy bear outside. They were sorry to learn a few years later that the factory and shop were closed and that the big teddy bear had been auctioned off. At The Meadow Inn they enjoyed a delicious dinner and then caught a taxi back to the farmhouse, since they were full and tired and felt that they couldn't face the steep walk back to Woodlands, especially those steps!!

They wrapped up the day with a liquid night cap and a crossword puzzle.

Tuesday

After a super English breakfast and a chat to Elloise about dresses and to Chris about ducks, they set out to walk to Madeley along the main road. On the way Chris and Elloise overtook them in their car, pulling up they kindly offered them a lift, which they happily accepted.

They were on a quest to try to find Mabel's cousin Dorothy, who Mabel hadn't seen for about ten years. Mabel knew the road where she lived so they set out to find it. From the shopping centre at Madeley they walked along Church Road, which curved back on itself, consequently they passed the barn where King Charles II spent a night hiding from the Roundheads in the 17th century.

They then came to the Church where they met the vicar who told them about a communal grave for men and boys who had died in a mining accident. He took them around the side of the church to the burial site which was being restored, so they stopped to learn a little of how the miners came to be killed. In those days they accessed the mine by way of a large chain which the miners hung onto. Apparently the chain broke and they all fell down into the pit and were crushed by the heavy links. They only had a quick look in the church as there were workmen in there, before continuing on their way.

THREE HAPPY WANDERERS

2003 June and Mabel with the big teddy at Merrythorpes

19. IRONBRIDGE 2003

Around the bend they passed a little pub which they noticed sold sandwiches and made a mental note to return there for lunch. Arriving outside Dorothy's house Mabel approached the front door wondering what kind of reception she would get from her cousin (or even if she would be at home). The door was opened and a surprised Dorothy appeared, holding an armful of bedding, and when Mabel explained who she was, she welcomed them all into her house and made them tea and coffee. She was delighted to be re-united with Mabel and was pleased to give them a guided tour of her very pretty garden. They spent some time chatting, but since Dorothy was in the middle of her household chores and they hadn't yet had lunch, they left for the pub, promising to meet up with her later on.

Retracing their steps to the pub which they had espied earlier, they entered to be greeted by a big black dog and his master the Landlord, with whom they got into conversation and it transpired that Dorothy's house had many years previously been a doctor's house. After ordering sandwiches and drinks which the landlord prepared, he showed them how he had trained the dog to eat pork scratchings only at his command.

After a pleasant interlude discussing music (Rod Stewart's album of Ella Fitzgerald songs was playing and June asked for information about it, as she said that her daughter would like it) they returned to Dorothy's house. She bundled them into her car and took them to a picturesque village, where they walked around for a while and she then drove on to the China Museum which was about to close, so they only had a quick look around before returning to Ironbridge and The White Horse Inn for dinner.

Mabel and Dorothy reminisced and Dorothy told them about a stone cottage which was nearby, where her grandfather had lived and Mabel recalled visiting as a small child. After dinner they walked up the road to have a look at it. Dorothy then dropped them off at Woodlands Farm and Mabel promised to send her some photographs of their visit and to keep in touch.

At the farmhouse, they got chatting to Elloise who told them about some of the countries that she had visited and the costumes which she had collected, and when June said that she kept a red dress on the bedroom door, just because she liked to look at it, Elloise said that she would get out some of her costumes for them to look at.

Wednesday

At breakfast next morning they met a lady called Terri from St. Albans who was staying there on her own for two nights, whilst visiting her sister in hospital. As she was by herself and feeling sad about her sister, who was very ill, they decided to take her under their joint wings and arranged to meet her for a cup of tea in the town later. They walked down towards the town and when they came to Hodge Bower they walked along to find Prospect House which was built some time in the 19th century for Mabel's great-great grandfather.

Retracing their steps they met up with Terri in Ironbridge town centre and went for a cup of tea (and no doubt a naughty cake or two) before heading out to Blists Hill Victorian Museum, where Terri left them to go and visit her sister. Making their way around the Victorian shops they came to a pub where they were entertained by a singer and pianist performing songs from the turn of the century.

The audience was encouraged to join in the sing-along and June was pulled to her feet by the singer to 'ride' around the room on 'a bicycle built for two'. After this thirsty work they went upstairs to the café and had lunch before continuing on their exploration of the museum's workshops. The first stop was the doctor's house and surgery, then the workshop making GEM's rocking horses, the fairground, the old schoolroom and the foundry.

They had arranged to meet Terri at The Meadow Inn for their evening meal, so realising that to walk into Ironbridge would be a long way, they decided to walk to Madeley instead where they thought they could catch a bus to Ironbridge. To their dismay, they discovered that there was no bus due, but they were given the phone number of a taxi firm by two ladies at the bus stop, so June phoned on her mobile and it duly arrived and ferried them to the inn.

After a merry repast and doing their level best to amuse Terri, she took them back to Woodlands in her car, thanking them for being so mad and cheering her up. She came into their room for a nightcap with Elloise who took a photo of them with Terri, which June later sent to her in memory of a mad few days.

To their surprise, when they walked into their room, there were several beautiful, exotic dresses draped around the walls with a note from Elloise, who had gone out, saying that they were welcome to try them on, so they had a few glasses of wine, screwed up their courage, squeezed in their stomachs and did just that.

They laughed *so* much trying on the dresses and taking photos posed in the outfits, they were verging on the hysterical when June put the belly dancers outfit on! What a fun evening they had!

19. IRONBRIDGE 2003

Thursday
They awoke to rain, so after breakfast they set off with cagoules and umbrellas to walk to Colebrookdale Cemetery to search for grave stones of Mabel's grandmother's family. They didn't find them, so walked on to the church where they were shown around by the warden's husband. Mabel looked through the church records and found the entry for the marriage of her great aunt and uncle, Dorothy's grandparents.

Still in the rain they splashed on to another little museum, where they had pasties for lunch before having a look around. They made their way back to Woodlands and divesting themselves of their wet clothes, made themselves presentable before going out to dinner.

In the evening Irene's friends Val and Dave, who lived not too far away in Telford, came to collect them in their car to take them to a pub for a folk evening. They invited them to take a look around the grounds, where they admired the pools, waterfowl and woodland. Whilst they ate dinner they were entertained by an Irish folk group and a young man with a beautiful voice singing and playing the guitar.

After a pleasant and relaxing evening Val and Dave delivered them back to Woodlands Farm and bade them farewell.

Friday
They walked down to Ironbridge and caught the 96 bus to Shrewsbury whereupon they looked around the shops, making their way across a bridge to the Tourist Information Office and found out where the antique shops were. There was a café called Oscar's in the centre so they had lunch there, a delicious cheesy lasagne and then feeling very full went off to explore the antique shops.

After this they made their way to the Abbey using the map that Mabel had purchased at the Tourist Information Centre. They looked around the Abbey and then found a café called the Courtyard where they had a cup of tea before catching the bus back to Ironbridge.

Climbing back up the steps they wended their way back to the house and in due course had a makeshift tea with bits and bobs that they had brought with them, along with a cake which Elloise had very kindly made for them.

Saturday
They packed their cases and when Fred arrived to take them home they showed him around the house and gardens and the secret pool. He then took

them to Shrewsbury where they re-visited the Abbey and then the Tourist Information Office, which is in the same building as Oscar's café where they went for lunch.

June took Fred to look around the Antique Centre, whilst Irene and Mabel went to browse around the shops, but before long Irene began to feel ill so Mabel took her back to the Tourist Information Office, where there were some toilets and Irene was sick and felt even worse. Mabel sat on the stairs for a while waiting for Irene and checking every so often to see how she was. When Irene didn't get any better Mabel got quite worried and waiting until she felt that Irene was well enough to leave, she hurried off to find June and Fred who were nearby in the Antique Centre.

After returning to see how she was they decided to take Irene home straight away, so Fred went to fetch the car (and drove the wrong way up a one way street to get closer) as it was parked quite a long way off and she wasn't up to walking far. Once in the car she started to feel a bit better and eventually fell asleep. It transpired about a month later that she had gall stones and was whipped into hospital and had an emergency operation to remove her gall bladder by micro surgery.

Despite the disastrous ending they all agreed that this had been a superbly enjoyable and very memorable adventure.

20. Anglesey & Dublin

28th August to 4th September 2004

They had often discussed the Isle of Man as a venue for an 'Adventure' but it always seemed too complicated or expensive (transport wise), so Irene suggested Anglesey as a possible similar alternative, (both being on the west coast of Britain). This was within easy striking distance for their two chauffeurs and offered the possibility of a day trip to Ireland, which none of them had ever visited and were interested in doing, so they all happily agreed to this and Irene set about looking for a farm for them to stay on.

Saturday
At 9.15am Buz drove Irene and Mabel to June's house where they climbed into Fred's car, and waving goodbye to Buz set off for Anglesey, stopping on the way at Llangollen for tea and cakes and a comfort break. After they had crossed the bridge over the Menai Straits and onto the island of Anglesey, they looked for somewhere to have lunch and found a pub where they enjoyed their meal before setting off to Fferan Fawr farm in the north of the island.

Irene had booked them in for a week's bed and breakfast, without realising that the advert '10 minutes to the sea' referred to the time by car, so when they saw the notice to the farm and drove up the track, they realised what a long way it was from the main road and even further from the sea!

Heather, the farmer's wife, greeted them with a cup of tea and showed them to their rooms, after which Fred took them to the shops and railway station to get some provisions, and help them to familiarise themselves with the area. Fred left for home early evening and after waving him goodbye and thanking him for bringing them, they took a stroll around the farmyard with its chickens, cockerels, cats and dogs, then they went indoors to get their bearings in the house, which was previously two houses and so quite a maze.

They entered the house through a large conservatory which was used as the breakfast room, and went through the farmer's wife's sitting room, where she did her ironing, and into a small hall with stairs leading off which led up to June's bedroom and bathroom. To get to Irene and Mabel's bedroom and their sitting room, they had to go back outside and in through another door next to the barn. The sitting room was immediately inside the door and led through to a kitchen which in turn led through to the barn and also had a back door leading out to a patio with table and chairs. The stairs led off the sitting room up to the bedroom, which had a sloping ceiling and a window which overlooked the garden and a lovely old apple tree in full fruit.

Using the provisions which they had bought earlier at the local shop they put together a meal of soup, cheese on toast and tea and sat at the kitchen table making plans for the next day, and as they were feeling a little weary they had an early night.

Sunday

Irene was up at the crack of dawn as usual and wandered down to the paper shop, taking photos along the way and stopping for a chat to the farmer.

They arrived at the breakfast table which was covered with a blue and white checked tablecloth, to find it laden with all kinds of home made jams, marmalade, butter, sugars, fruit drinks and fresh fruit, and there was a side table which was filled with every sort of cereal.

Heather produced a wonderful full English breakfast, which was happily devoured, and they then set about tasting the lovely preserves on toast, washed down with lashings of hot tea. During the meal they were joined by a family, Sue and Mark and their little daughter Grace, who they got to know a little better over the next two days.

Although the weather was cold, overcast and windy, wrapped up warmly in cagoules with scarves gloves and boots (not forgetting their walking sticks) they set out along the farm track to the road heading for the sea. They found their way to a beach and promptly named it 'five house beach' and walked along the shore watching the large variety of seabirds and exploring the rock pools along a rocky promontory. The rain ceased after a while and although it was still very windy they found it quite exhilarating and pressed on in the hope of finding somewhere to get a cup of tea.

They were disappointed when they arrived at a car park where they had spotted a large white van, only to discover that it just sold seaside paraphernalia, so headed off towards another likely looking building across the sand dunes and after quite a trudge found that it was just houses, without a café in sight! Some time later after battling against the wind they espied The Maelor Lake Hotel which appeared to serve meals, so they entered in happy anticipation only to find that the hotel had fallen into partial disuse, and the proprietor only seemed to be interested in drinking with the locals. He did however oblige them by making a pot of tea, and they refreshed themselves whilst chatting to him and the only other customer.

Later on, when they came across windsurfers on the beach at Rhosneigr, they felt that the proprietor was missing a great business opportunity, with his large building so close to the beach and lake, with very few facilities for the surfers locally.

They set off again in search of lunch and followed the signs to Rhosneigr and found a pub Tofarny Mor serving meals, so they availed themselves of Sunday lunch in the restaurant. Prawn cocktails were followed by roast beef with all the trimmings, after which they staggered to the beach, and since the sun had come out, sat and did crossword puzzles and sunbathed in a spot sheltered from the wind.

After a good long rest, they started to make their way back to the farm, but were diverted by a sign reading 'home made cakes' and were tempted into a little teashop where they had tea and cakes, covered with hot custard. Continuing on their way they had almost reached the entrance to the farm track, when it began to rain heavily, so they sheltered under some trees, where June demonstrated the 'Doctor Doctor' line dance and tried to teach it to Irene and Mabel but to no avail, but at least they had a laugh at their antics (and probably so did anyone else who saw them!).

When the rain had ceased they walked slowly back up the long hill to the farmhouse where they dried out and changed their clothes, by which time it was early evening and they made themselves a scratch meal from their larder, which they sat and ate in June's bedroom, with a few glasses of red wine. They then did crosswords puzzles, recounting the events of the day, and after their exertions, they fell into their beds and had no trouble falling asleep.

Monday

Over breakfast Irene recounted her early morning walk, where she had photographed some council houses, an old mill tower base, a steaming manure heap, and the farmer's wife's 'girls' (a herd of Friesian cows). During breakfast Grace appeared at the table with a butterfly painted on her face, and Irene couldn't resist taking her photo. After their 'full English' breakfast, Heather

THREE HAPPY WANDERERS

2004 *Irene, June and Mabel and a millstone, Anglesey*

2004 *Molly Malone statue, Dublin*

20. ANGLESEY & DUBLIN 2004

cut up a whole fresh pineapple (which Grace had requested) and shared it between them.

Whilst June and Mabel prepared sandwiches for their picnic lunch, Irene photographed Heather with the farm dogs, before they set off to walk to Cable Bay. It was overcast and cool (but later on the sun came out and they were able to shed their coats). Walking along the beach heading for the bay they were fascinated by the seabirds feeding on the rich harvest of the sea.

Further along the coast they came upon an intriguing large green mound, which they felt compelled to explore, so they clambered up the winding path towards it and found that it was a Neolithic burial chamber circa 2500BC. They were amused when Mabel pointed out a notice which stated *'It is an offence to injure or deface the monument as it is in the care of the Secretary of State for Wales'*.

There were bars across the actual chamber, but they were able to go a little way in and take photos of one another, the large rocks, standing stones and boulders, after which they pressed on to Cable Bay where they removed their coats, ate their sandwiches, and sunbathed on the grassy cliff overlooking the bay. They did a few crossword puzzles to keep their brains working, which reminded them that they were in need of a cup of tea, so they set out to try to find their way back to the farm by an alternative route.

They walked for a very long time; probably a couple of hours, in what they thought was the right direction. Across the fields they could see their farm's buildings, but couldn't find a way through to them. The track seemed to stretch endlessly in front of them and they didn't see a soul to ask the way, but at last they came to a cottage and June asked an old man standing in the doorway if he could direct them to the farm. He said that there wasn't a way across the fields so they had to walk around the fields and onto the road where, after a very long time they came to the railway station, which they recognised, and passing through the level crossing were able to make their way back, arriving at the rear of the farm exhausted and thirsty.

After a reviving cup of tea they agreed that they had walked enough for one day, so decided to make their own evening meal instead of going to the Tofarny Mor as planned, so they made do with cheese on toast, followed by a cake which Heather had made for them. In the evening they sat chatting in the lounge with Heather and Grace's mother Sue, drinking wine and Southern Comfort, and generally putting the world to rights. After a very pleasant interlude they realised that it was getting late and finally retired at 1am.

Tuesday

They had an early breakfast with Sue, Mark and Grace who were leaving for home that morning. After waving goodbye to them they sat chatting to Heather for a while and said that they would like to go to Dublin on the ferry from Holyhead for the day. Heather, who knew the train and ferry times, said that they would have difficulty in tying them together and that they would arrive back at the farm very late with no means of transport from the railway station. She offered to take them to Holyhead in her car and collect them again at the end of the day, but they would have to make an early start, so they gratefully accepted her kind offer.

They decided to stay around the farm for a while and as it was a lovely day, they sat in the sun and looked around the garden at the varieties of apple trees and visited the new born puppies in the barn. There were 15 of them and the mother dog had placed them in three little groups – she must have felt overwhelmed at having to feed so many! At lunch time they made sandwiches to eat sitting in the garden. Mabel's chair had a rain water puddle on it which she didn't notice until she sat in it! She had to dash indoors to change her wet trousers, and this was then referred to afterwards by Irene and June as 'when Mabel wet her trousers'.

They enjoyed a lovely relaxing day, doing a quiz, taking it in turns to set questions which they hoped would puzzle the other two, Irene and Mabel had a game of scrabble, while June chased the beautiful cockerel amongst the bushes trying to get a good shot with her camera. Both June and Irene took pictures throughout the day, especially when the RAF fighter planes came zooming low over the top of the house, shattering the peace and quiet. The first time that this happened they scared the living daylights out of them and the farmyard fowl, which scattered squawking into the barn.

Feeling refreshed after a restful day they smartened themselves up and set off at about 7pm for the two mile walk to the Tofarny Mor pub, where they had dinner and a few relaxing drinks, before wending their way home in the dark with the aid of Irene's torch.

Wednesday

After an early breakfast Heather ran them to Holyhead where they caught the Stenaline ferry to Dublin. They strolled around the deck looking at shops and cafes, and after a cup of tea they went out of a rear door to watch the bow waves and get some fresh air. They landed at Dunlaughaire and made their way to the railway station where they boarded the train for Dublin. The train stopped at lots of little stations and they had no idea where to get off, so they asked another passenger who told them that they should alight at Tara Street, which they did.

On reaching the main road they saw a notice for open top bus tours and decided to take one, purchasing tickets for a tour which was running in about half an hour, which just about gave them time to replenish the 'inner woman'. They made their way to a pub off O'Connell Street where they had sandwiches and tea before dashing back to catch the tour bus at 12.30pm.

Climbing up to the top deck they had a great view of the city as the guide pointed out places of interest along the way, including amongst other things the Cathedral, statues, churches, the university and the Guinness factory. There wasn't time for them to get off the bus to look around as they needed to get the early ferry in time to meet Heather at Holyhead.

Alighting from the tour bus they made their way back to O'Connell Street and took photos of an enormously tall monument, The Millennium Spire, statues of James Joyce and Molly Malone.

June recalls telling Irene that she wasn't sure what the new 'no smoking' law covered, and whether the streets were considered 'a public place'. The law had just been enforced and since no-one seemed to be smoking in the streets she didn't know. It felt strange, but very pleasant for non-smokers to be in places where smoking was no longer allowed.

Keeping an eye on the time, they found a café where they could have tea and scones before returning to Tara Street Station and catching the train back to the ferry. As it was getting near to tea time, they had fish and chips on the ferry, and very nice they were too! They had pleasant crossings on both trips and really enjoyed them. When they reached Holyhead June phoned Heather to say that they were back, and they sat under a clock with statues on it while they waited for her. It was at this point they realised that they had all been to Ireland, for the first time, and had not partaken of a pint of Guinness!!

They arrived back at the farm at about 7pm, so after an easy day on their feet, went for a walk around the farm followed by the cat, and admired (and took photos of) the glorious sunset. Later on they sat in the lounge doing metal puzzles (exercising their brains you see) and watched a James Bond film on a video which Heather had loaned to them.

Thursday

On Irene's early morning walk and photo opportunity, she again spotted the old mill and mentioned it at breakfast, where they had been joined by a regular visitor to the farm called Mike. He offered to run them to the mill in his car so off they all went and arriving at the mill they took pictures and Mike took one of the three of them by a mill stone. A lady came out of the old house and pointed out that it was private property, so shamefacedly they got back in the car and directed Mike to 'five house beach' where they watched some canoeists surfing the waves.

After a while they decided to go to RAF Valley to take close-ups of the stealth bombers, where the three friends went for a walk around the perimeter of the base while Mike went off on his own. They noted the sign *'Police Dogs – halt if challenged'* and speculated upon what they would do if this should happen? Run? Freeze? Or offer them biscuits?! They picked and ate blackberries along the way and after stopping for a while on a grassy knoll to eat their sandwiches, from which vantage point they could observe the comings and goings of the aircraft. Since this was the closest they could get to the planes they turned around and made their way back to the wooden bridge.

They were just contemplating the rather long walk back to the farm, when Mike reappeared and offered them a lift. He asked them if they would like to go to Beaumaris (on the other side of the island) and they were very happy to jump at the opportunity, since it was a long way and they had no car.

Arriving at Beaumaris they stopped at a café near to the castle where they sat at an outside table, and whilst they were awaiting the arrival of their tea and scones, they snapped away with their cameras at the antics of a seagull trying to get a drink from a bucket. After their enjoyable repast they strolled through a park and leaned on a rail watching the boats on the Menai Straits and taking pictures of the two bridges which span it. Mike then took them across one of the bridges to the mainland, and across the other bridge back onto Anglesey. On arrival back at the farm, they thanked Mike for a most enjoyable day and for being such good company, before washing and changing their clothes and setting off on the trek to the pub for dinner.

Friday

After another magnificent breakfast they set off on the long walk down the farm track, across the main road, and along to Rhosneigr, which took a few hours, so naturally by the time they got there it was lunch time. They found a fish and chip shop and took their hot packages to the beach, where they sat in the shelter of a wall, as it was windy, and consumed them with relish whilst watching sail boarding and windsurfing on the sea. The sea was rough and choppy, which made it very exciting to watch, especially when the sail boarders did somersaults. After a while they started to feel a bit cold, and as the wind was blowing sand over them, they took themselves off to the little teashop and had tea and home-made cakes with hot custard again.

On the way to Rhosneigr they had noticed a small lake, so thought that they would explore it on the way back. Arriving at the lakeside, they crossed a wooden footbridge and proceeded to walk around the lake; it was still very windy and the water was whipped into foam around some little inlets. Irene and June took photos of the wildflowers along the way, contrasting with the rippling water slapping against the banks of the lake.

They came to a path leading away from the lake and feeling adventurous they followed it, not knowing where it would lead them. At the side of the path there was a notice informing them that the lake was a David Bellamy Conservation area. The path led them on to a deserted derelict stone-built cottage where the roof had fallen in and it looked very sad. They imagined people living there in years gone by and tending their orchard which was now very neglected. They trudged through the overgrown orchard, and came to a stile leading into a field; they had just clambered over it, when about half a dozen dogs rushed up to them barking madly. Bravely they brandished their walking sticks at them and carried on through the field, stopping to talk to several horses behind an electric fence.

Wondering how they were going to find their way back to the road, they came at last to a cottage with a gate leading to the road with a notice stating 'Parking Forbidden'. A little further along the road they saw a sign to the Maelor Lake Hotel, so knew that they were going in the right direction, and eventually found their way back to the farm.

They got back about 5pm, and after a short rest, they showered, changed their clothes and set off again en route for the Tofarny Mor restaurant where they enjoyed an excellent dinner. June had a lamb shank (her favourite), Irene a large steak and Mabel had lasagne with garlic bread. After relaxing for a while they summoned up their energies for the long walk back to the farm and started walking along the road in the dark by torchlight. They saw the headlights of an approaching car and were very relieved to find that it was Heather, who was worried about them, and had set out to look for them. She very kindly gave them a lift, for which they were mightily grateful.

When they arrived back at the farm they abandoned their plans to do their packing and fell wearily into their beds.

Saturday

They enjoyed their last breakfast with Heather, whom they now regarded as a friend, and packed their bags before Buz arrived to take them home about 10.30am. Heather made him a cup of tea, after which they gave him a guided tour of the farm and its animals, and loaded their bags into his car. With very mixed feelings they bade Heather goodbye, thanked her for all her kindness and generosity, and set off on their journey home.

They had planned to stop in Llangollen for lunch, but it was very busy and crowded with traffic, so they drove on and eventually came to The Aqueduct Inn, which overlooked the Pont-Cysyllte Aqueduct. After they had lunched there, Buz drove them down to the bridge, parked up, and they all strolled over the aqueduct, watching the narrow boats drifting along beside them, exchanging pleasantries with the bargees. They bought ice creams at the opposite side, and walked back eating them and enjoying the sunshine.

At the end of the day, upon arriving home, and thanking Buz for a safe journey, they all agreed that although it had been quite tiring, it had been a smashing 'Adventure'.

21. Highley, Severn Valley

29th August to 5th September 2005

This year they decided to take advantage of the kind offer by Irene's friends Brenda and Ray for the use of their log cabin in Highley near the Severn Valley Steam Railway. Shortly before they were due to go on their adventure Mabel was taken ill and was in hospital with polymialgia, so Irene and June reluctantly decided to go, hoping that Mabel might be able to join them during the week.

Bank Holiday Monday
On a lovely sunny morning Buz and Irene arrived at June's house at 9.30am and promptly returned to Irene's house to pick up her walking stick (a very important item!) before setting off for Highley. They made very slow progress getting to Bewdley as the traffic was typical of a bank holiday! Eventually they stopped at a pub just outside Bewdley and had lunch before carrying on into the town where they couldn't find room to park as it was packed out with holidaymakers.

Since there was nowhere to park they decided to press on to Highley and after driving along the side of the signal box on the railway station (which seemed a very odd thing to do) they came to a lane which led up to a field. The cabin was situated immediately to the right hand side of the field and discreetly distanced from its next door neighbour. As they drove up they were welcomed by Brenda and her family who made them feel at home as they proffered them cups of tea. They spent some time chatting before they took their leave and headed back home. Buz stayed for a while longer and left about 7.45pm, hastily departing as they started to prepare dinner which was curry with naan bread. He hates curry!

After dinner they sat out on the balcony and soaked up the last rays of the sun, listening to the birds' evensong and the breeze sighing through the apple trees whilst watching out for squawking pheasants as they scuttled across the field and darted into the surrounding hedges and trees. It was a perfect end to the day and they sat and talked about Mabel, hoping that she was recovering and would be able to join them later in the week.

Tuesday

It was a gloriously hot morning so they sat outside on the balcony to eat breakfast and think about where to spend the day. They decided upon Bridgnorth so gathering up their cameras and walking sticks, set off down the lane to Highley Station. There they caught the steam train after picking up timetables and leaflets for places of interest and purchasing tickets from the uniformed station master. Shortly afterwards the big old black steam engine puffed its way alongside the platform and squealed to a halt after tooting its whistle as it approached the station. Clambouring aboard the newly varnished, wooden coach carriages, they positioned themselves by the windows the better to enjoy the view.

The view was indeed splendid as they swished past the farmers' fields with sheep and cattle contentedly grazing along the banks of the River Severn. There was a patchwork of fields separated by hedgerows and generously dotted with trees and wildflowers. Predominant amongst the flowers was the pale cerise coloured rose bay willow herb (otherwise known as fireweed because cinders from the engines would set fire to the grass along the side of the tracks where the seeds had been blown by the passing of the trains). Wherever they go they always seem to come across this stately and beautiful wildflower. They also passed a golf course and the Severn Valley Country Park on either side of the track where you can flag the train down at Halt.

Arriving at Bridgnorth they strolled around the town and found a cosy café where they enjoyed lunch. Afterwards they mooched around the shoe shops looking, without success, for a long handled shoe horn for Irene's brother and then turned their attention to the antique and charity shops. Wandering around the town they took photos of the many and varied multicoloured hanging baskets. The alleyways were bedecked with rows of baskets and tubs overflowing with petunias, fuchsias, begonias, geraniums and a multitude of other annuals. There was a very interesting black and white gabled building set in the middle of the High Street on its own little island. This was originally the Corn Exchange and is now the Town Hall and Assizes Court open to the public. So they wandered in and looked around the various rooms containing stained glass windows, heraldic shields, mayoral or civic robes and ancient items of weaponry. There was no one else around, so June tried out the Judge's chair and demanded 'silence' from the imaginary members while Irene banged the gavel. This was thirsty work so they trotted off to find the town hall's tea rooms and indulge in tea and cakes before making their way to the train station where they caught the 5.25pm train to Highley.

Arriving back at the cabin they had cottage pie with home grown runner beans from Irene's garden, then relaxed doing crossword puzzles and reading in the evening.

Wednesday

It was a lovely hot sunny day and while Irene was cooking bacon and eggs June phoned Doug to enquire about Mabel. She was feeling a bit better and hoped to leave hospital the following day. Pleased with that good news they gathered up their sticks and bags and set off to walk to The Severn Valley Country Park. From Highley Station they turned left at the pub and walked alongside the river until they came to the old bridge. Crossing over they headed up to the visitors centre where they asked the ladies who were serving behind the counter how to get to Alveley village. As they made them a cup of tea they explained that they planned to have lunch in The Three Horseshoes, feeling a bit guilty that they weren't eating at the centre. Following their directions they came to a large field full of wildflowers which banked steeply up towards Alveley. Puffing their way up the hill they came upon a stone memorial to the miners.

They stopped to rest and take photos since there was a wonderful panoramic view of the Severn Valley. Continuing on they passed through a gate and turned left along the lane to the village, but to their dismay discovered that the pub was closed. In desperation they tried the village store but that was closed too! Since they were getting very hungry by this time they took a few quick photos of the church and surrounding houses and headed speedily back to the visitors centre. They were glad to find that they could still get something to eat as it was long past lunch time, making do with sandwiches, crisps and cups of tea.

After lunch they walked back to the river where they saw a group of workmen building a new bridge alongside the old one. Stopping to talk to them they discovered from the young crane driver that a kingfisher caught and ate its breakfast near the bridge each morning. He said that it perched on the same post on the riverbank every day and that he got there early to watch it before the other workmen arrived and disturbed the peace. He told them that he was a city boy who had never spent time in the countryside and was fascinated by the wildlife and scenery. He was hoping that the job would last a long time as he was usually employed in towns and cities and that it was a joy to come to work each day. His enthusiasm was catching as he appeared to be making a real study of the things that he was observing each day. They were delighted to have had the opportunity to chat with him and have often wondered whether he changed his lifestyle to accommodate his new found passion.

As they walked back along the riverbank dark clouds were gathering above and it was clear that they were in for some rain, so they stepped out a bit sharpish since they didn't want to get wet! No sooner had they got inside than the heavens opened and they sat and watched the storm lashing the trees and bushes with the lightning illuminating the field and the other cabins. They heard one enormous crack of thunder with a simultaneous flash of lightning and knew that something very nearby had been struck.

Hoping that the rain would have ceased by the following day, they continued to prepare and eat dinner which was chicken and mushroom stir fry and rice, and tucked in with relish since lunch had been somewhat sparse. The storm eventually abated and they retired for the night early in peace and quiet.

Thursday

Perhaps because they went to bed early, June was the first one to get up at 7.30am in the morning (which is a very unusual occurrence) and walked around the field checking to see whether the storm had caused any damage. There was nothing seriously damaged, just a few branches and lots of leaves. Irene was surprised to find her friend up first when she was greeted with a cup of tea in bed! Happily the weather had changed back to sunshine and clear skies, so after breakfast they set off to catch the train to Bewdley. Arriving at Bewdley Station they were very taken with the public conveniences on the platform, so stopped to take photos before crossing the railway bridge and walking into the town.

After a short stroll along the river bank and a mooch in the charity and antique shops on the main road, they went to the fish and chip shop by the river bridge and ordered lunch. Since it was a lovely day they sat outside to eat, and watched the comings and goings of the swans, ducks and geese, with the gulls dive bombing all and sundry and hunting for chip scraps. Once

21. HIGHLEY, SEVERN VALLEY 2005

replete they headed back up the hill to the museum and visited the various workshops. They were particularly interested in the making of clay pipes and their history.

Making their way around to the rear of the museum they wandered around the small formal garden before heading out to the park. The pond was particularly beautiful, edged with numerous plants, shrubs and ornamental trees and containing a flotilla of pretty pink and white water lilies. After a walk around the pond they found a bench and sat watching the frogs hopping about on the lily pads and the ducks waddling in and out of the pond, apparently oblivious to the dangers of the marauding children who had arrived with their parents. Their peace and quiet having been shattered they took themselves off and made their way back to the river where they sat and enjoyed a cup of tea, while watching the waterfowl. Passing under the bridge they came upon a paved area where flood barriers were being built as a precaution against the houses and businesses being flooded as they had been recently.

Ambling along to the station they caught the train back to Highley and walked to the cabin where they prepared salad with jacket potatoes, ham and cheese. After a very pleasant day they rounded it off by playing the card game 'Bezique' before retiring.

Friday

After breakfast they set off in bright sunshine to find Highley Country Park which they had seen signposted by the station. Making their way up the slope, through the woods, they emerged into a large open space with grassy hills leading up to a huge wheel perched on the top. Trudging up the hill they arrived at the wheel which, it transpired, was part of the winding gear from the now defunct Highley colliery and had been set in stone in the park as a memorial to the miners who had worked there. Nearby there was a pit trolley which was full to overflowing with purple petunias. They stopped to admire the view and the flowers and after taking a few photos moved on through the park, passing the toilets (and making good use of them). Leaving the park by the large wrought iron gates they emerged onto the road which winds up to the village.

Continuing up the road they came to Smoke Alley which, it was clear from the map of the village in the cabin, was a short cut from the station to the centre of Highley. There was a lady in the garden of the first cottage that they came to and she came over to talk to them as they had stopped to admire her absolutely stunning garden. Half the garden consisted of a huge vegetable and

2005 *Cattle in the River Severn near Arley*

2005 *Church House, Highley*

21. HIGHLEY, SEVERN VALLEY 2005

fruit patch and the other half was lawns and flower beds, with at least half a dozen hanging baskets and tubs around the front and side of the house. They were quite overwhelmed at the amount of produce in the vegetable patch and the great variety of plants and shrubs on the ornamental side. They told the lady that they had never seen such a fabulous cottage garden and got chatting about the flowers and shrubs which she told them was the part of the garden which she tended. She then called her husband over and they chatted to him about the vegetable patch which he looked after and was clearly closer to his heart than the flowers. They had quite a long chat since there was so much to admire from the abundance of brightly coloured flowers through to the ornamental stone wall and neat lawns. After asking if they might take some photos they wandered about the garden happily snapping away while the lady told them that they had won a prize in the Britain in Bloom flower competition.

When they mentioned that they were on their way to have a look around Highley, the lady asked them to go into her cottage so that she could give them a leaflet showing places of interest in the village. She pointed out the section referring to Smoke Alley, telling them that the sandstone cottages date from 1800 and would have housed quarrymen and their families. Thanking her for the leaflet they took their leave and carried on their way, stopping next at the parish church of St. Mary's.

Approaching the church they stopped to admire the lovely old black and white gabled building standing next to it. They later learned that this late medieval house was the original home of the first priest and they wondered when it had started to lean to one side, hopefully not when he was living in it! Entering the cool confines of the church they admired the stained glass windows and made a mental note to return for a longer visit. They wandered around the rear of the church and to their dismay came across a barn full of chickens, which smelled awful and looked even worse! They were very distressed to see the conditions that the hens were being kept in, cooped up in the old barn and hoped fervently that they were allowed to roam about sometimes.

Leaving the churchyard they walked along to the centre of the village where they came upon a metal statue in the form of a miner in a cage in the pit shaft, with a clock on the top. There was a bench very close to it, so after a quick wash and brush up in the new brick-built conveniences, they sat down and ate their packed lunches in the village square, where they had an excellent view of the Clee Hills.

THREE HAPPY WANDERERS

When they had finished lunch they crossed the road and entered Silverdale Street where they were very pleasantly surprised to see a long row of hanging baskets full of colourful flowers attached to the walls of the terraced houses. There were also tubs and troughs in between which were overflowing with multicoloured blooms. Seeing a lady up a step ladder weeding one of the baskets they stopped to congratulate her, and the rest of the residents, on the wonderful display of flowers which greeted you as you entered the street. Another lady joined them and between them they told them about the joint efforts of the street's occupants in the planting and upkeep of the flower displays and the allotments on the opposite side of the road. They hadn't noticed the allotments and when they turned around to look at them they were very impressed with their abundance of produce and the orderliness of their layout. The ladies explained that they belonged to the street's residents since they had no back gardens. If any of the residents were not able or interested in tending their plots or putting up hanging baskets, other people in the street would step in and do them.

After a very interesting chat to the two ladies, they took their leave of them and with their directions to them to head for the donkey bridge, they set off up the road and on the right hand side of the row of houses they found a stile on the edge of a field. Clambouring over the stile they spotted the diagonal track which they had been told to follow across the field, so they wandered along it looking at the many species of wildflowers along the way. When they came to a gap in the hedge they found themselves entering an alleyway at the rear of a housing estate. Emerging into Redstone Drive they then turned left and saw a lady mowing her lawn. They stopped to ask her which was the path to the donkey bridge and she pointed out a very narrow overgrow track opposite her bungalow. After a pleasant conversation about gardens and plants they set off once again in their quest.

They were very glad that they had brought their walking sticks with them as the path was very narrow and overgrow with stinging nettles. Bashing their way through the waist high nettles they eventually came to Netherton Lane which they crossed and continued along a track which had the golf course to their right. After a while they came to a wide road which they later discovered was Bind Lane, so continuing down the lane to the left they arrived at a ford. Not sure whether they had passed the bridge they asked a Japanese family, who were taking photos, if they knew where the bridge was. They indicated to them that they had indeed passed the spot where they should have turned off, unfortunately they had just come down a steep hill, so had to trudge back

21. HIGHLEY, SEVERN VALLEY 2005

up again. The whole area was rich woodland with thick, high trees and bushes, so peering into a gap they spotted the sign 'Donkey Bridge' and let out a cheer. According to the leaflet that they were using as a guide the Donkey Bridge was about 300 years old and had recently been restored to its former glory. As the name implies it was a packhorse bridge and was constructed from red sandstone having twin arches which span the Borle Brook.

After taking a few photos they headed back up Bind Lane and turned left into Woodhill Road. They had noticed in their leaflet a sign to The Garden Village and assuming that it would be a pretty area with hanging baskets such as they had seen in Silverdale Street, decided to do a detour to look at it. It was in the area where they planned to have their evening meal, since The Malt Shovel had been recommended to Irene by Brenda and Ray, the owners of the cabin. The road stretched out before them and seemed to go on forever (they had been walking for a very long time) and they were glad to reach the area called Garden Village. Walking around the small housing estate they searched for something resembling a garden or a village and were disappointed on both counts! All they found was a row of concrete built shops with not a flower in sight.

Making their way back down the main road they first came to The Castle public house where they studied the menu before going to look at The Malt Shovel which wasn't far away. There were tables and chairs outside which overlooked the Clee Hills and since it was promising to be a lovely sunset, they settled upon having dinner there. They ordered food and sat outside with their drinks, waiting in eager anticipation for the sunset, along with several other customers. They were not disappointed as it was a glorious and spectacular sight as the sun sank slowly behind the Clee Hills, washing them with a gold and orange hue.

When they had eaten their dinner and drunk a few more glasses of wine they decided that it was much too far to walk back to the cabin. They went into the bar and asked the landlady if she kept the phone numbers of local taxis and if they could use her phone. She laughed and said that there was no chance of getting a taxi at that time of the evening as they had to come out from Bridgnorth. They must have looked very despondent at the thought of walking all that way back because she disappeared into the rear of the pub and returned with the good news that her husband was prepared to run them home. In the event it was the lady who ran them home whilst the man shut up shop, they had mentioned that they knew Brenda and Ray and wondered if that was why they got a lift.

As they drove along the Bridgnorth Road they realised just how far it was to the station, especially at night and in the dark after a hard day's walking! After thanking their rescuer as she drove off and being thankful to be back at the cabin, they fell into their beds and slept soundly.

Saturday

Arising refreshed from their well deserved sleep they treated themselves to a delicious bacon and egg breakfast, sitting outside on the balcony, enjoying the rural view as they ate, since it was a beautiful sunny day. Setting off with their trusty walking sticks they strolled down to the station and saw a Thomas the Tank mask on the front of a steam train. The train was full of children and their parents enjoying a trip on 'Thomas' so they took a few photos and moved on. Passing The Ship Inn, which was in a very derelict state, they discussed, as they walked along the riverbank towards Arley, how they would renovate it and serve delicious tempting meals.

Strolling along the edge of the river they happened upon various farm animals, first coming to a handsome chestnut horse and stopped to admire his glossy mane. Irene promised to bring him an apple next time they came that way and they walked on enjoying the sights and sounds of the river, stopping to take photos of a herd of cows which had come down to the waters edge to drink.

Continuing on their way they came to a large sloping field where sheep were grazing. June was walking ahead along a narrow path when she came quite close to a large sheep with black tipped ears. Naturally she stopped to say 'hello' and the sheep stared at her and stamped its two front feet! She fell about laughing and Irene bringing up the rear wondered what all the kefuffle was about. When June explained and pointed out the bad tempered animal, Irene took a photo in the hope that it would repeat its performance.

Pressing on they came to a big tree on the edge of the riverbank, which appeared to have been struck by lightning, it was broken in two and there was a strange bright orange substance inside it. On closer inspection they observed that the base of the tree was smouldering and they didn't quite realise at first that it was on fire! They concluded that this may have been a casualty from the storm three days previously. It was hard to believe that it could still be burning, but it was, and in a valiant effort to dowse the fire Irene poured the water from her drinking bottle over it. June promised to share her bottle of water so that Irene wouldn't dehydrate as a result of her sacrificial act!

21. HIGHLEY, SEVERN VALLEY 2005

Just as they were about to continue on they saw a Severn Valley volunteer jogging past, they called to him to show him the damaged tree and ask if there was someone that they could report to that it was still smouldering. He came over to have a look and said that he would let the forestry commission people know. Thankful that they were relieved of the responsibility of having to do something about it, they went on their way.

Coming to the railway bridge where Irene wanted to get a shot of a steam train going over it, they sat down on the riverbank and watched the river drifting past and listened to the odd biplane murmuring overhead. It was all so peaceful and tranquil, until June happened to look up and see a very menacing looking figure on the opposite bank. Irene had wandered off at this point to await the hoped for train, so hadn't spotted the man staring across the water and giving June the creeps. He was wearing shorts and a tee shirt and sunglasses, all very correct for a hot sunny day, but why was he wearing gloves and looking as though he was trying to conceal the fact by holding them behind his back? At one stage he appeared to be searching for a way down to the river (which was quite shallow at this point) as though he was planning to cross it. There were no houses or signs of human life anywhere near and it was quite scary! Irene re-joined June and both took photos of the man who, by this stage, had taken on the persona of a serial killer. They heaved a sigh of relief when he turned around and went back the way he had come.

Brave as they were, they didn't fancy continuing on towards Arley in case they met up with him somewhere along the way, so turned around and sauntered back to Highley. Back at the cabin they cooked a lovely meal of steak and jacket potatoes and relaxed with a few glasses of wine, mulling over the day's events. After a few more glasses of wine and a game or two of cards they retired to bed, all thoughts of serial killers dismissed from their minds!

Sunday

Another lovely sunny morning so they decided to go for a ride on a train to Hampton Loade, have Sunday lunch at the pub there and endeavour to walk back. After breakfast they optimistically set off in their shorts and tee shirts, their trusty walking sticks in hand, and caught the train to Hampton Loade passing through Halt. When they arrived at the station there were lots of people wandering around and sitting about enjoying the sunshine, many eating ice-creams, and 'train spotting'.

Making their way to the pub they realised that they may not be able to sit outside in the sun as the garden area was packed with families, obviously enjoying a day out. In the cool interior of the pub they ordered their roast beef dinners and relaxed with pints of lager and lime whilst they waited for their lunch to arrive. They waited for quite a long time as there were so many people to serve, but it was no great hardship, sitting drinking lager and putting the worlds to rights!

After lunch they walked back along the riverside seeking shade wherever possible since it was very hot, enjoying the beautiful scenery and counting their blessings that they live in such a lovely country. They went back to the cabin and after cups of tea set about making a start on packing for their departure the following day. The evening was spent relaxing on the balcony with glasses of wine, watching the sun go down and doing a crossword puzzle, before retiring.

Monday

They got up bright and early, breakfasted and cleared away so that they would be ready for when Fred arrived at 10 o'clock. Greeting him with a cup of tea they sat for a while on the balcony and discussed what Fred might like to do for the day. He decided that he would like to walk to Arley and have lunch there. Once again they were blessed with a lovely sunny day as they strolled along the riverbank passing the chestnut horse, where Irene apologised for forgetting the promised apple. When they came to the burnt out tree Fred was just as staggered as they had been to find that there was still smoke emitting from it. They looked for the black eared sheep which had stamped its feet at June a few days before, but couldn't find it.

They took some lovely photos of a herd of cows drinking from the riverbank and were quite glad to be on the opposite side of the river when they noticed a massive white bull in amongst them! The herd looked so attractive because the cows were all different colours ranging from white through creams and browns to black.

Pointing out the spot where they saw the 'serial killer' they continued on to Arley and were very glad to see The Harbour Inn come into view. Hungry and thirsty they went in and ordered BIG drinks from the landlord to quench their thirsts whilst perusing the menu. They settled on steak and chips which they thoroughly enjoyed, before making their way up the hill to Arley station, where they caught the train back to Highley. When they arrived in Highley they took Fred along Smoke Alley to see the wonderful garden which they had admired earlier in the week. Both the man and lady were in the garden and they came over to the hedge to have a chat. After due inspection and

21. HIGHLEY, SEVERN VALLEY 2005

admiration they walked up to the main road and crossed over to the church where (in a very proprietorial manner) they showed Fred around.

After a stroll around the village, they made their way down the hill passing through The Country Park and re-visiting the wheel and the wagon full of petunias, on their way to The Ship Inn over the railway line. The pub was closed (again!) so they had a look at the river and Fred chatted to the fishermen sitting on the bank. Returning to the cabin they had a cup of tea and a slice of cake and then packed the bags and boxes into Fred's car ready for the journey home.

They set off about 8 o'clock but didn't get very far! After bumping down the lane to Highley station they could hear something banging on the bottom of the car. Fred drove on a few yards to the station car park and pulled up to inspect the exhaust pipe, which was hanging loose. He spotted some wire in a small fenced off area, so climbed over and picked up a piece to try to tie the exhaust pipe back on. After several futile attempts to make it secure he decided to call the A.A. on his mobile and get some professional help. By this time it would have been about 9 o'clock and was quite dark, when suddenly several police cars swooped into the car park with their blue lights flashing. They assumed that they had come for them, since there was no-one else around and Fred had climbed over the fence by the station workshop. Expecting them to come rushing over they sat and waited in trepidation, but when they produced bags of fish and chips and lounged against their car bonnets eating them, they realised that they were not there on their account!

After a while one of the officers came over, curious no doubt as to why they were just sitting there at that time of night, and asked if everything was alright. When they explained their predicament he sympathised and told them why they were there. He said that they were on a training exercise from Manchester seeing how fast they could get to Highley, and which was the quickest route. After consuming their chips they all piled into their vehicles (about 5 of them) and zoomed off, leaving them to the eerie atmosphere of the deserted station. About an hour later the welcome sight of the big yellow A.A. van hove into view and they were pleased to know that rescue was in sight. The A.A. man was very pleasant and made the exhaust pipe as secure as he could, after inspecting the underside of the car for any other damage.

Thanking him for his help they set off to Bewdley, with him following to ensure that the pipe stayed on, before he turned off to go home. By this time they were starving, since they had planned to eat back at their homes, but that was several hours before! Deciding that the fish and chip shop was probably still open as it was, by this time, about 10.30pm, they drove to the shop by the river and bought their supper. Sitting in the car they enjoyed the fish and chips very much, as the smell of the chips which the police officers had been eating had given them an appetite.

They set off for home about 11.00pm and arrived back at Irene's house at midnight. They regaled Buz with the story of the breakdown (they had phoned him earlier to explain the situation and tell him not to worry when Irene didn't turn up at the expected time).

All in all it was an adventure in itself, and another tale to add to the stories which they would relate to Mabel whom they hoped would join them the following year. Although they had really enjoyed themselves they had missed having Mabel with them and felt that she would have loved it too.

22. Dolgellau

12th to 16th August 2007

Mabel had been ill, and in and out of hospital over the previous two years, so as she was now starting to feel a little better, she said that she would like to tentatively embark upon another 'adventure'. In 2006, since Mabel was still feeling not quite herself, they took their men folk and all went instead on a 1940s weekend in Cambridgeshire.

Irene enquired from her friend Brenda if her cabin on the side of the river Severn at Bewdley was free for them to visit and she said that it was alright for them to go from a Monday to Friday, so Irene booked it up for them.

In the meantime there were horrendous floods, washing away the banks of the Severn in the Bewdley area and destroying part of the railway track and embankments on the Severn Valley Railway. The whole of the area was devastated and it was some months before it was restored. Although the cabin was not affected, the garden was under water and they decided that it was best not to go until the railway track was repaired and they would be able to travel on it.

June's childhood friend Pauline had been offering her the use of her cottage in Wales for many years, but June had never got around to accepting the offer so, as they were now in need of somewhere to stay, she contacted Pauline to see if her cottage was available. It transpired that it was only available for two days, so they decided to take them and also book bed and breakfast somewhere close by for a further two days. Fred searched the internet and found a place which looked as though it was quite close to the cottage, so he booked it for them.

Thursday
At the crack of dawn (well actually 9.30am) Buz set off with Irene, June and Mabel and their luggage packed into his Ford Focus and they all headed for

the Welsh border in high spirits, despite the overcast weather. As they neared Dolgellau they were on the look out for an old bridge on the Towyn road where they had to turn off for the cottage, which was in a row of listed stone built cottages.

Upon arrival they unloaded their luggage, explored the interior and sorted out who was sleeping where. June's bedroom had a balcony which looked down over the living room and which later on clearly showed the bucket which she took up with her, as the toilet was downstairs and she didn't fancy going down the steep stairs in the middle of the night! Irene and Mabel's bedroom (with single beds) overlooked the back garden and wild flower meadow.

Downstairs, the living room had a comfortable settee and armchairs grouped around an open fireplace with a dining table and chairs set close to the window, which was overlooking the road. A small modern kitchen was situated at the far end, a lobby led out to the bathroom and the back door which opened onto a tiny patio which was shared with the cottage next door. The garden overlooked a brook flowing through a delightfully pleasing wildflower meadow.

Having found their bearings they had a cup of tea, and Buz drove them into Dolgellau where they found a small bakery shop with a few tables, so they bought home-made Welsh cakes and Cornish pasties and sat and had their lunch.

Buz then took them to find where they were going to stay for the last two nights, it was a lovely big old farmhouse set in beautiful gardens secreted behind high hedges and trees, and would be difficult to find if you didn't know that it was there. The owners were not in, so Buz took them back to the cottage and departed for home.

After waving him off, they took the path along the side of the row of cottages which led to the river and a path going to the town. The narrow path opened up past a small fast flowing stream and following the pathway to the right by the bridge they emerged from the trees into a park with a large grassed area where there were men playing cricket near a sports pavilion.

Wandering into the town they were on the lookout for charity shops, as they wanted to do a small jigsaw puzzle. Finding one in a toy shop, and having purchased it, they went off leaving Mabel's umbrella behind which they retrieved a couple of days later. They had a look around this pretty market town to suss out places to eat for the following day and discovered that the pubs did not serve meals on a Sunday, so they realised that they had to find somewhere that did.

22. DOLGELLAU 2007

2007 *Singing in the rain, Dolgellau*

2007 *The Square, Dolgellau*

It had started to rain and as they saw a bus going in what they thought was the right direction for the cottage, they hurried up to it and asked the driver if he was going along the Towyn road. When they described where they wanted to go, he recognised the description of the cottages and confirmed that it was along his route. Gratefully they clambered aboard and sank wearily into the seats, relieved that they didn't have to walk back up the hill.

Arriving back at the cottage they heated up Irene's delicious stew and dumplings for dinner, washed down with a few glasses of red wine, before making a start on the two-dog jigsaw puzzle. And so to bed!

Friday

Since it was pouring with rain and Irene had come back from buying the daily paper soaking wet, they decided to wait until the rain had eased off a bit before going for a walk. They occupied themselves by doing jigsaw and crossword puzzles and reading the newspaper. As the rain showed no sign of abating they made a decision to don their macs and boots and brave the elements, so setting forth with umbrellas at the ready they headed for the path at the side of the cottages, and walked along the side of the river on the Mawdach trail towards the bridge at Bont Y Wernddu.

Irene pointed out that the river had risen since she had walked along it earlier in the day, and had taken a photograph of a large rock in the river with writing on it. She took another photo at a similar time the following day which showed that it had risen by at least a foot.

It felt like they were walking alongside a river in a wood, as there were trees either side of them for a good part of the way, but now and then there would be a clearing and they saw sheep grazing in the fields. At one point they came to a picnic table where, despite the rain, they decided to stop and rest. Irene did them a little cabaret of 'Singing in the Rain' complete with large striped umbrella. They had been walking for an hour by this time, so they thought it best to turn back, as another hour in the pouring rain splashing through the puddles, would be quite enough! On the way back Irene took another photo of the river from the bridge, and again commented on the height of the water.

After divesting themselves of their extremely sodden clothes and putting on dry ones, they had a salad lunch and much welcome cup of tea, before setting about trying to dry out their clothes. June started mopping out the shoes with paper towels and Mabel finished them off with the hairdryer, while Irene wiped their cagoules and trousers and hung them around the room.

22. DOLGELLAU 2007

This task completed they continued doing the jigsaw puzzle, until they wanted to go for dinner, when they phoned for a taxi which took them to The Unicorn pub in the town where they enjoyed lamb shanks. They had a sheet of paper with a pub quiz on it, so they did the quiz just between the three of them, before phoning for the taxi man to come and take them home since they were very tired and decided to have an early night.

It was still raining!

Saturday

They were relieved to wake up to a nice sunny day and after breakfast they packed their bags, washed up, cleaned the house, stripped the beds and awaited the arrival of Mr Williams in his car. He had kindly offered to collect them, in order to save them having to carry their bags up the hill to his house, they piled their bags into his car and Mabel sat in the front seat, while Irene and June were directed by Mr Williams to a metal gate across the road in a wooded area.

Venturing forth, they saw that the overgrown area near to the gate opened out into a path and clearing which came out at the bottom of his garden. An ornamental archway covered with laburnum led through to a more formal part of the garden, then past a greenhouse at the side of a gravel drive leading to the front door of the house. Reunited with Mabel they entered the old converted farmhouse, which was a beautiful building with a lovely old wooden staircase leading to a sitting area with their bedrooms leading off.

After unpacking their bags and having a chat to Mrs Williams, they walked down to the town along the road and had a good look around the church, restaurants, cafes, pubs, charity shops and the antique shop where Mabel bought a rose bowl to take to a lady in Switzerland.

Making their way towards the river they came to an area with flower beds and finding a large tree stump they sat down and admired the view which included Cader Idris, the highest mountain in the area. Walking along the river, in the playing field area that they had passed through on Thursday, Mabel and June decided to have a lie down on the grass and make the most of the sunshine.

They rested by the river for a while and when they fell asleep Irene wandered off to take photographs of children playing rugby. Irene was just walking back to the two prone figures when she saw a dog charging towards them, it appeared to be oblivious to the obstacles in its path and continued racing at full tilt, rushing between them at a mad dash. Startled at the noise and movement

Mabel and June awoke wondering what on earth was going on; sadly it was all over so quickly that Irene missed out on a very funny photo opportunity.

Before making their way back into the town Irene took June and Mabel across the field to take their photos sitting in the stone circle of some ancient standing stones. They passed a grave yard and a wall with a line of bright blue kettles on it, which they couldn't resist photographing, before buying ice creams from a little kiosk, and proceeding up a narrow alleyway which led to the church and another graveyard clearly much older than the first one.

Making their way back to the main market square they went to The Bistro for their dinner, which they all agreed was excellent, and with full tummies they plodded up the hill to the bed and breakfast and slept soundly after the day's exertions.

Sunday

Breakfast was cooked and served by Mr Williams, the local historian, previously a head master and one time mayor of Dolgellau, who told them some of the history of Powys Castle, and so they decided to visit it on the way home.

Walking towards the town they caught the bus to Fairbourne, and riding along looked at the shops and followed the miniature railway along the front towards the little station where they got off, went into the café, and had a snack and drink. They waited a little while for the ferry to take them across the estuary to the seaside town of Barmouth.

Sliding down the shingle they climbed into a dinghy with an outboard motor, along with several other people, and Mabel reminisced about going on this ferry about 40 years earlier with Doug and their children. The young ferryman told them that it would have been his grandfather running the ferry at that time, and later his father took over before passing the job onto him, but he only did it for part of the year as he owned and managed some pleasure boats in Spain.

When they alighted at Barmouth they headed for the beach and wandering along gathering shells, they talked about the time they took the Home-Start families there on a day trip and recalled all the fun they had with them, most of the children had never been to the seaside before and some of the parents too. (They had played happily on the beach, running in and out of the sea, jumping over the waves and squealing with delight, in between building sand castles, bouncing on trampolines and riding the donkeys. The mums spread out a delicious picnic and the children sat on a car rug and happily tucked in. They all fell asleep in the coach going home!)

22. DOLGELLAU 2007

After a while Irene decided to hold a competition for the prettiest and most unusual shells so they stepped up the search and hunted amongst the rock pools in earnest. The judging was carried out on a wall on the promenade, where they spread their shells out and after much discussion June was declared the winner by mutual consent.

This exertion reminded them that they were in need of their afternoon cup of tea, so they wandered along the main road until they found a little café, where the lady was about to close, but agreed to serve them if they didn't mind her clearing up around them. They were happy to eat their cakes and drink their tea, whilst chatting to the proprietor as she cleared things away.

They looked around the town, and explored the antique shop before heading to the bus stop by a building with a huge dragon on the front, to await a bus back to Dolgellau. While they were waiting a police car drew up and a police woman got out and started talking to a lady at the bus stop, it appeared that she was giving the officer some information about a crime, and they were fascinated listening to this conversation, which whiled away the time, as they had quite a long wait for the bus and it had started to rain and became very chilly.

During this time a man came and stood in the queue and joined in with the conversation, it was apparent that he was very drunk and when the bus arrived and drew past the stop for the driver to take a break, before embarking upon the journey to Dolgellau, the drunk started to verbally abuse the driver because he wouldn't let them on the bus and they were all cold and shivery.

The police officer had left by this time and they were getting concerned at the man's behaviour, which got worse when the driver finally allowed them to get on the bus, but wouldn't let a youth on who had no money. The drunk was arguing with the driver but he eventually paid for the youth, who appeared not to know him, as they sat separately and Irene was worried in case the drunk sat next to her; it was quite a diverting episode.

Alighting at Dolgellau they headed for The Ship hotel and shaking off the raindrops divested themselves of their wet clothes and settled themselves into comfortable seats with much welcomed drinks in front of them. After studying the menu they looked up and to their surprise saw the drunk from the bus stop join a woman who had been sitting there for a while on her own. It was obvious that they had not met before, and had met by mutual agreement via a third party.

The room was quite small and they were all sitting facing the couple and could not help but hear their conversation (they considered themselves to be students of human behaviour, others may take the view that they were just plain nosey!). The thing that surprised them was that he appeared to be completely sober, whereas an hour before he was falling down drunk. He seemed to have smartened himself up a bit, and ordered two pints of water for himself and a drink for the woman.

She paid for the drinks thereafter as he said that he had no money and would pay next time. Shortly after she made an excuse and left and he was clearly surprised as he must have thought that they were going to spend the evening together. This was their entertainment, while they ate their delicious sea bass, and drank a few glasses of cheer.

June phoned the taxi driver that they had used on Friday, who duly arrived and drove them (probably a little puzzled) to a different house from the last time. Once back at the house they divested themselves of their wet clothes and laid them out to dry. Whilst Irene and Mabel relaxed in their room June had a nice long soak in a hot bath before retiring.

Monday

After one of Mr Williams's breakfasts, they packed their bags and waited for Fred to collect them and take them home; when he arrived they took him on a tour of the gardens and showed him the fast running stream which ran along the side of the property. Mr and Mrs Williams offered them all tea, so they sat chatting in their lounge and they told them about the history of the house and its renovations and how they had developed the gardens. Irene was particularly intrigued by the bread oven in the fireplace which was an original feature of the house.

They bade their hosts farewell and set out to show Fred the cottage which they stayed at for the first two days. They then headed off towards the estuary and walked across the toll bridge at Bont Y Wernddu which is only used for cars and small vehicles, where they all admired the view, especially the cows, before returning in the car to Dolgellau. Once there they looked around the town, showing Fred the antique shop before setting off to Welshpool, where they went for lunch at Evans bakery.

After lunch they visited Powys Castle (the only castle in Wales built by the Welsh) and after a good look around followed by tea and cakes in the refectory, they were allowed a quick look at the gardens as it was approaching closing time.

As they set off for home they promised themselves to return and explore these exquisite gardens in more depth and hopefully with better weather, maybe on another 'adventure'?

23. Highley, Severn Valley

13th to 18th July 2008

They had planned to go to Highley the previous year, but due to the terrible flooding in the Severn Valley area and the damage it caused to the railway track, they had to change their plans. Since the repairs to the line had been completed by the summer, they decided to ask Brenda and Ray if their cabin was free for a few days in July and since it was they took advantage of their generosity.

Sunday

The original plan was for Fred to take them to Highley and Buz bring them back, but Buz kindly offered to give Doug a day out, so they all went together. Irene and Buz arrived at June and Fred's house at 10.30am in their car, bringing Mabel and Doug, and with June in Fred's car, they all set out in convoy for Bridgnorth.

When they arrived at Bridgnorth they went into the Antique Centre and had a good mooch around, Mabel bought a lovely little Minton jam pot as a gift for her friend in Switzerland who was delighted with it. June bought a small willow pattern teapot, a bed sheet and a ceramic wall plaque of a toucan depicting the Guinness adverts (the latter being a present for her daughter whose birthday was at the end of the month). Doug bought a book by Sir Arthur Conan Doyle, and they all agreed that the Centre had some beautiful items.

After lunching in the Centre's café they walked along to the bridge where they stood admiring the view of the river Severn. It was a lovely sunny day so June and Fred opted to go for a walk along the river, whilst the other four collected Buz's car and drove off to Highley Station, stopping along the way to look at an old ferry boat raised up on a platform structure at Hampton Loade. They discovered that the ferry had been operated for many years by two sisters who lived nearby and who also sold eggs and jam, but now it had become a monument to a past way of life.

Arriving at Highley, Irene and Mabel sat by the river chatting to the locals and watching the fishermen whilst drinking lager and lime outside The Ship Inn. This was built in 1770 and was the first public house to be built in the area to provide the miners at Highley colliery with somewhere to slake their thirst. Meanwhile Buz and Doug visited the newly opened Engine House at the Severn Valley Railway Visitor's Centre and perused the exhibits for an hour or so.

June and Fred in the meantime were walking along the riverbank at Bridgnorth admiring the vast range of wildflowers and enjoying the sunshine (it had been raining most days the previous week) before setting off to re-join the others at Highley Station. As they arrived the other four were just setting out to collect the cabin keys from Brenda and Ray who were staying at their other cabin near Bewdley, so they took a look at The Engine House (which was just closing) and wandered along the lovely old platform by the station and down the slope to The Ship Inn (which had also just closed)!

When Irene, Buz, Mabel and Doug arrived at Brenda and Ray's they were welcomed with cups of tea whilst they admired Ray's catch of the day, a big barbel fish (described as two feet long – a fisherman's tale?). On returning to Highley Station and driving past the signal box and along a track ascending to a large open field edged with a variety of cabins in all shapes and sizes, they met up with June and Fred who were absorbed in watching the antics of a pair of male pheasants challenging one another and eventually disappearing into the bushes amidst a flurry of feathers and with a great deal of squawking!

The girls' bags were duly removed from the cars and unpacked and after settling them in the men folk departed for their homes, whilst they prepared and ate a light tea and sat chatting about the war and reminiscing about their childhood experiences before retiring. June was in the double bedded room, with Mabel and Irene sharing the room with the two single beds, both rooms had shower and toilet rooms, so they felt that they were all very well provided for.

Monday

Since Irene had injured her knee a couple of days previously and didn't feel like walking too far, they all sat outside on the raised wooden veranda after breakfast (just cereals – since they didn't want to put on any more weight – their 'full English breakfasts' being a thing of the past) recounting some of

23. HIGHLEY, SEVERN VALLEY 2008

their exploits on previous 'Adventures'. There was a variety of birds darting across the field and flitting in and out of the trees and when a goldfinch landed in the cabin's guttering and started drinking the rainwater they got the bird books out and spent a pleasant hour or so identifying some of the birds that they were watching.

They decided to have lunch and venture out as far as the railway station, so after a quick cheese on toast June took Mabel further up the field to show her some of the other cabins, as it was all new to her, while Irene started to walk very gingerly down the lane.

There is a way down some steps from the top of the field leading down to the lane, which Mabel and June were heading towards, when they met a lady called Josie who asked if they were looking for someone. June explained that they were looking for a cut through the trees and fields going up to Highley village, as it was a long way down to the station and back up the hill to the village. Josie said that there was no way through as there were houses and a golf course in between. She offered them a lift to the village as she was going to collect her grandson from school. Mabel and June explained that Irene was making her way slowly down the lane and that she would probably be glad of a lift to the village as she couldn't walk very far with her knee being so sore.

All three descended some steps to the lane, where Josie's car was parked, and encountered Irene. After explaining to her about the offer of a lift, she was very pleased to accept (since she had only planned to go as far as the station) and they all piled into the car. Josie dropped them off in the village and kindly offered to give them a lift back in half an hour's time if they wanted it. They thanked her but declined, as they wanted to explore the village for a few hours and June and Irene wanted to show Mabel some of the places that they had visited three years before, when Mabel had been too ill to go with them.

They began by taking a look at the clock sculpture by David Howorth which was erected in 1999 and was located in the village centre and features a life-sized miner in a cage at the pit bottom, whilst the winding tower features an abstract design to incorporate the clock. In the square containing the clock there is a much appreciated bench and some splendid public toilets surrounded by tubs of colourful flowers, which they understand are planted and tended by enthusiastic gardening volunteers.

From there they crossed the road and walked along a row of terraced houses which were all beautifully decorated with hanging baskets, flower tubs, troughs and window boxes. On the opposite side of the road there were allotments all the way along, and a lady who they stopped to talk to told them that they belonged to the householders. She said that they never got much work done on them, as when they got together they kept stopping for a chat. There was a real sense of community and the spirit amongst the residents was quite infectious. Mabel and June stood chatting to another lady about the floral decorations and how everyone who was able, took part in preparing the street for the village gardens and flowers competition, which was due to be judged the following week.

Irene had decided to go back to the station, so June and Mabel (after looking across the fields and deciding that a walk over there was a bit too far) proceeded down Church Street and into the churchyard of St. Mary's Church. They duly admired the very well maintained small Norman church and the medieval church house, the home of the original priest. After a short detour around the rear of the house, where June and Irene had previously been upset to encounter an old shed crammed full of chickens, June was relieved to discover that the shed was empty and the chickens gone.

Thus curiosity satisfied, they strolled amongst the graves looking at the old headstones, crosses and ancient memorials on the way towards the exit gate, which brought them out onto the main road. Almost opposite the gate is the early 16th century Manor House (the original centre of the village) and they stopped to admire it with its sign 'Circa 1520'; it is indeed a beautiful example of a half timbered Tudor house. When they saw the 'for sale' sign in the garden they fanaticised about buying and living in it!

Walking back towards the village they stopped to talk to a lady at 'Valrosa' who was pruning her roses, she said that she herself looks after the flowers by the church and the ones by the statue of the miner in The Village square. She was quite upset that the village has been re-designated as a town since a new housing estate was built, thus increasing the number of people on the electoral role. It transpires that The Village cannot be entered in the 'Britain in Bloom' competition as a village any more, however the villagers are objecting to the change of status and trying to reverse it. She said that they cannot compete with towns like Bridgnorth, where the council pays for the flowers and their tending, whereas the villagers provide their own flowers, and volunteers plant and water them. She told them that the lady in Smoke Alley (who June and Irene had met three years ago on a previous 'Adventure') is called Jasmine, and that she plants and looks after the flowers at either end of Smoke Alley. Saying 'goodbye' to her they set out along Smoke Alley where they saw Jasmine talking to another lady over the top of her hedge.

23. HIGHLEY, SEVERN VALLEY 2008

When they drew near the other lady had moved on, and they said 'hello' to Jasmine and June asked her if she remembered Irene and herself taking photos of the house and the magnificent flowers in the garden three years previously. She did remember and even recalled where they were staying. They had quite a long chat about the gardens and Jasmine agreed with the lady at 'Valrosa' that the plants were suffering from a lack of sunshine this year. June told Jasmine that she had brought with her some of the photos which she had taken three years ago of Jasmine's garden. She asked if she would like them and when she said that she would, arranged to drop them off in the next few days.

Taking their leave they carried on walking down towards the station and taking the 'short cut' through the woods eventually lighted at the station, where they spotted Irene walking across the railway line and heading for the platform. They followed her across and whilst telling her about their encounter with Jasmine sat awaiting the arrival of the last train of the day in order to take photos as it approached and departed.

This done, they all wandered back up towards the cabin and turned right to look for a right of way to take them across the railway line and down to the river, which Josie had told them about earlier. To their surprise the house which they had previously thought was just around the bend, was in fact on the other side of the track, so they crossed the line, looking very carefully both ways in case a train was coming – although they would almost certainly have heard it. They walked along the side of the track to the house where (after their dog's vociferous welcome) Brian and his wife came out to talk to them. They are friends of Brenda and Ray, the people who own the cabin that the three friends were borrowing, and which Brian had previously done some extensive work on. Three years ago he had repaired the door lock when June and Irene were there. He explained to them how to get down to the river and across to the Severn Valley Country Park at Alveley, which was very helpful, because that was what they planned to do the following day.

They said goodbye and retraced their steps across the track and, spotting a gap in the bushes, resolved to investigate it from the other side (by the cabin) to ascertain whether it may be an overgrown pathway. This did indeed appear to be the case, so they decided to use this 'secret' path the following day.

That evening they had a delicious cottage pie (which Mabel had prepared beforehand at home) with glasses of red wine and cups of tea.

After dinner they attempted to do The Ultimate Puzzle by Mr Lee Willcott (which June's son John had given her for Christmas) but after much crawling about the floor re-arranging the pieces, they gave up after only managing one solution out of the forty eight. They opted for playing cards instead and June and Irene taught Mabel a version of Rummy which she had not played before and as usual when they play games, she went on to beat the other two! June then wrote up the diary for the day and they all retired for the night.

Tuesday

After breakfast they set out to walk to the Severn Valley Country Park at Alveley, where they proposed to have lunch at The Visitors Centre.

On the left hand side the cabin is an old orchard, there was a gap in the trees which made them think that there had been a cut through there previously. So taking their trusty walking sticks, they bashed aside the stinging nettles and flattened the grass and weeds which revealed metal steps. This confirmed their suspicions and they soon formed a neat little pathway which would be a short cut for them through to the train track, hereafter referred to as their 'secret path'.

Crossing the line they walked a short way along, hastily jumping into the shoulder high stinging nettles lining the track as a train came thundering towards them, steam whistle blowing. Expecting to be admonished by the train driver, they looked suitably shamefaced, but he just gave them a cheery wave as did some of the passengers. Dusting themselves off, and applying docks leaves to the nettle stings, they continued along the track until they came to a gap in the hedge. Squeezing through, avoiding nettles and brambles they emerged into a field, and walking along the side of the hedge they looked out for the large oak tree, where Brian had told them to turn right.

When they came upon a large oak tree they were unsure which way to go, as there appeared to be two small pools in their way. They found out later that they should have turned right there and would have been able to get past the pools to get to the river. Continuing onwards they followed a track which led them into a wooded area and appeared to head towards the river, this was a lovely walk and all was well until they hit a large mud patch. They couldn't avoid the patch without climbing back up the hill and trying to find another way down, so they decided to take on the challenge of negotiating the slick, since they never seem to do things the easy way.

Slowly they advanced towards the deep red oozing clay and tentatively prodded the ground with their walking sticks to try to find a firm patch to tread on. Irene's stick sank into the mire and was sucked out minus its rubber ferrule and not being prepared to leave it behind she valiantly plunged her

23. HIGHLEY, SEVERN VALLEY 2008

2008 *Guard and Engine, Highley Station*

2008 *Silverdale Street, Highley*

hand into the goo and hooked it out with her finger. As she carried on ploughing her way through the mud pool, she was quite a sight with one muddy finger held aloft with an even muddier ferrule on the end of it. She tried to convince the other two to get as muddy, by saying that it was as smooth as silk and felt lovely on her hands!

June and Mabel held on to one another crossing a particularly wet patch, where Mabel nearly left her shoe behind (this was prised out of the mud by Irene with her stick) and June only just managed to retain one of her trainers which was being sucked off her foot as she ploughed forwards. It was extremely funny and would have warranted a place on the TV programme where they show video clips of people doing ridiculous things!

All three of them emerged with very muddy footwear, Irene's walking boots were twice their normal size due to the caked on mud, and as soon as they were clear of the 'slick' they endeavoured to scrape off some of the mud, they must have been quite a source of amusement to other walkers, all of whom had clean boots!

When they finally reached the riverside, they saw a picnic table and benches and sat down with twigs and grass to clean the worst of the clay off, and lighten their load! A couple who were walking past with their dog stopped to commiserate with them and told them about an easier way to get back. After a short rest they made their way along to the bridge, but despite their best efforts they still looked as though they had been in a bog and they continued trying to clean their footwear up at every opportunity when they came across a tuft of grass or nice sharp stone.

Crossing over the new bridge, June and Irene explained to Mabel that it was still being built the last time that they came (in 2005) when they had walked across on the old bridge, chatting to the workmen who were building the new one and who told them where the kingfisher perched in the mornings on its fishing expeditions.

The old bridge was built in 1937 for the purpose of transporting coal from the colliery at Alveley to the railway line. Trams pulled by metal cables carried the coal across the bridge from the east to the west bank of the river Severn. The good coal was loaded onto trains and the rubbish was swung back over the river to be dumped as spoil heaps, which are now the grassy hills of the country park. The new bridge is a replica of the old one and was opened on 15th December 2006 and is called 'The Highley and Alveley Bridge'.

On the other side they paused to take photos of the statue of a knight, before pressing on towards the Visitors Centre nestling amongst the hills,

23. HIGHLEY, SEVERN VALLEY 2008

which are now covered in a profusion of wildflowers and offer panoramic views of the river valley below. Catching their breath after the climb, they sat for a while admiring the view and watching the golfers in the distance, before continuing up to the Visitors Centre, which they were very glad to see as they were more than ready for their lunch!

To their dismay they arrived at The Centre only to find that it was closed on Tuesdays (and Mondays) and all hopes of lunch disappeared. The saving grace was that the toilets were open and they could get a drink of water from the tap. There was also an excellent device for cleaning mud off boots, made from two brushes and a broom handle, so they set about scraping some more of the mud off their boots, before resting on a bench and discussing what to do next. The options were, either to go on to Alveley village and hope that the pub there was still serving food, or return to The Engine House at Highley Station.

Irene and June on their previous visit had found the pub in Alveley Village closed – on a bank holiday – and so were all of the shops, so no food on that occasion either. There was another possibility, which was to walk into Highley village and buy sandwiches from the supermarket (as they knew that there was nowhere serving food at that time of day). They decided to do the latter, so after a short rest, a shared banana, a drink and a loo visit, they headed back down the hill to the bridge, crossing over and taking the track into Highley village.

The track lead into a road which was very long and steep and Irene had set off ahead of the other two, who, had she been with them, would have been tempted to investigate a caravan site to see if there was a shop open. Getting very hungry and thirsty Mabel and June came upon the golf club, they wondered if non-members/players could use their bar, however Irene was too far ahead for them to call her back to go and enquire. They found out the following day, when in conversation with a lady walking her dog beside the river, that non-members would be served, so they made a mental note for future reference.

Huffing and puffing up the hill Mabel and June eventually arrived in Highley where they caught up with Irene and turning into the square made good use of the bench and toilets, before purchasing sandwiches and drinks from Costcutter. Crossing the road, they walked along to the church via Birdcage Walk and finding a couple of benches settled down to eat their lunch amidst the gravestones. It was a gloriously sunny day and they were so pleased that it hadn't rained as had been forecast, and they felt very thankful to be sitting in the shade of this lovely old church, enjoying the peace and quiet, along with their sandwiches.

After lunch they made their way out of the churchyard, across the road and into Smoke Alley where they met up with Jasmine again, so they stopped to chat for a while, and promised to return with the photos. Carrying on down the road towards the station, they came to the entrance of the Highley part of the Severn Valley Country Park, where they were impressed by a police notice on the gate warning that; 'Antisocial Behaviour will not be tolerated'. Passing through the gateway into the car park, they made good use of the toilet facilities.

A man, who (it later transpired) was one of the park's volunteer workers, was filling a watering can from a tap, and watering the tubs of flowers adorning the area. Moving on, they entered into a large grassed and well tended area with trees and shrubs, and on a small hillock there was a large mining wheel sculpture, which is dedicated to over one thousand miners who worked at the Alveley mine between 1879 and 1969. Strategically placed and angled to display it to its best potential, it dominates the whole area quite dramatically alongside a large coal truck which was full of purple petunias.

As they approached it, they met the volunteer again who was watering the numerous plants in the massive coal truck, whilst his two dogs waited patiently nearby. June got chatting to him about the flower festivals and after a while he offered to take a photo of the three of them by the big wheel, as Irene had tried to take one on delayed action without success. Thanking him and saying 'goodbye' they gathered up their bags and walked through the park and on down through the woods to the station, where they sat and watched the last train of the day arrive and depart, as had become their custom.

When they got back to the cabin Mabel and June flopped down on the grass and lay in the sun, soaking up the last rays of the day, while Irene (bless her) made cups of tea. Once revived June made a delicious stir fry and rice dinner, after which they did a 1988 crossword puzzle, some of the clues from 20 years ago seemed very strange! June then wrote up the diary and they happily retired for the night.

Wednesday

After breakfast they decided to let Brian know that the kitchen water-heater was leaking quite badly, so they called at his house and asked if he would pop up and take a look at it, as he normally did the maintenance in the cabin. He agreed to do this, and they arranged to let him know when they got back.

23. HIGHLEY, SEVERN VALLEY 2008

Walking around the rear of his garden, they headed down towards the river and climbed over a wire fence to reach the pathway, where they met a lady who told them of an easier way down!

Off they set to Arley, passing The Ship Inn and the time of day with other hikers and dog walkers as they went, the sun had really started to warm up and they began shedding jackets and rolling up their trouser legs to cool off a little. They all agreed that it was an idyllic rural English scene, with cows, sheep, birds, trees and wildflowers in abundance and fishermen dotted liberally along the riverbank.

At this point the River Severn is quite fast flowing and they wondered how the fishermen managed to catch anything – they spoke to a very friendly man who said that his sons came fishing with him, which they thought must be very satisfying for him, knowing that he had passed on his skills to another generation. At one of the many stiles along the way, they got chatting to a volunteer ticket collector who warned them that the path ahead was very muddy near the river and told them of an alternative route, avoiding the mud.

They came upon a burnt out tree, which Irene and June had spotted burning after a lightening strike, when last there three years before. It had been smouldering when they went past and they had stopped to see if they could do anything (there had been a terrific thunder storm the previous night). Irene had sacrificed some of her drinking water and when a Severn Valley Volunteer came along they had pointed it out to him and he said that he would report it to the relevant authorities.

At the next stile, they met a group of women hikers, who were amazed that Mabel was in her 80s when they saw her clambering over it. They were on the circular walk which took them through Highley, Alveley and Arley; the friends confessed that they could no longer manage such long walks. Eventually, they hit the muddy patch, which looked as though it had been caused by cows trying to get down to the river, they had missed the alternative route and didn't fancy turning back, so stepped gingerly around the very wet parts and managed to scramble up the bank holding onto tree roots to get past the bad patches. It was nowhere near as bad as the clay-like mud of the day before last, so they got through comparatively unscathed.

When they came to the river they saw a fisherman standing in the water with a small floating platform holding his fishing tackle; Irene asked if he would mind if she took his photo, as it was quite an unusual sight, and he was quite happy to oblige. They were glad to see Arley come into view as they were getting hungry, so they were pleased to find that The Harbour Inn was still open for lunches. The landlord Mike welcomed them in with a smile, and three very kind customers vacated the comfortable arm chairs, so that they could sit on them (they must have spotted the look of exhaustion and desperation on their faces!)

Mabel ordered fish and chips, Irene had chilli bowl with naan bread and June chose liver and onions followed by caramelised apple and custard and they all thoroughly enjoyed their meals, even Irene who got showered with salt when a customer was passing and tripped up throwing his condiment tray into the air! They sat in the arm chairs for a couple of hours resting their weary bones after the long (for them) hike.

Just before five o'clock they made their way up the steep hill (this is when they really appreciate their walking sticks) leading to the station. They aimed to catch the last train to Highley and whilst they were waiting took photos of Arley Station, which is very picturesque with its hanging baskets and pretty flower laden tubs adding to the scene.

They boarded the lovely old steam train with its varnished wooden carriages and signs telling them that it was The Royal Scot and entered a carriage with a side corridor. This reminded them of post war holidays when everyone was desperate to have a few days at the sea side and they had to crush as many people as possible into the carriages whilst those who couldn't get in sat on their suitcases (those little brown cardboard utility cases) in the corridor.

As they neared Highley Station they enjoyed hearing the shrill sound of the steam whistle, warning the signal man of the train's approach. He was standing on the track as the train drew to a halt and he then exchanged 'tokens' or 'keys' (which are contained within 'the staff') with the train driver. Once the 'token' has been passed to the man in the signal box and slotted into the token box, it then allows the signal man to change the signals in order for the train to proceed. After watching the last train of the day depart and chatting to the station master who got Mabel a bottle of water from the little station shop, they made their way back up the lane and June called into Brian's to let him know that they were back, while Irene and Mabel attended to a very important matter, making cups of tea!

Brian came and took away the boiler, returning with it later on and informing them that it was irreparable, so from then on they had to boil the kettle for hot water. Later, they started on the jigsaw puzzle that Mabel had brought with her, of the Crab Inn in Shanklin which they had admired on a previous adventure, before having a light supper of cheese, biscuits and salad and retiring for the night.

23. HIGHLEY, SEVERN VALLEY 2008

Thursday

It was quite a pleasant day with sun and some cloud cover but still warm enough not to take their coats with them, as they walked the track to the station after breakfast and caught the 10.45am train to Bewdley. The original plan was to walk from Arley to Bewdley so that Irene could photograph a steam train crossing the Victoria Bridge, in order to replace a fading poster on her landing wall of which she was very fond.

After the exertions of the previous day Mabel felt that it would be a bit too far for her, and Irene's knee was quite sore, so they decided to have a gentle stroll around Bewdley instead. Finding themselves a side corridor carriage again so that they could further reminisce, they headed for the ancient and historic town of Bewdley that nestles alongside the river Severn which has overflowed into the town many times during the past few years.

Upon alighting at the station, they saw several old carriages which were being used as shops to raise funds for the Society, so had a mooch around and made a few purchases before setting off on the twelve minute walk to the town centre. Irene's knee was quite sore by now, so she opted to sit by the river after a quick walk around part of the museum and was quite happy watching the antics of the Canada Geese who were avidly defending their territory against intruding male geese and any other waterfowl that they perceived as a threat.

Meanwhile, back at the museum, Irene hoped to obtain leaflets from the Tourist Information Centre (only to discover that the members of staff were on strike as part of a protest by local council workers). Mabel and June made their way around the various workshops stopping to watch a demonstration of clay pipe making. Clay pipes were made for use in the area for several hundred years and in addition to using them for smoking tobacco they were also used by children to blow bubbles. After looking around the many interesting exhibits such as rope making and other arts and crafts and peering into the spooky cells (the old town lock up) they commented upon the injustice of being transported for life for stealing a chicken from some wealthy land owner. June had her photo taken sitting in the stocks, but it would not have been much fun to be locked in them in the 1800s.

Emerging from this gloom they appreciated the serenity and peace of the gardens which consisted of vegetable and herb plots, formal flower beds and a large pond with lilies, bulrushes, water iris and a female mallard duck with five ducklings. They watched the antics of the ducks for a while; two of the ducklings kept escaping from Mom and dashing about in the pond exploring the weeds whilst she sat upon three of her brood (to prevent their escaping?)

By this time it was getting way past lunch time and they thought that they should return to Irene who had been patiently sitting watching the water life and the local bikers for quite a while and was getting a bit cold. They all went into the famous fish and chip shop (they had intended eating their fish and chips by the riverside in true traditional style out of paper with their fingers). What a delicious treat, the batter was made from gluten free flour on this particular day, and very crispy it was too! Irene felt that she should start walking back to the railway station as she was limping quite badly which slowed down her progress.

Meanwhile June and Mabel walked along the side of the river going through the arches and looking at the newly paved area and the flood barriers which have been put in place after the very severe floods of 2005. They talked to a man who lived in the area which was flooded, and he was quite blasé about it, saying that he had been flooded fourteen times and accepted that if you live on a flood plain it's par for the course. They tried to figure out what the names on the floor in the block paving represented, some of them were nautical terms and one, Sabrina, they were told by the local man, was the Roman name for 'Severn'.

Wandering back up the road to the Antique Centre they had a quick look around before setting off to rejoin Irene at the station, where she had been chatting with a Birmingham couple. They all caught the last train back to Highley and agreed that the museum at Bewdley was well worth another visit, and there was a lot more of the town to be explored in the future.

Once back at the cabin they continued doing the jigsaw puzzle (in an attempt to complete it before leaving the next day) into the early hours of the morning, pausing only to have a snack and the odd glass of wine.

Friday

After breakfast they made a start on packing their belongings and tidying up the cabin since this was their day of departure, then they sat outside on the veranda once again with cups of tea to discuss the plan for the day. Their musings were interrupted as they were compelled to stop now and then to watch the prolific birdlife flitting about the trees in the field which was spread out in front of them, with an occasional squawk from one of the pheasants.

Earlier in the week they had promised to go back to Smoke Alley and take the photos to Jasmine which June had taken on a previous adventure, so they decided to start the day by visiting her, then going on to The Engine House. They were saving this visit for a rainy day, and coincidentally, it did rain whilst

23. HIGHLEY, SEVERN VALLEY 2008

they were in there. Reluctantly leaving the birdlife behind at the cabin they gathered up their walking sticks, cameras and the photographs and set out for Smoke Alley.

Walking through the station they found the little white gate leading to the woods, headed up the track which leads onto the road to the village and then turned right into Smoke Alley. Jasmine tends the most beautiful garden stocked full of a wide variety of colourful flowers in all hues, and not a weed in sight! The lawns too are immaculate and the hanging baskets decorate the house to perfection with their fuchsias and trailing lobelia to name but two of her many plants. Then there is the vegetable garden (not a 'patch' which you might expect in a garden, but a whole extra garden) which is enough to make your mouth water, with its beans, peas, potatoes, cabbages, onions, carrots and many other vegetables including salad, which is her husband's domain.

They passed a lady along the Alley who stopped to chat and she told them that she had always lived in the village and wouldn't want to be anywhere else, she appeared to be very contented and looked healthy and sprightly so they were amazed to discover that she would shortly be 90 years of age! She said that she had worked for 70 years in a Kidderminster carpet factory. It never ceases to surprise them when they meet such lovely and interesting people on their journeys.

Arriving at the hedge which borders Jasmine's garden they spotted a man working in the vegetable patch and asked him if she was about, so he called to her and she came over to speak to them. When June gave her the photographs she was absolutely delighted and called her husband over to look at them. He introduced himself as 'Willie' and he too was very pleased with them, but declared that 'it is a waste of time growing anything that you can't eat!' They suspected that he was just joking, since he tended the vegetable garden whilst Jasmine looked after the flower garden, both of which, they told them, were a delight to the senses. June said that she admired their garden so much that she has one of the photographs of it as the screen saver on her computer and sees it every time she switches it on.

After a pleasant chat Mabel and June followed Irene back along the Alley where they found her chatting to the man who had been working in the garden when they arrived. They made their way down the hill to the Country Park and made good use of their conveniences before wending their way through the woods to The Engine House, just as it began to rain!

The Engine House had only recently opened, having been delayed for almost a year due to the severe storms and flooding which had devastated the whole of this area the previous year. Their first stop was the café since it was lunch time and they were feeling a bit peckish, but they didn't want to eat too much as Irene was making a steak dinner in the evening, so Mabel and June settled for mushroom soup while Irene had lasagne, with the obligatory cups of tea. Thus replete, they wandered around the museum admiring the huge steam trains, which have been beautifully restored and renovated by an army of volunteers since 1962 when the Severn Valley Railway organisation was formed.

They boarded the mail train sorting carriage, which was the actual one involved in the Great Train robbery and felt that they were entering into a significant part of Britain's history. They recalled it as being a serious and sad event, where the train driver was badly injured and later died as a result of his injuries. This event has often been portrayed by the media as a daring act and the robbers have almost become cult heroes, but this attitude takes no account of the devastation to the lives of the train driver and his family.

They all watched the video of John Betjeman reading the poem 'Night Mail' by W.H. Auden about the advent of the steam train and its affect upon the lives of many people. Irene and June put on tan coloured cow gowns and played at being postal sorters on the mail train while Mabel looked on in amusement.

There was much to be admired and learned as they spent a happy couple of hours wandering amongst the huge locomotives, railway vehicles and artefacts, soaking up the history of the railway and Highley. It is thought that Highley was probably named after a Saxon called 'Huga' over 1000 years ago, at which time the Anglo Saxons made a clearing in the Wyre Forest, building their houses around the church.

In 1086 Lady Godiva, who was a wealthy and powerful woman, owned much property in the West Midlands area, including Highley. It is said that she wanted to make her tyrannical husband Leofric the Earl of Mercia, lower his tenants' taxes (the Heregeld), so for a bet with him she rode naked through Coventry on Market Day on horseback, her modesty only covered by her long golden hair. She won the bet and he freed the people of Coventry from paying the hated tax.

In 1862 the railway and station at Highley were opened, and later in 1880 the Highley mine was developed and became very successful so terraced houses, shops, and a Methodist chapel were built to accommodate the miners' families.

Leaving The Engine House they were very pleased that the rain had stopped as they walked back to the cabin where Irene prepared a braised steak

23. HIGHLEY, SEVERN VALLEY 2008

dinner while June and Mabel fitted a few more pieces in the jigsaw puzzle and finished packing before doing some more cleaning. Unfortunately they didn't have time to finish the jigsaw puzzle, so Mabel picked up the pieces as carefully as she could and said that she would finish it off at home so that they could take a photo of it since it was a reminder of a previous 'adventure' on the Isle of Wight.

After they had eaten and cleared away Buz arrived to take them home. They gave him the dinner which they had saved for him, which he ate whilst they busied themselves completing the cleaning. He then helped them to pack the car before they locked up and took their leave of this very pleasant little holiday home, hoping they may be able to return again some time soon.

They agreed that the time had flown past so quickly as it always seems to when you are enjoying yourself, and they looked forward to their next 'adventure'…wherever that would be?

24. Highley, Severn Valley

12th to 19th July 2009

After much debate they decided to return to Highley again and Irene asked her friends if their log cabin was available in July. It was, so Fred and Buz were press-ganged into chauffeuring once more. Fred offered to take them as he wanted to visit his grandchildren in Colchester for the rest of the week and be able to spend the following weekend with them. Buz was happy to bring them back, so it worked out quite well.

Sunday

Irene and Buz picked Mabel up and rendezvoused at June's house at 10am on a bright, sunny morning. After much juggling of their personal bags, walking sticks, bedding bags, cool boxes and food boxes, Fred managed to get most of it into the boot, with Irene and Mabel separated by a pile of bags on the back seat and June's legs wrapped around a rucksack. Waving goodbye to Buz they set off at 10.30am and headed for Bridgnorth, intending to stop there for a while, but the car was so full of luggage it was decided that it would be prudent to go straight to the cabin and unload.

Arriving at Highley Station and driving along in front of the signal box, they received some very curious looks from people on the platform awaiting the steam train. They must have wondered what on earth they were doing (except the locals of course who would know that there was a field beyond the station yard with a row of cabins in it). They started to feel at home in the now familiar setting when bumping their way up the track (Fred's Mondeo springs have never been the same since). The Adventure in 2005 was when the exhaust pipe fell off!

After unpacking the car and stowing the perishables into the fridge they set off again and returned to Bridgnorth, parked the car and looked around for somewhere to have lunch. They settled upon The Old Castle where they wined and dined before strolling along the cobbled streets of this historic town with its half-timbered shops. Making their way to Bridgnorth Antique Centre they whiled away a pleasant hour casting their eyes over the furniture and bric a brac of yesteryear. Irene was delighted to have found and indeed purchased some Denbyware 'Greenwheat' plates to add to her collection.

Fred drove them back to the cabin about 4 o'clock where they all enjoyed cups of tea and Mabel's delicious home-made scones, eaten out on the balcony since it was a beautiful sunny afternoon. Fred then set off back home and they waved him goodbye as he bumped back down the track.

They decided to lie outside in the sun, so June produced a large bedspread (which she had brought from home for this purpose) and laid it on the grass outside the cabin. Mabel and June spread themselves out, complete with pillows, and settled down for an afternoon nap, whilst Irene opted to sit in a garden chair. Funnily enough Irene was the one who fell asleep while Mabel and June reminisced about previous adventures amongst other things.

Rain clouds began to loom so they beat a hasty retreat into the cabin, gathering up their pillows, bedspread and clothes as they went. After a reviving cup of tea they set about organising their bedrooms, there was a lot of chatter and laughter and they soon relaxed into adventure mode. Full up from their cooked lunch earlier and not feeling like another full meal, Mabel suggested having June's home-made carrot and coriander soup accompanied by Fred's home-made bread for supper. Once eaten and cleared away Irene and Mabel started to sort out the edge pieces of a jigsaw puzzle, whilst June played a few games of Spider Solitaire on her laptop before proceeding to type up the day's happenings. In previous years she had made notes in her diaries but having acquired a laptop for Christmas, decided to record each day's events straight onto it, to save time later when she came to type them up. Although they hadn't done much walking, they were very tired and had no trouble falling asleep.

Monday

Irene woke the others with mugs of tea and re-arranged the table and chairs on the balcony whilst Mabel and June eased themselves into the morning. They all enjoyed breakfast together al fresco listening to the birds and watching the pheasants scurrying about the field. About 11 o'clock they ambled down the track to Highley Station equipped with walking sticks, cameras and bottles of water. Deciding to take the risk of getting wet if it rained (which of course it did) they left their cagoules behind, relying upon their recently acquired hooded fleeces. However, the morning was bright and sunny with blue skies and fluffy white clouds and they bought tickets for the steam train to Arley, proposing to walk on towards Northwood Halt where the Victoria Bridge spans the River Severn. Irene had a large thirty-year-old poster at home of a steam train, chugging its way across this bridge, it was looking the worse for wear so she wanted to replace it.

Alighting from the train in Arley they asked a railway volunteer worker which would be the best side of the river from which to photograph the bridge in question and he directed them to the path on the nearside of the river. They headed downhill from the station past The Harbour pub, resolving to return there for lunch since they had enjoyed their meal there last year.

Finding the path and clambering over this adventure's first stile, they felt a bit stiff and creaky and helped each other across in the knowledge that it would get easier as the week progressed. The wild flowers and grasses were lovely, flowing and rustling as flurries of breeze passed over them, with the fields to the right of them and the river with its occupants (ducks, swans and fishermen) to the left, it was indeed a peaceful and idyllic scene.

The undergrowth was quite tall and they came upon one of the bridge's archways sooner than expected, so passing underneath it and continuing along the riverbank they kept looking back to find the best view to take photographs. The bridge was partially obstructed from view by the foliage, so some time was taken walking backwards and forwards to get the shot of the bridge which Irene was trying to achieve. Having established the best position, they realised that there was still about an hour to wait until the train was due to pass by.

Settling down amongst the shrubs and wildflowers they refreshed themselves with their bottles of water, using the convenience of the bushes as and when the need arose. It was a very pleasant interlude watching the canoeists drifting with the current, and gulls wheeling about overhead and diving under the bridge. During this time they noticed the inscription on the bridge which told them that it was built in 1861 by Messrs Brassey Construction Company and designed by John Fowler (engineer).

They heard the train whistle first at the Highley incline, then at Arley Station and waited in eager anticipation as it got nearer, listening for the next whistle as it came around the bend approaching the bridge. When it hove into view they clicked away like mad, hoping to get the ideal shot of the train with its steam trail drifting behind it and the sun reflecting on the red and cream coaches.

24. HIGHLEY, SEVERN VALLEY 2009

When the train disappeared from view amongst the trees on the opposite bank they gathered up their bags and sticks and headed back along the trail to Arley. After a while it began to rain and even with their hoods up it was decided that it would be prudent to shelter for a while. Finding a suitable tree they watched the fishermen casting their lines and the swans, mallards and coots drifting into the bank-side searching for a tasty morsel. They passed a few hilarious minutes revising the steps to the line dance 'Walking after Midnight' which June had taught Irene and Mabel on a previous adventure in Twynings.

When the rain eased off a little, they continued on their way and headed straight for The Harbour Inn where they divested themselves of their wet jackets and put them on the backs of their chairs to dry. They were welcomed by Mike the landlord who remembered them from the previous year when they had fallen exhausted through the pub doorway, having walked all the way from Highley. Once again they collapsed into the armchairs by the fire and gratefully consumed the shandys which he set before them. They ordered hot beef and chicken sandwiches and a bowl of chips (for sharing) from the landlady Sandra and they were absolutely delicious! A very happy hour was spent chatting with the landlord and eating their lunch before setting off again.

June and Mabel had never walked around the village of Arley, so it was decided to chance the weather and go sightseeing. Strolling down the hill they crossed the footbridge over the River Severn and turning right came to the village shop and post office. This had been The Nelson public house when Irene used to go there as a child with her parents. On the opposite side of the road was a café with picnic tables and since it was a bank holiday and nothing was open they sat a while looking out over the river and watching the boaters.

Re-tracing their steps to the bridge they turned right and walked along a small beach where they watched children playing with their dogs, whilst their parents were 'messing about in boats'. On the edge of the beach there was a little bench where Mabel sat awhile whilst Irene and June took photos before they all set off up the hill towards the church. They passed by several architecturally interesting houses, including Arley Tower (a folly) built by Viscount Valentia to block the view of the castle from its neighbours. The castle was originally Viscount Valentia's manor house and was demolished in 1962, leaving the grounds, now an arboretum open to the public. Arriving at the entrance to the Arboretum they were sorry to see that this too was closed and made a mental note to return on a day when it was open (not Mondays or Tuesdays).

Continuing on they came to St. Peter's church with its 800 year old nave and even older Norman carvings above the pulpit. They were quite pleased to be able to dodge into the church as it had started raining and they hadn't taken their macs with them. The church was built from the local sandstone which was mined from Hexton's Quarry thus, despite the time differences between additions to the building; the stone remains the same colour. The majority of the monuments and wall tablets are memorials to the various Lords of the Manor of Arley from the twelfth to the nineteenth centuries.

When they emerged from the church the rain had eased off slightly, but the cows in the field just beyond the cemetery were still lying down! Hurrying down the hill to the bridge they thought that they might need to find somewhere to shelter if the rain came on any harder. Pressing on to The Harbour Inn, they stopped in the porch to shelter for a few minutes as the pub was closed. Mabel was concerned that they might miss the last train of the day so started to make her way up the hill to the station while Irene and June chatted to a lady who was leaving the pub.

Re-united on the platform they all took photos of the train and the station and realised that it was the same engine and carriages which they had seen crossing the River Severn at Victoria Bridge earlier that day. They caught the train to Highley and alighting at the station decided to go to see whether The Ship Inn was open, but as usual there was no sign of life, so they sat and watched the ducks on the river. Suddenly there was a loud squawking, fluttering of wings and splashing as a group of ducks on the far bank fled into the water when a small animal scattered them in their panic to escape from it. June spotted the animal which looked remarkably like the one which she had seen and photographed on the railway track the previous year, and which the three of them had tried in vain to identify. She went to the edge of the bank and asked one of the fishermen if he knew what the animal was, and he said that it was probably one of the wild mink which inhabit that stretch of the riverbank.

Since the pub was closed they headed back towards the cabin. As they passed by the signal box the signalman came out and stood at the top of the steps. He looked quite friendly so Irene asked him whether he might spare the time to show them the internal workings of the box. He was more than happy to accommodate them and they climbed up the steps as he welcomed them in. He introduced himself as Brian and said that he, like all other operators, was a volunteer and that he was an optician by profession.

He explained that he was waiting for the last train of the day from Bridgnorth to Kidderminster to pass through and had time to tell them how the signal box worked. He was, he said, only qualified to operate the Highley box and would have to be re-trained to operate any other box on the line. He showed them the machine in which the single track token is placed to register that a particular train was in the station. The token was handed over by the train driver to the signalman who duly registered it. It all seemed very complicated to them and they were not surprised to find that the volunteers have to go on a course to learn all of the ins and outs. Brian was very careful to register all the details of his actions in the ledger. They spent a very interesting and informative fifteen minutes and left thanking Brian for taking the time to explain things to them and being so kind and patient.

Waving him goodbye they wandered back up the lane to the cabin and after the obligatory cups of tea, heated up the beef stew and dumplings which Irene had prepared at home. They had worked up quite an appetite so greatly enjoyed this delicacy!

After dinner June recorded the day's events on her laptop, whilst Irene read a book and Mabel did a Sudoku before they all retired for the night.

Tuesday

It was a very wet morning but Irene decided to walk down to the station and on to the Engine House to enquire about opening times. She walked down the hill with the lady who had given them a lift into the village the previous year and who offered to do the same again if they wanted to go out at three o'clock when she was going to collect her grandson from school. Irene thanked her for her kind offer and said that they would see what the weather was like later. June and Mabel having seen the rain, rolled over in their beds and went back to sleep. About ten o'clock when Irene returned she roused her friends with mugs of tea and set about getting breakfast ready. After eating and clearing away, they made up packed lunches in the hope that the rain would ease off and it would be possible to go for a walk later.

Whilst it was still overcast they made use of the time by transferring the photographs which they had taken so far on their digital cameras onto June's laptop. By 1.30pm the rain had stopped so they set off to the village in the hope that they might do the walk to the Donkey Bridge if the rain kept off.

Making their way past the station they toiled up the hill and turned off into Smoke Alley, wondering whether Jasmine would be in her garden and sure enough there she was hanging out her washing. She came over to the hedge to chat to them and Willie, in his vegetable patch, came to say hello. Discussing the weather and the gardens, Willie said that despite the recent drought he never watered his vegetables, which surprised them as they had all been watering their beans and tomatoes almost on a daily basis. Jasmine offered to give them some garden peas for their dinner and they explained that they were just setting out for a walk and asked if she would mind them calling in for them on the way back. She said that would be fine and they said farewell and continued on their way to the village shops where they bought crisps to go with their packed lunches.

Sauntering back along the road they turned into the alley which brought them out close to the church gate and passing through looked for a bench to sit on whilst eating their sandwiches. Since the benches were all rain soaked they looked for one which wasn't too wet and dried it off with some kitchen roll (which they just happened to have with them). They settled down to eat, and as they were finishing their lunch a lady, who had been tending her husband's grave, stopped to talk to them for a while.

As the sun was shining and they were hopeful that the rain would keep off, they set off to walk to the Donkey Bridge making their way along Silverdale Street. There they met up with two of the ladies who tended the Street's allotments, they were Ann and Brenda and they explained how they organised the barbecues and communal social gatherings. They appeared to be amongst the prime movers in organising the street for the village's annual floral competition, the judging for which was due to take place on the following evening. Silverdale Street has won the best terraced street prize in previous years and the residents take great pride in the general upkeep of their houses and allotments.

It suddenly began to rain quite heavily and they bade them a hasty farewell before scurrying off to find shelter in the local teashop on the main road, but on arrival found to their dismay that it was closed. Nearby they spotted a pub called the Bache Arms and hurriedly ducking into the doorway made a quick decision to go in and ask if they could have a pot of tea to warm them up.

Shaking off their wet cagoules they piled in through the door and were greeted by the landlord who must have been amused at the sight of three sodden ladies spilling into the bar. They asked for cups of tea and he obligingly said that he would put the kettle on and make them a pot straight away and that he would bring it to them. He invited them to make themselves at home, which they did, by spreading their cagoules around the room to dry, draping them over fixings on the walls. The landlord, who introduced himself as Mark, said that the room was about to be refurbished so not to worry about their dripping coats as there were no other customers to be disturbed by the sight of them.

24. HIGHLEY, SEVERN VALLEY 2009

He returned after a while with a big old crock teapot, cups and saucers and poured them steaming hot drinks which were greatly appreciated. As he wasn't busy he stopped to chat to them and explained that he had only been there for two weeks and had great plans for the pub which had been closed for some time after the death of the previous landlord. He intended providing facilities for children, a restaurant, bar meals, a function hall and a games room. He planned to have live bands, and provide food and drinks for special functions in conjunction with the Severn Valley Railway. His enthusiasm was infectious and they could well see that he could make the pub into a real asset for the villagers and holidaymakers. They said that they would be interested in eating there when visiting Highley as there wasn't anywhere else to get a meal within easy walking distance of the cabin, other than the two take-aways. At this point he said that they were quite welcome to take food in to eat on the premises until he had the bar meals up and running. They assured him that they would spread the word about his plans as they wandered about chatting to people locally.

They sat drinking tea and doing a crossword puzzle until the rain eased off a little, then gathering up their walking sticks and donning their now dry cagoules bade farewell to Mark, assuring him that they would be back again to take advantage of his hospitality during the week. Discovering Mark was another of those serendipitous moments in their adventures.

Walking briskly down the road they made their way to Smoke Alley to go to Jasmine and Willie's house, to collect the peas which Jasmine had offered them earlier in the day. She invited them to come in, sit down and chat for a while with her and Willie. Telling them about Mark's plans for the Bache Arms they also mentioned that they had never managed to find the Ship Inn by the station open. Willie said that it wasn't open until about seven or eight o'clock and stayed open until the early hours and that it was generally the locals and fishermen that frequented it. He said that he didn't go there any more and he thought that there may be a change of ownership in the near future. At this point it started to rain very heavily and Jasmine dashed outside to fetch in the washing. She came back in with a big bag containing peas, potatoes and a huge lettuce and asked her husband if he would mind giving them a lift back to the cabin. He happily acquiesced and they bundled into his car trying to dodge the raindrops. They insisted that he dropped them off before the now very muddy track as they didn't want him to damage the suspension on his car.

Hurrying up the track they shared the load of the huge bag of vegetables between them and were glad to be back in the cosy cabin where Mabel heated up a delicious cottage pie whilst June and Irene shelled the freshly picked peas to accompany it. They retired that night hoping that the weather would improve by the following day.

Wednesday

Unfortunately they awoke to another very wet morning but after breakfast, stoic as ever, Irene wandered down to the station and watched the trains for a while. June showed Mabel how her laptop worked and between them they edited some of the photos which they had taken in the previous couple of days. Mabel then played a game of 'Patience' on the computer and before long Irene had returned and they all had bacon rolls for lunch.

Mabel was feeling a bit tired and decided not to go out for a walk so Irene and June, with one eye on the weather, set off for Highley Country Park. Passing through the station they walked up the lane and into the park, it had turned into a lovely sunny day so when they arrived at the top of the hill June lay down on the grass for a quick sunbathe whilst Irene busied herself with her camera.

After a rest they walked out through the gates and up the road where they encountered a man, just off the lane by the golf course, in a wheelchair who was listening to the radio programme 'Classic FM'. They chatted to him for a while and recited poems such as Wordsworth's "Daffodils" and William Henry Davies's "Leisure". He told them that he had lived in the area for a very long time and enjoyed it greatly: he regularly sat in that spot and enjoyed the peace and quiet.

They wished him 'good day' and strolled down the road where they entered the country park gates and started walking towards the big wheel memorial on the hill. As they got closer, they recognised the volunteer gardener who had kindly taken a photograph of them the previous year. He was sitting on the bench with his dogs lying companionably at his side and they were pleased that he recognised them and asked where Mabel was. They chatted with him for a while and told him about the book that they were writing of their adventures, and asked for his name to go in the book. He told them that his name was Phil and that he walked his dogs on the hill every day as he lived locally. Just then a man and woman walked up and greeted him; he introduced them as a local councillor and his wife. They all started walking down the hill together, chatting about the difference in the status of Highley which had happened during the past year, and the councillor said that one of the advantages of being a town rather than a village was that they received more government funding. They said farewell at Phil's back gate as Irene and June continued on down the hill to the station.

Irene crossed the track just as the gates were about to close pending the arrival of a train which she wanted to photograph. June got chatting to a lady with a beautiful collie dog called Boris. She, it transpired, lived next door but one to Jasmine and Willie. Her name was Maureen and she told June how much fun they have on their 1940s weekends when the locals (and visitors) get dressed up in clothes relating to that era. They all go on a specially commissioned steam train to a dance in Bridgnorth with big band music and have a great time. They also help out on the station with refreshments when the re-enactment of the World War II battle is in progress. When Irene crossed back over the track and joined in the conversation she agreed with June that it would be something they would like to do the following year.

There was an American woman photographer who was giving the Station Master palpitations as she kept walking onto the line as the train was approaching. The signalman shouted at her from his box and there was a general consensus that some people were not safe to be out!

On their return to the cabin they found that Mabel had had a good sleep and was feeling refreshed. The other two related their afternoon's events over tea consisting of salad; followed by apple and blackcurrant crumble and custard (Irene had stew and a roll). Unusually for them they watched television for a while and June typed up the diary with the day's events before retiring to bed.

Thursday

They awoke to a lovely sunny day and after an egg and bacon breakfast set off to walk to Alveley Country Park. Crossing the train track near Brian's house and finding the gate open which leads to the river, they decided that it was alright for them to go through. Brian had told them previously that they could go this way although it was private land, since they were staying in Ray's cabin and he was known to the landowner. They encountered the man who owns the land and explained who they were. He was happy for them to use this short cut as they were Ray's friends and would respect his family's privacy. Apparently people walk through his garden sometimes and have even stopped to have a picnic there in the misguided belief that it is public land. They told him that they were from Birmingham and he said that he was born there and was a scrap metal merchant there for most of his working life, before retiring to Highley where he owns riverside land, several properties and fishing rights.

After a very interesting chat they continued on their route along the riverbank towards the bridge spanning the Severn by Alveley. Making a slight detour to look at the area which was a mud slick and where they got stuck the previous year, they were surprised to see that the muddy patch was still there, but relieved that they didn't have to manoeuvre around it this time! They took a few photos and continued on their way, crossing the bridge and panting their way up the incline towards the Visitors Centre. There was a bench very strategically placed to sit and watch the golfers down below, which had a panoramic view of the area surrounding Highley, so they parked themselves for a while and took photos.

Once rested they carried on up the hill until arriving at the Visitors Centre where Irene bought a book of walks around Highley and they all refreshed themselves with cups of tea in the café. Leaving the Centre they made their way towards Alveley through the car park and along the lane until reaching the gate to the flower meadow. Passing through the gate they slowly made their way up the steeply sloping field stopping to admire the abundance of wild flowers, multi-coloured butterflies and insects (some of which they had never seen before). At the top of the field they stopped at the memorial stone to take pictures of the flora and fauna and admire yet another panoramic view of the Severn Valley.

At top of the field they turned left through a gate and along the lane towards Alveley taking delight in the drifts of poppies, knapweed, lady's smock and corn-cockle in the hedgerow. Emerging onto a main road they encountered a lovely little Primitive Methodist Chapel built in 1862. They stood and admired it for a while then turned left into the village and soon arrived at their destination, The Three Horseshoes pub.

This attractive white painted brick inn was built in 1406 and is the oldest pub in Shropshire, and they were glad to enter through its portals in search of sustenance. They were greeted by a young lady behind the bar who devastated them by informing them that they weren't providing food but that they could buy drinks. This was very puzzling since there was a large table with a substantial looking buffet on it. She explained that this was a private function for a group of campanologists who were having their summer outing, and therefore she was unable to provide the pub's usual lunches. The bell-ringers were gathering up their belongings and appeared to be about to depart, so they said that they would be quite happy to have the remains of their buffet, but the barmaid said that health and hygiene regulations would not allow her to do that as it had been lying on the table for some time.

24. HIGHLEY, SEVERN VALLEY 2009

It seemed that they were fated not to eat in this pub, since in 2005 Irene and June had trekked across from the country park, only to find it closed. June related this sad tale to the lady and, crestfallen, they picked up their drinks and stepped outside, where they found a table which was close to a field with some beautiful chestnut horses in it. Almost immediately the lady came over to them and said that she had persuaded her husband to rustle up some sandwiches for them if that would suffice. They hastily acquiesced and placed their orders, then sipped happily on their drinks in the knowledge that food was about to appear. The sandwiches when they arrived were an ample reward for their wait; they were accompanied by salad and crisps and were enjoyed enormously.

After another shandy each and a chat to the horses (and of course the usual photo shots) they took their plates back into the bar and got chatting to the barmaid. Her name was Lianne and she looked very much like a young version of Toyah Wilcox, she said that she had been told this before. They said that they were staying near to Highley station and she replied that she had been there to the 1940s weekend the previous week and that it had been lots of fun. They said that they were contemplating going to the next one, as she was the second woman to tell them what fun it was.

Bidding her farewell and promising to return they wandered along to The Church of St Mary The Virgin, admiring the cottages around it. A notice board informed them that this ancient parish church was 850 years old and that the Parochial Parish Council was requesting donations towards its upkeep. Irene spent a while absorbing the atmosphere of this charming old building and marvelling at the skills of the men who made the stained glass windows and the artistry of the stonemasons. In the meantime Mabel and June remained outside and got chatting to a delightful lady in her 70s whose name was Anthea. She told them that she walked all around the area and had that day walked from her home in Bridgnorth. Irene came out and joined them and they were all impressed with the distances which she attained and felt that she was very brave to go walking about on her own.

She set off to catch the train from Highley back to Bridgnorth as it looked as though it was going to rain. As they waved her goodbye the Church Warden appeared from around the side of the church and stopped to talk to them. He asked if they had seen the animal carving on the stone roof, they all looked up to try to figure out what it was, as the warden said that no-one was sure, it could be a dog or a fox, but there was no record in the church about it. They took some photos to try to discern what it was in close up, but came to no conclusions. The Warden asked if they had been into the church and since June and Mabel hadn't, offered to show them around. Irene strolled through the churchyard and looked at the gravestones, reading their inscriptions.

Meanwhile the Warden was explaining to the other two that the church council were considering re-ordering the church by removing the pews and floor tiles and replacing them with chairs and carpet. June told him that the church in her village had done that and after twenty years of constant use the chairs and carpets were looking the worse for wear and in need of replacing. She doubted that the re-ordering had been cost effective and urged him to advise the church council to proceed with caution. After admiring the stained glass windows and the stone carvings June and Mabel made their way back outside to re-join Irene, leaving the Warden to lock up the church for the day.

Walking back the way they came they were on the look out for a nature reserve which the lady in the Visitors Centre had told them about earlier. After descending through the field of wildflowers and turning right along the lane they came upon the gate to The Nature Reserve. It was starting to rain, so spotting a bench which was partially sheltered by trees; they sat there for a while and watched the antics of the ducks and moorhens on the pond. Curiosity soon got the better of them and (perhaps thinking that they would provide them with lunch) they soon drifted over to see what was on the menu, but unfortunately they didn't have anything to give them. Completely unafraid of them the ducks came up quite close onto the bank and proceeded to preen and quack amongst themselves, seemingly oblivious to their presence. Two ducks appeared to be having a chat when an angry looking drake appeared over the side of the bank, squawking furiously and flapping his wings he drove them off the bank and sent them scudding back into the pool. Other than this amusing incident it was a very peaceful and relaxing scene. There was a background of bulrushes, reeds, great willow herb and various other wild flowers which attracted bees, butterflies and dragonflies. The lovely pink and white water lilies floating on this very pretty pond complemented this idyllic spot. After a stroll around the pool it began to rain more heavily and they were forced to put up their umbrellas and take their leave of this magical spot and head back past the Visitors Centre, down the hill, across the bridge and through the woods to their cosy cabin.

After a reviving cup of tea June prepared dinner which consisted of steak, jacket potatoes, mushrooms and tomatoes. This was cheerfully consumed by all, accompanied by a bottle of red wine which complemented the meal perfectly.

24. HIGHLEY, SEVERN VALLEY 2009

They decided to watch TV for a while but the reception was really bad, so they had a game of rummy which much to her surprise (because Mabel usually beats the other two at games) June won. She then transferred the day's photographs onto her laptop and typed up a few notes before joining the others doing a quiz which Mabel had brought with her. They happily whiled away an hour or so before retiring.

Friday

They fancied a cooked breakfast since the weather was dull and overcast so over sausage, eggs and beans discussed the plan for the day. It was decided that they would catch the bus into Bewdley (using their bus passes) and return to investigate the museum which they had only visited briefly the previous year. Since it was quite likely that it would rain they put on the caps which June had brought back from her holiday in California.

Hurrying off to catch the bus by the café on the main road, they passed by the country park and along Smoke Alley which was unusually deserted. The number 125 bus was due at 12.25pm, but in the event they need not have hurried since the bus was late. The journey was quite pleasant, passing through a rural area before arriving in Bewdley High Street. They alighted outside a shop called 'Cheep and Cheerful' where Irene bought a spatula for use in the cabin.

Making their way to the museum, they had cups of tea in the café and used their toilets. Deciding to return later to look around the museum they wandered across to the charity shop where they mooched about for a while before moving on to the antique shop. They had an interesting conversation with the lady shop assistant about Franz china. She said that she couldn't get hold of enough of it as it was very much in demand.

Wandering down to the river they passed under the bridge where a cormorant, perched on a small ledge at the base of the centre pillar, was flapping around and attracting much attention from passers-by. They stopped to watch it for a while expecting the bird to dive into the river in search of a fish, but it just clung steadfastly onto the stone. A man who was feeding the pigeons told them that the cormorants were coming in from the coast and moving down the river, which he hadn't known to happen before. The pigeons seemed to be very tame as they were literally feeding out of his hand and they appeared quite relaxed. After a while they walked back under the bridge to the fish and chip shop and went into the cafe adjoining, where Mabel had carrot and coriander soup followed by Bakewell tart and custard. Irene had

THREE HAPPY WANDERERS

2009 *Bridgnorth steam rally*

2009 *The girls in daft hats, Bewdley museum*

scampi and chips, June had cod and chips with mushy peas, and they all had cups of tea.

It started to rain so they sat chatting to some of the other customers whilst drinking their tea, and to their surprise realised that they had been sitting there for over an hour and a half. Reluctant to leave this dry cosy spot they dragged themselves out and went back to the museum where they made their way around the various workshops. They also watched a video on coracle-making which was very interesting as, on an earlier adventure in Ironbridge, they had watched a coracle race on that part of the River Severn. Coracles it would seem were originally used by poachers to move their booty from the woods and rivers downstream, so that they would make their escape by floating quietly away from the game keepers and water bailiffs.

In another room the history of the River Severn was displayed on posters around the walls. There were also models of the types of craft used to transport imports and exports to and from the Bristol Channel. There was a section, clearly meant for children, where they spotted some funny hats and couldn't resist trying them on, which resulted in them being convulsed with laughter at the sight of themselves in the mirror. June found a tricorn hat; Irene's hat looked like that of a garden gnome and Mabel's was a woolly hat which resembled the one which Compo wore in 'The Last of the Summer Wine'. It was so funny that they could barely contain themselves and kept shushing one another in case someone heard them and came to see what all the racket was about! After taking some photos of one another they made a hasty visit to the loos before they had an accident. When they look at those photographs now, they still laugh at their daft antics.

The next workshop visited was that of a man who made stained glass items such as panels, windows and other ornamental artwork. They were very impressed by the skill and expertise of the craftsman and reluctantly departed as the museum was closing for the day. A member of staff was making her way around the various workshops and locking the doors. They asked if it was still possible to go into the gardens at the rear; she said that they could and let them through to take photos of the pond and look around the herb gardens. This was a very pretty garden and they wished that they had longer to spend in it.

Exiting the gardens by the rear gate they found themselves in what was originally Upper Street (now re-named High Street). This was a fascinating street containing a Baptist church, a Methodist church, a Family church, an Anglican church, a Meeting house and a school. They were so surprised to see all of these buildings in one street that they were determined to return and investigate the area further.

They strolled down to the bus stop and waited for the bus to Highley which was 20 minutes late, not an uncommon occurrence they were told by some locals who were also at the bus stop. They got off the bus near the Bache Arms and went in for cups of tea and while waiting for their pot of tea to arrive Irene and June did a spot of line dancing on the lovely old oak floor. The Landlord Mark sat and talked to them about his plans for the pub and about the changes which he had already made and asked them what they thought of them. Rested and refreshed they walked back to the cabin via Smoke Alley.

June had brought a beef stir-fry with her from home, so she heated it up and cooked rice to go with it for dinner. It was delicious and was accompanied by a bottle of red wine. After dinner she transferred the day's photos onto her laptop and typed up a few notes whilst Mabel and Irene washed and dried the dishes and cleared them away. A pleasant evening was spent relaxing, reading and doing crossword puzzles whilst chatting about the day's events and how interesting it had been despite the inclement weather.

Saturday

It was a lovely sunny morning so, over breakfast, they agreed that it would be an ideal day to visit Bridgnorth for the 'Rally in the Valley'. This is an annual steam rally which is held in a field along the riverbank. They caught the train from Highley and upon reaching Bridgnorth, a kind gentleman whom they had been chatting to on the train, showed them the way down from the station to the bridge over the river, which was a much quicker route than they would have taken. Turning right out of the station they descended a flight of steps, turned left, then shortly after turned right and followed the road around until arriving at the river bridge. They left their guide at this point, thanking him for being so helpful and wishing him a pleasant day.

By the side of the bridge there was a group of Morris dancers, known as 'mummers' who black their faces for their performances. With the river behind them and the decorative and colourful troughs of flowers along the sides of the bridge it presented a striking backdrop to the whirling dancers. These were both male and female, which is not always the case with Morris dancers since at one time they were traditionally all male. The band, dressed in the same brightly coloured outfits as the dancers, played accordions, violins, a banjo and a clarinet. They played very lively music which, mingled with the stamping of the clogs and clashing of the dancers wooden sticks, blended into

24. HIGHLEY, SEVERN VALLEY 2009

a soul stirring cacophony of sounds. They could have lingered here all day but since there was a lot to see, reluctantly tore themselves away, crossed the bridge and descended the steps to the riverbank.

Along the way they passed a large plaque with a picture of a steam engine on it commemorating the site of Hazledine's foundry, which produced the first steam locomotive in the world to haul fee- paying passengers. It was built in 1808 and was designed by Richard Trevithick using local labour under the supervision of the engineer John Rastrick.

A ten minute walk brought them to an open field where the Rally was being held, they paid £3 each (concessions) and later agreed that they had had more than their money's worth. Making their way towards the arena they passed steam rollers, steam organs, agricultural vehicles and traction engines which would have been used as generators at fun fairs in the earlier part of the twentieth century. They were all building up a head of steam before their parade, which they watched later in the arena. Then they wandered along looking at the classic cars, keeping their eyes peeled for a 'Moggy' like June's and Jaguars like Irene and Buz's and the one which Mabel and Doug used to own. They duly spotted them amongst the assorted collection of motorbikes, vans, caravans, military vehicles, massive fairground trucks and a circus caravan.

They admired the immaculate glossy red paintwork of the caravan and peeped inside to look at the raspberry coloured oil lamps and the tiles which were covered in red roses behind the highly polished black lead stove on which stood a shiny kettle. At the far end there was a bed with a multicoloured patchwork quilt draped over it, and the windows and the glass panels around the mirror were a work of art with their elaborate engravings of flowers and bows.

Near to the caravan there was a Fairground Steam Organ churning out its unique music which reminded them of their childhood visits to the Onion Fair in Aston Park, Birmingham. They stopped to listen to the jangling music and watch the colourful figures adorning the front of the organ; the man had a baton in his hand and appeared to be conducting, whilst the two women either side of him in belly dancers outfits, held bells and strikers which they clashed together, adding to the cacophony.

They walked back to the arena, through a maze of stalls which sold everything from canal art to burgers, on their way to watch a parade of heavy horses in the arena. Fascinated by his skill they stopped for a while to watch a blacksmith clashing his hammer onto the anvil whilst making tools.

They found a good spot to see the Shire horses parading around with their owners, some pulling carts and farming machinery. First of them into the arena was a pair of magnificent dark brown and white Clydesdales in their decorated harnesses pulling a farm trailer. Second was a pair of lighter brown working horses pulling a plough with a man perched precariously on the back and next came two women leading a rich chestnut coloured Suffolk Punch and her foal which was only a few months old. The Master of Ceremonies explained that there would be more horses there on the following day as most of the local working horses were away at a Shire Horse Show in Wales. He went on to say that all working horses had originated from the French Destrier horses which were used in battle and bred as big strong animals in order to support the weight of their rider's armour as well as their own. Working horses were employed for pulling drays, coaches, milk floats and other delivery vehicles as well as long carts loaded with timber or hay and many other goods.

Suffolk Punches are distinguishable by their broad rumps and lack of feathering around their fetlocks. The feathering was bred out as it became a problem when the horses were ploughing through heavy clay soil. The pretty little foal was very cute and the crowds were delighted by its frolicking as it followed its mother around.

It was time to eat so they found the open marquee where they had seen people eating earlier. They found a table and went off individually to the various food stalls to choose their lunch. Irene had a Chinese beef chow mein and Mabel and June had hot pork baps and shared a plate of chips. They thought that it was a good idea to have many food outlets and one large seating area where you could sit and watch the Morris dancers perform on a wooden stage. After lunch they made their way around to where the horses were stabled and admired and photographed them at close quarters.

They then returned to the arena to watch the parade of steam engines, which was truly a remarkable sight as they lumbered past them with black smoke billowing from their chimneys and the sound of the steam hissing and spluttering. There were about fifteen huge engines followed by a similar number of tractors (mainly Massey Fergusons) and it was indeed a spectacular sight (and sound!) especially when they all blew their whistles together as a finale. They exited the arena within a few feet of them and as they rumbled by they appreciated the sheer magnitude of them and the amount of time and effort required in their maintenance and upkeep.

In need of some refreshment they went back into the marquee for a cup of tea and were delighted to see that a group of performers which they last saw at Blist Hill on their Ironbridge Adventure, were setting up their equipment and getting ready to begin a 'sing along'. They were always happy to join in a sing along, especially if the songs were from the thirties and forties since they knew the words to these! So whilst enjoying their tea they also joined in the singing and since not many other people appeared to know the words the performers concentrated their attention on them and they almost felt part of the group!

After about half an hour of exercising their lungs, the singers and pianist bowed out and several groups of Morris dancers began preparing for their show by spreading sand on floor, before entertaining the crowd with their lively jigs. Some of the groups were just men, some just women, but mostly there were both. The clashing of sticks and crashing of clogs on the wooden floor along with the music from the band and the shouts of glee from the dancers made for a very lively performance indeed.

The friends were having such a lovely time and were reluctant to tear themselves away, but needed to leave in time to walk to the station to catch the train. They left wishing that there was time to stay and listen to the band called The Plonkers which they had watched setting up their musical instruments, and who looked like they would be a lot of fun.

Making their way back to catch the train they could hear the jolly sound of the band and the hissing of the traction engines fading into the distance and being replaced by the whistle of the steam engine as they neared the station. Relaxing on the train they reflected upon the amount of enjoyment derived from the day and what good value for money it had been. Alighting at Highley Station they happily, if wearily, trudged back up the lane to the cabin, where they looked out all of the bits of food left over from various meals and produced a tasty scratch supper. Relaxing after their meal they played cards and retired to their beds early.

Sunday

As they had hoped for some sunny weather on their last day they were disappointed to wake to a wet and miserable morning. After breakfast they packed their bags and the food boxes and cleaned the bedrooms and bathrooms. By this time the rain had stopped so they decided to try to walk to the Donkey Bridge which June and Irene had walked to previously. On the way to the village they did a detour along Smoke Alley to thank Jasmine for the vegetables and say goodbye for another year. When they knocked on her door and explained where they were headed for, to their surprise she said that she used to live near to the Donkey Bridge as a child and her family owned a donkey. She went back into the house and produced a copy of a leaflet with a photograph of her donkey on the back page. Jasmine then offered to give them some cuttings of penstemons which they had been admiring in her garden, so they waited a while as she took the cuttings and they bore them away wrapped in tissue paper and placed in a plastic bag.

Waving farewell they carried on towards the church and walking along Church Street, on the corner of Silverdale Street and saw Phil, the man who waters the plants in the country park, coming towards them on his bike. He stopped to talk to them and noticed their caps which had emblazoned across the front 'Alcatraz Psycho Ward Outpatients' and asked if they had been to Alcatraz. June said that only she had been, and when he said that he had been to San Francisco she asked if he had been across the Golden Gate Bridge. He said that he hadn't and they had a chat about the places which they had visited there, before he cycled off.

They headed for a stile on the corner of Silverdale Street and to their dismay spotted a herd of bullocks grazing nearby. Not fancying walking through them, they retraced their steps back to the church and found a way around passing by some allotments and arrived at the gate to the field with the bullocks in! Since there was a massive muddy pool surrounding the gate they realised that there was no way that they could get through to the field which they needed to cross. So, retracing their steps yet again up to Silverdale Street they arrived at the field with the bullocks in, but this time they were further away from the stile, so they scrambled over and hurried along the edge of the field hoping that they wouldn't notice them.

Having made it to the other side of the field without incident they darted swiftly into the alleyway which took them into a small housing estate where they asked a lady the way to the Donkey Bridge. A man who was cleaning his car came over and directed them and they set off again crossing a road into an overgrown field and down a very narrow muddy track. It started to rain so while sheltering under some trees they noticed three youths playing rugby. They watched them for a while finding it hard to believe that they would carry on playing as by this time it was raining heavily and their clothes were soaked. They couldn't decide who were the craziest, the youths for continuing to play whilst drenched to the skin or them for standing and watching! At this point they decided to abandon the attempt to reach the Donkey Bridge and with umbrellas up and heads down trudged back up the muddy slope, through the estate and along the alleyway. The bullocks were still there waiting to greet

24. HIGHLEY, SEVERN VALLEY 2009

them but looking considerably more bedraggled than before! Since they were attempting to shelter under the trees on the side of the field the friends took the path diagonally across the middle to the stile. One large white bullock ambled over to inspect them and they beat a hasty retreat over the stile. Once reaching safety they stopped to take photos of the sharp horned bullock, which now looked quiet amiable.

Hurrying down Silverdale Street they quickly shook out their brollies and dived into the Bache Arms where Mark greeted them and promptly went off to put the kettle on. He was clearly beginning to understand the needs of these three particular customers and when asked said that he was more than happy for them to eat their packed lunches there. Divested of their wet cagoules they settled down to enjoy their sandwiches and the very welcome pot of tea which Mark duly produced. He then returned a while later with a bowl of delicious steaming hot potato wedges for them to sample as he wanted to gauge whether this would be something that he could cook for his bar snacks. They were in full agreement that they would be popular and told him that they had enjoyed them very much.

Mark's wife Sam came over to speak to them, she was holding a little girl of about twelve months and they were surprised to learn that she had several other children as she didn't look old enough. She chatted to them about their future plans with the pub, saying that they were on a trial period with the new owners, and that if they made a success of it they may be kept on, which is what they wanted in order to be able to settle down there with their children. Promising to return on their next visit to Highley they said goodbye and set off in the rain with umbrellas aloft.

Back at the cabin they packed up the food boxes and finished off cleaning the kitchen and at 5.30pm Buz arrived to collect them and they all had a cup of tea before transferring their bags and boxes to his car. About an hour later they set off and drove through a heavy storm with black thunderous clouds overhead, to be rewarded later on by a beautiful rainbow. On the way home they talked about returning the following year and were keen to try to go when the Severn Valley Railway held their 1940s weekend. Jasmine's neighbour Maureen had captured their interest, when she talked to them about it at the station one day when walking her collie dog Boris.

Despite the fact that the weather hadn't been very kind to them, it hadn't prevented them from getting out and about and enjoying themselves. They had met some new and interesting people and renewed their acquaintances with some of the locals who they were beginning to think of as their friends.

25. Torbay

10th to 17th July 2010

Whilst they were writing about their adventures they all felt that they would like to return to Torbay and re-visit some of their favourite places that they had been to in the nineties. Also to see a few that they would have liked to have had the time to visit but never managed to fit in. Some years ago June and Fred had been to Torquay and found a nice friendly looking family run hotel on Cockington Lane. They thought that they would like to stay in that area as Cockington Village is one of their favourite places and the gradient is not too steep (unlike their previous accommodation on Braddons Hill Road). The hotel which they decided upon was Lanscombe House Hotel (which they remembered as a tea shop) so it was booked and they all started saving their money and looking forward to the adventure.

As things turned out, the week before they were due to go Mabel had a repeat dose of Polymyalgia which she had previously suffered from in 2005 and since the medication interfered with her warfarin dose, she had to attend the clinic on Wednesday to have it checked. She felt that she could not stay for the week as it was important to attend the clinic, but since they all wanted her to have a break and she wanted to go, a compromise was reached. Buz (who was taking them) very kindly offered to stay an extra night thus giving Mabel two days with them. So it was decided that she would go, and then return with Buz on Monday night.

Saturday

At 9.15am Irene and Buz collected Mabel from her house and drove on to June's house to pick her up. Once all of the luggage was safely stowed in the car, they waved goodbye to Fred. He was going to his daughter's house, returning on Wednesday then coming to join them on Friday, before bringing them home on Saturday.

25. TORBAY 2010

2010 *Irene, June and Mabel by Brunel's statue*

THREE HAPPY WANDERERS

Heading for the M6 they started on the journey south, stopping at a motorway service station to have a picnic. They found a very pleasant spot, clearly set aside for family picnics, and joined several families with children playing happily in the sun. They were quite happy being entertained by the children climbing a huge tree, as well as admiring the scenic view. After lunch they continued on their way, doing crossword puzzles to pass the time.

When they came to Shaldon they stopped in a car park on a cliff overlooking the estuary and looked at the view for a while. Pressing on towards Watcombe they went to look for Brunel Woods which are situated in a small housing estate opposite the lane leading down to Watcombe beach. Parking on the street they entered the gate to the woods and walked up a slope until they came to a clearing.

There they found the statues depicting Isambard Kingdom Brunel's life, known as 'Brunel's Dance'. Buz had heard about this collection of wood carvings and as a Brunel fan was very pleased to see them for the first time. He was particularly struck with the centre piece, a 58 foot totem pole illustrating Brunel's engineering skills and he lay on the ground (to look up without getting a crick in his neck) in order to try and work out where the various bridges were shown on the pole.

They took photos and chatted to a family who had also come to look at the statues, and they learned that there had been some restoration work done on the statue of Brunel including a replacement nose (which apparently only lasted a few weeks). Leaving the clearing they walked back through the woods to the car and set off to look for The Giant Rock. Crossing the Teignmouth Road they drove down Watcombe Beach Lane which was very narrow and stopped at a car park where they had seen the Victorian turning circle and The Giant Rock on a previous visit. June, Irene and Buz got out of the car and walked across to the woods to read a notice about the valley of the rocks and The Giant Rock, Mabel came over to look at the notice while Buz and June went a short way into the woods to see whether they could see the Giant Rock, but it was completely covered with grass, bushes and trees.

At first they couldn't find the turning circle, but as they were about to leave the car park spotted an old five barred gate overgrown with weeds and large nettles. June got out of the car to investigate but couldn't get very far past the gate because the brambles were so high and prolific. However she recognised an old signpost marked 'picnic area' but sadly the picnic area was nowhere to be seen as the whole site was neglected and overgrown. Mabel and June recalled reading a notice in 1994 to the effect that European funds had been

25. TORBAY 2010

used to restore the turning circle and install a picnic area, it seemed so sad and wasteful that Torbay council had failed to maintain the site.

Leaving the car park they headed back to the main road up Watcombe Beach Road and turned left towards Babbacombe where Buz went in search of the flat where his Dad had lived. They stopped for a while to reminisce and peeking into the back garden Buz was quite upset to see that the weeping cherry tree planted in memory of his mother was no longer there.

Continuing on through Babbacombe and Torquay to Cockington they found Lanscombe House Hotel, where they were greeted by the proprietor Leon Butler who gave them a very warm welcome and asked if they would care to have a pot of tea and a rest after their long journey. They carried their bags up to their rooms, Irene and Buz in the double, with Mabel and June in the twin bedded room. Strolling out to the garden they sat in the sunshine at a white wrought iron table and were served with tea and biscuits by Leon. They looked around the garden and were pretty sure that it was here that they sat many years before and had a cream tea in a tearoom. Leon later confirmed that it was indeed a tearoom a few years previously and that the entrance to the garden was via a large wooden gate which they could see had been padlocked and had roses growing over it.

They decided to go into Torquay and have a fish supper overlooking the harbour, but first have a quick look at the village, the cricket pitch and the manor house, Buz having never been to the latter two. They drove up to The Court and found a small car park just outside the gates to the grounds where they left the car and strolled around to the upper lodge cottage. They stopped to admire the view of the cricket pitch and surrounding woodlands with the Court and the church nestling in the landscape.

After pointing out the places of interest to Buz they re-traced their steps to the car and set off for Torquay via Cockington Lane. It was difficult to park near the harbour, so Buz dropped them off by the quay and close to the shops and cafes and went to find a parking place. They wanted to try to find the fish and chip shop which they had been to before, but couldn't be sure whether the one which they chose was the same one, as it had been many years ago! Mabel and June then sat looking out over the harbour at the mainly blue and white pleasure boats bobbing about, whilst Irene was taking photos of 'street furniture' for a competition, while they waited for Buz to return from parking the car.

Meeting up at the café they entered, seated themselves at a table and ordered fish and chips and mushy peas. These were eaten and enjoyed with great relish and they felt well satisfied as they strolled along the new bridge that spans the harbour, which they had not seen before. After passing the pleasure boat area they came to a part of the harbour where there were fishing boats, with their tackle of nets, ropes, lobster pots and buoys piled up in a colourful display along the quayside. The layout along the front had been changed since they were there last, so they took their time getting their bearings and trying, to no avail, to find out where they would go to catch the ferry to Brixham. Buz said that he would go and collect the car and they thought that it would be easier if they walked part of the way up the hill towards where the car was parked. They waited outside a big church which is now used as a 'Rainbow Funhouse' and were shortly picked up just as the temperature was starting to drop and the evening was getting a bit cool.

They returned to Cockington via Seaway Lane and approached the front door of the hotel, keys at the ready. Irene tried her set first and couldn't gain entry, then Buz tried without success, then June tried with her set of keys and Mabel's assistance, but also with no success. They admitted defeat and rang the bell to summon Leon, who explained that they needed to pull the door towards them as they turned the key. Lesson over, they went up to their rooms and put the kettle on as they were all in need of a cup of tea by this time. Buz went downstairs and sat in the lounge reading the newspaper while the ladies sat chatting in Mabel and June's room drinking tea, before retiring for the night.

Sunday

Waking to a lovely sunny morning Irene greeted June and Mabel with cups of tea in bed before they all met up in the dining room, where they enjoyed full English breakfasts. They decided to spend the day at Brixham and Berry Head, but first they would go to Cockington village and The Court so that Buz could look at the craft centre and the organic garden. Parking in the same place as the previous day they walked through the gate into the grounds and to their surprise realised that you could in fact park within the grounds. They didn't recall seeing cars in the park on previous visits.

Strolling across the cricket ground they made their way to The Court and after a quick look inside they sat outside whilst Buz inspected the café and shop. They were looking at the carriage horses and were impressed by the sight of one of the drivers teaching his small grandson how to steer the horse and carriage, it was nice to see that he was passing his skills on to the next generation.

25. TORBAY 2010

Irene had to drag Buz out of the manor house, as they had limited themselves to a one hour visit, since they knew very well that they could have happily spent all day there. Making their way around the side of the house Irene and Buz went into the craft centre to watch glass blowing while June and Mabel walked on up to the walled organic kitchen garden where Irene joined them shortly afterwards. The team of volunteers had changed since they were there last, and were overseen by a paid warden employed by The Torbay Coast and Countryside Trust, to promote conservation in the Torbay area. After a short rest they left the garden and met up with Buz by the craft centre, he had been enjoying watching the skills of the glassmakers and had bought Irene a paper weight. He walked back to the car park to bring the car a bit closer so that Mabel didn't have such a long walk.

Buz then drove them to Paignton to have a look at the house where his parents lived over fifty years ago. After a short nostalgic detour they set off for their intended destination of Berry Head where they headed for the café on the top. They all had delicious meals before going outside to bask in the lovely warm sunshine and the gentle breeze as they wandered around the fort ruins taking photos. They eventually came to a spot that they were searching for where they had lain, many years before, on the edge of the cliff watching the seagulls wheeling around and having fun on the thermals. Irene sat on the bench where she had sat previously whilst June and Mabel got as close to the edge of the cliff as they dared, but felt that they couldn't get as close as previously as it was making them feel giddy!

After lying on the grass for a while they all made their way back to the car and drove down to Brixham where Buz parked the car near the sailing club. Mabel was feeling a bit tired from her exertions on Berry Head, so opted to stay in the car and have a little nap. Irene, Buz and June strolled along the harbour wall and up to The Golden Hind, where they bought pots of dressed crab and consumed them whilst watching the 'tourists' milling around the old galleon. Thinking that they had left Mabel for a long enough rest, they walked back to the car where she was happily doing a crossword puzzle.

Re-joining their friend they set off for Cockington and went straight to The Drum Inn for dinner. Whilst having their meal they noticed that there was to be a quiz in the pub on the following Wednesday night, so June and Irene made a mental note to eat there and join in the quiz. After the meal, as they were sitting chatting, Mabel said that she was feeling cold and as the temperature had dropped quite drastically after a lovely hot day, they agreed with her but were not unduly alarmed.

When she started to shiver they realised that there was something wrong, since it was not all that cold. Ushering her out to the car June wrapped her fleece around her but by the time that they had got to the hotel Mabel's teeth were chattering and she was getting quite distressed. They got her upstairs to the bedroom and popped her straight into bed (clothes and all) wrapping her in the two duvets as they looked around for some other way of warming her up. The hotel's policy was to have the towel rails switched on during the day so that guests would have nice hot towels to return to in the evening. Irene spotted the warm towels and brought them into the bedroom where they wrapped them around Mabel in an attempt to stop her shivering. June put her beach towels onto the rails and Irene went into her bedroom to get the towels from her bathroom. All wrapped up like a mummy Mabel lay trying to get warmed up, but it was about and hour before she stopped shivering and a further hour before she was comfortable enough to go to sleep. Irene stayed with June until Mabel fell asleep as the two friends were very concerned for her and considering getting a doctor to come and see her. She then had a very good night's sleep with June waking up at regular intervals to peer at her and make sure that she was okay.

Monday

After breakfast Buz said that he would take Mabel straight back home, but she said that she felt well enough to go for a drive on Dartmoor and return home as planned later in the day.

Buz drove them to the moors via Totnes and as they passed over the top they spotted a group of Dartmoor ponies grazing peacefully on the side of the road. They stopped the car and June and Irene stealthily approached the ponies which appeared to accept their presence without batting an eyelid, it was only when Buz walked towards them that they became restless and skittish before settling back down as they seemed to accept his presence too. There were about thirteen of these beautiful animals including four foals and their colours ranged from white through tan and all shades of brown to black. They allowed them to get quite close up to them and take photos, so when another car stopped and other people started to walk towards them, the friends left.

Passing through the beautiful scenery they crossed a bridge at Venfod Reservoir and headed towards Hay Tor, an interesting cluster of huge granite rocks where they stopped and had a walk around in the sunshine. The panoramic view from the Tor was stunning and it was clear to see why it was a popular spot for motorist and walkers alike to have their picnics there.

25. TORBAY 2010

2010 *Dartmoor ponies*

Seeing other people with their refreshments they decided it was time for them to have a cup of tea, so continued on their way, stopping at the first pub that they came to which happened to be The Forest Inn at Hexworthy. Sitting outside in the sun they appreciated the pots of tea whilst admiring the pub's hanging baskets which were draped with bright red begonias. After a short rest, they once again continued on their way to Dartmoor where they all got out of the car to have a short walk along the river bank and watch the antics of the children scrambling over the rocks and thoroughly enjoying themselves.

Returning to the car they drove a couple of hundred yards to Badgers Holt restaurant where they had an excellent lunch and afterwards walked around outside looking at the impressive collection of domestic fowl. There were many groups of foreign school children enjoying the delights of the restaurant and they thought what a lovely part of the country it was to show off to visitors.

Their last port of call was to be Widdicombe in the Moor (where the folk song 'Widdicombe Fair' originated from). Of course they sang the song as they approached the village and suspect that is what most people (in their age range) find themselves doing. It was a very picturesque village complete with village green, Norman church, Sexton's Cottage and Church House, now a National Trust Property and used as an information centre, shop and village hall. The latter has a torpedo standing on a plinth outside it from the Second World War, this was awarded to the villagers for their important contribution to the war effort when they gathered sphagnum moss from Dartmoor and sent it to the fighting forces to be used as field dressings for the soldier's wounds as it has healing properties.

There is a granite plinth on the village green which was presented to the parish of Widdicombe in the Moor by Francis Hamlyn Esquire of Dunstone Court in 1948. It depicts the village name and an etching of the grey mare (from the folk song) complete with its 7 riders. This was undoubtedly the focal point for the many Japanese tourist and their cameras as they arrived by the coach load.

The splendid pub sign also depicts the horse and riders but is misleadingly called 'The Old Inn'. They were running out of time, so didn't manage to go into the pub or the magnificent church. Reluctantly leaving this lovely old village they headed back to the hotel, detouring at a farm shop so that Mabel could buy some of their home cured bacon to take back to Doug. They all bought a few treats from the farm shop whose assistants had kindly kept open for them to choose their purchases. They then went on to Cockington where

25. TORBAY 2010

they three had a cup of tea and a chat in the hotel bedroom whilst Buz had a nap before the long drive home.

At 7.30pm (in the rain) Irene and June waved Mabel and Buz off as they started out for home, then settled down with the crossword book and a small snack for supper.

Tuesday

It was overcast first thing and they wondered what they would do for the day. They had an answer phone message from the night before from Buz saying that they had arrived home safely with no incidents. It seemed a bit strange just the two of them sitting down to breakfast. Paula waited on them as usual with Leon in the kitchen cooking his perfect English breakfasts, and it was no hardship to linger a while finishing off the contents of the teapot.

Whilst checking through the front door to see what the temperature was like, they bumped into Leon who told them about some of the local walks and gave them some guides, one of them being a murder mystery. They took these back to June's room and thought that they would like to do the mystery one when Fred came to collect them. The other walk went across Thornhill Brake which is an area of shrubs and wildflowers, so they decided to take this route to go to Torre Abbey which they thought they would visit as the weather looked as though it might rain and an indoor activity would be a good idea.

Gathering up their raincoats, umbrellas and walking sticks they crossed Cockington Lane and found the gateway leading to Thornhill Brake, they were glad that they had put their trainers on as there was a bit of red Devon sandstone mud to be negotiated. They climbed up the bank and found that it was a popular place for owners walking their dogs, who exchanged cheery greetings with them. It was a very pleasant open area and they were surprised that they had not discovered it on previous visits, as it was clearly a shortcut to Seaway Lane which they had often taken back into Torquay. Leaving the Brake via a stile they emerged at Vicarage Hill which is a continuation of Seaway Lane which they followed, only stopping to don their Macs as it had started to rain.

They turned off to go in the direction of Torquay train station and when they arrived they walked across the bridge to the café as they were getting a bit wet and felt in need of a cuppa. Finding themselves a corner table they shrugged out of their wet Macs and June discovered that hers was leaking and no longer doing the job for which it was intended! Two hot mugs of tea revived them and they were soon on their way again, pleased that the rain had stopped and following the directions of the man in the café to Torre Abbey.

Before reaching the Abbey they came upon an American theme café and bar gardens, so stopped to look at (and photograph) the statues of famous stars such as Marilyn Monroe and Elvis Presley. It was a fascinating place and they said that they would like to dine there, but it was only open in the evening and was quite a walk from Cockington. Irene stopped to take a photograph of a cat when it suddenly jumped onto her back, giving her a bit of a fright. They seem to have disturbed the 'guard' dog that was barking furiously, so took their leave and continued on their way.

When they arrived at the Abbey they stopped to take photos of the stone swans adorning the grand pillars of the gateway to the Abbey grounds, then they continued on down the drive and, seeing a large wooden door open leading to the gardens, passed through and were confronted by the Palm House. This large greenhouse was full of tropical and semi-tropical plants with a fish pond sporting lovely lilies as well as koi carp and goldfish. There was an abundance of bougainvillea and large tropical ferns which bought back memories of holidays in hot foreign parts. Irene stayed there for a while, whilst June wandered off to look at the cactus house. Meeting up again they headed for the house as it was threatening to rain again. They passed some statues of horses made out of what they assumed was wicker and stopped to take photos as Irene was looking for a good photograph for a competition where the subject was 'texture'.

Passing through the doorway of the 800 year old Abbey they approached a lady at a counter taking entrance money. She was quite surprised that they had arrived through the gardens; apparently they had entered through a staff gate instead of the main entrance where they should have paid to get in. They duly paid their fees and headed straight for the café and toilets. After a comfort break they perused the menu in the café and opted for the Cornish pasties which looked very inviting. After lunch they proceeded to make their way through the Abbey, starting on the ground floor, admiring the paintings, carvings and statues.

They were particularly struck by two paintings which were situated near to one another and which June recalled herself and Mabel commenting upon on the 1995 Adventure. One painting depicts a very wealthy family picnicking on a spacious lawn with chubby, healthy looking children playing happily. The other painting shows a poor family in a cottage kitchen with the mother sitting at a table in an attitude of despair, head in hands, having just read in a

25. TORBAY 2010

newspaper of the likely death of her soldier husband in a fierce battle. Two boys are shown sitting on the floor and (ironically) playing at battles with their toy soldiers, oblivious to their mother's distress, while the older daughter appears to be aware of the possible tragedy awaiting their family. The contrast between the two families is stark and makes evident the plight of poor families when they lose their breadwinner.

Making their way upstairs they came to a very pretentious exhibition of modern art purporting to be a psychological forest. The expression 'Emperor's New Clothes' came to June's mind and she wrote this in the book which was asking for the public's responses to the exhibition. 'From the sublime to the ridiculous' was another saying which could be applied here. In the modern art section there was a model of a man reclining in an armchair, the whole thing was made of cardboard. This was very striking and skilfully made and warranted more than just a quick glance. In this section there were also some fun items, a chair hanging from the ceiling, which by perpetual motion, kept changing its shape and a wooden model called 'Running Machine' which showed 16 wooden shoes in the form of two wheels rotating on axles when pushed and looking as if they were running. Another model which they admired depicted a panoramic view of a city at night with blue and white lights and electrical components representing the buildings (some of them being tower blocks).

They stopped to admire the striking sculpture of 'Othello', a painting of a small girl holding a present and a large oil painting of sailing ships at sea in a gale. Descending the magnificent oak staircase they found their way into the old catacombs (known as the vaulted cellars) which originally stored food and drinks for the monks and later occupants of the Abbey. As they exited the Abbey at this point, they saw a model of a huge colourful caterpillar adorning the side wall, made primarily from plastic bags, created by local school children and students in one of the workshops.

They wanted to see inside The Spanish Barn and wandering over noticed that there was another modern art exhibition in there and as they entered they were told by a lady attendant not to take photographs of the exhibits, since Damien Hurst who was the main exhibitor was 'positively paranoid about having his work photographed'. They re-assured her that their interest lay in the barn itself and that they were not remotely interested in looking at two encapsulated halves of a cow, revealing its innards. Whilst they could appreciate that this may be of interest to an aspiring vet, it was not their idea of art!

Wednesday

After a delicious bacon and egg breakfast and since it was a lovely sunny day they walked to Cockington village shops where they mooched amongst the brasses in the forge, before making their way around to the mill stream. They were delighted to find that a family of moorhens were ducking, diving and dabbling and they were happy to while away some time watching their antics. Strolling past The Drum and up onto the cricket field they made their way to The Court where they sat outside watching the horses pulling the carriages and their passengers boarding and alighting. One of the horses started to behave in a very skittish manner and the passengers (a lady and man with three small children) were looking a bit apprehensive. The mare was looking very unhappy and kept tossing its head and flicking its ears and generally stamping about, but eventually settled down with much soothing from its lady driver and continued with the ride.

Walking around the side of The Court they came to the crafts studio in the Stable Yard, a series of craft shops with artisans demonstrating their skills to the visitors. The first studio that they visited was the glass blowing where they saw paperweights being made and were fascinated by the techniques employed. Next they moved on to watch the man making rocking horses. He was repairing a large white Victorian horse and told them that he had found what he thought was a christening gown and a drinking vessel in a secret compartment in it. Apparently he asked the present owners whether they wanted him to remove these items, but they said to leave them where they were. This idea of a time capsule was new to Irene but June explained that she had bought a miniature horse for Fred and his too has a time capsule in. They deduced that this must be a tradition with rocking horses.

Leaving the craft studio they went through a creeper covered archway into the rose garden, a large walled garden full of roses and they wondered whether this might originally have been a fruit or vegetable garden for the manor house. Walking through the garden they left through another exit which upon turning right led them to the stables. Walking past the stables (which only had one horse in) they went around to the entrance of the organic garden and stopped to look at an old cider press which had been re-located to this area.

Passing through the gateway they emerged into the walled garden and wandered around inspecting the vegetable plots and comparing the size of the onions with the small ones that they had grown back home. They noticed some very bright yellow foliage and went over to see what it was and whilst chatting to a couple of the young work experience volunteers asked them

25. TORBAY 2010

about the black pods which were growing on the plant with yellow foliage. They had never seen them before and the two young volunteers didn't know what they were called either, so Irene went off and asked Steve the head gardener who told her that they were called Mrs Caruthers' Purple Podded Peas.

They found a couple of pods so took them home to show Mabel and see whether she recognised them (later when they asked her about them she said that she had never seen them before so they decided to plant them and see what happened). New additions to the gardens were Medieval Medicines, a herb border, marigolds, sunflowers, poppies, leeks, lettuces, radishes and runner beans. They took time to go into the small thatched shed which sat against a wall in the corner of the garden next to a lean-to wooden shed named 'Gardener's Delight'. Irene had never been into the thatched shed since it had always been closed when she was there, whereas June had been in with Mabel when Irene was unable to come with them and when it first opened. The sign on the wall informed them that it was a Thatched Cobb Shed and upon entering it June was surprised to see that the ears of corn were still attached to the thatch as she expected them to have been eaten by field mice or squirrels.

Leaving the walled garden they went around to the rear of The Court and entered the early Norman church, the Parish Church of St. George and St. Mary which nestles on the side of a bank. They decided to count the number of birds carved into the long wooden screen which spans the width of the church in front of the altar. In The Court a notice board said that there were 12 birds in the screen, the leaflet in the church said that there were 16 and the murder mystery trail leaflet said 14. In the event, they counted 15 birds, so concluded that the church had the correct number and that there was one which was eluding them.

Feeling in need of a drink they went to The Court and had a cup of tea, sitting outside and watching the horses and carriages as they drank. After a pleasant interlude they headed for the Gamekeeper's Cottage (its present name is 'The Rabbits'), originally it was where the warriner lived and tended the colony of rabbits which were kept on the hillside by the cottage as fresh meat for The Court before pheasants became fashionable food for the upper classes. There was a group of school children with their teacher playing trust games on the grassy area to the side of the cottage and they reminisced about playing these games with the inner city children that they had taken away to Malvern for many years.

Following the path through Manscombe woods they passed the two small lakes and climbed up a long steep hill through the woods. They emerged at the crest of the hill where, leaning on a five bar gate they looked out over a panoramic view of Torquay. They picked out the bay, the harbour and a very grand looking house (which they passed later on). This path led to an alleyway and they eventually emerged into Manscombe Road, which was part of a fairly new housing estate. Having had their curiosity satisfied as to where the track in the woods led, they decided to carry on this way and try to make their way through the housing estate to the town centre of Torquay.

Having walked a few hundred yards they came upon a Water Board man sitting in his van looking at a map. They stopped and asked him if he could direct them down to the coast road leading into Torquay. He consulted his map and showed them the route to take before driving off. Weaving their way through the estate they arrived at the main road and sat down for a rest on a bench overlooking the seafront on the corner of Cockington Lane.

After a while they were joined by a large man with a long white beard and hair, dressed in a long cloak and carrying a staff who they nick-named Moses as he looked like their idea of the biblical character. He was waving to the passing vehicles, and people in cars and buses seemed to know him and were waving back. Before they had time to pluck up their courage to speak to him it started to rain, and since there was a bus shelter nearby they made a dash for it. It was just as well that they did, as within a few minutes it was pouring down and people appeared from seemingly nowhere to take cover from the downpour.

By this time they had decided to catch the bus rather than walk into the town, and after a half-hour wait and listening to much grumbling by their fellow queuers boarded the bus sighing with relief as they sat down. It was about 3.15pm by this time, so alighting from the bus in the town they dived into the nearest café and ordered cream teas (after all they had missed lunch!). Once replete they set out to find the Tourist Information Centre where they were lucky enough to encounter a very helpful young man who guided them through the maze of bus time tables to get them to and from Babbacombe Theatre. They planned to go to see the show 'The Laughter Party' the following evening and booked the tickets through him as he wished them a pleasant evening.

It had stopped raining by this time so they strolled along to Debenhams where there was a sale on. June wanted to buy Irene a top for her birthday (the previous week) and it wasn't long before Irene spotted something that she liked. June had been looking for a pair of burgundy coloured gloves for a long time and was delighted to find a pair in the sale. Purchases completed, they then caught the bus to Cockington Lane and walked up the lane to the hotel (hoods up as it had started to rain again). Back in their rooms they put their feet up for a while and relaxed with a cup of tea before getting changed to go out to dinner.

They walked along the lane to The Drum Inn and asked which area the quiz was to be held in, so that they could be close enough to see and hear the question master. Having chosen their table they ordered dinner (Irene had beef burger and chips and June had chicken pie and chips). The meal was excellent and they were seated close to the bar so could refill their drinks without moving from the table. The Quiz was great fun and they felt that although they didn't win, they didn't disgrace themselves either!

Strolling back to the hotel they agreed that despite the showers they had had a lovely and interesting day, which they rounded off with a nightcap in their rooms before falling into their beds.

Thursday

Over a tasty fried breakfast they discussed where to spend the day, and since it was raining thought that they would catch a bus to Goodrington and hope that the weather would clear up later (as predicted by the weather forecast). They walked along the boardwalk which runs adjacent to Cockington Lane, which was a bit slippery due to the rain, but a very pleasant walk amongst the trees and wild flowers. At the bottom of the lane they crossed the main road on the sea front and caught the bus to Goodrington.

They asked the bus driver to let them know when they reached the Goodrington stop and settled back for the ride. Admiring the scenery along the way and chatting about this and that they didn't notice that they had sailed past Goodrington and when speculating amongst themselves as to whether they had passed the stop, a lady behind leaned forward and told them that they were way past the stop and well on the way to Brixham. They shrugged their shoulders and settled for going to visit their favourite harbour rather than getting off the bus and finding their way back to Goodrington.

Alighting from the bus in Brixham they were very pleasantly surprised at the rise in temperature; it had been windy and wet in Torquay and was a lovely sunny day here. Strolling down from the bus stop to the quayside, they happened to pass a shop which sold nautical gear and since June was on the look out for a new waterproof walking coat, popped in for a quick look. She soon found just what she was looking for, a bright red coat so that Fred could spot her amongst the crowds at classic car rallies.

Continuing on they came to the harbour area and felt in need of a little refreshment, so wishing to sit where they could watch any action that was occurring by The Golden Hind, they waited for a few minutes to obtain a suitable table outside in a very busy café overlooking the galleon. Once their tea was in front of them they sat back and allowed themselves to be entertained by the antics of a family who had disembarked from the ship and were dressed as pirates, who were clearly celebrating someone's birthday. A group of students dressed as Pierottes emerged from the rear of a van complete with their musical instruments and proceeded to play 'Happy Birthday' encouraging the onlookers to join in, which of course they did.

Mindful of the fact that they were going to the theatre in the evening, they walked along to check the ferry times, and found that the 1.30pm ferry was due to depart. The young lady at the kiosk phoned through to the ferryman and asked him to wait for their arrival before sailing. They hurried as quickly as they could along the breakwater and arrived slightly out of breath to be hailed by the ferryman who kindly helped them aboard. It was a very pleasant crossing which got progressively choppier as they neared Torquay and indeed when they alighted

2010 *The Golden Hind, Brixham Harbour*

25. TORBAY 2010

onto the pier were momentarily non-plussed at the strength of the wind and had to hang onto the rail. They were also puzzled as they knew that last time they had caught a ferry to Brixham they had set out from the part of the harbour by the Tourist Information Centre and they now found themselves on a very long pier (which they had never noticed before) and heading for the Princess Theatre.

They couldn't get over the fact that they had never seen this pier before and they decided that this structure had been hidden from view by hoardings and recently renovated, as all the rows of iron seats ranged along each side of the walkway were sparkling white, in excellent condition and looked freshly painted. As they puzzled over this they walked towards the bistro attached to the theatre and wandered in to have a look at the menu. Homity Pie caught June's eye and Irene fancied Nachos and Chilli, so they found themselves a table near the window and overlooking the harbour. Towards the end of their meal they noticed that it had started to rain, so decided to catch the bus back to Cockington. In the event, they had missed the last bus to Cockington Village so caught the one passing the end of Cockington Lane.

They had no choice but to walk along the lane in the rain to their hotel, however the weather helped them to make the decision about whether to get the bus to Babbacombe in the evening or order a taxi. When they arrived at Lanscome House (dripping wet and looking very bedraggled) Leon met them in the hallway and they asked him for a phone number for the local taxi firm. Once in June's bedroom and divested of their wet outer garments Irene made a cup of tea whilst June phoned the taxi company. Since they didn't have to start getting ready to go out for a good hour or so they had a little nap.

Waking refreshed and raring to go they got showered and changed and armed with umbrellas they ran through the downpour and piled into the taxi. Once in Babbacombe they arranged with the taxi driver to be collected at the end of the show. Picking up the tickets from the box office they made their way to their seats and settled down to an evening of superb entertainment. The show was called 'The Laughter Party' and was a variety show in traditional seaside fashion. The dancers, singers and comedy turns were all excellent performers and appeared to be enjoying themselves immensely and so the atmosphere was infectious and they had a very enjoyable evening.

Despite the continuous downpour and dodging the rain they even had an entertaining ride home in the taxi, when the driver told them about his friendship with a male member of the cast who had asked him to go to London with him to be his driver. Over a light supper they recalled the acts and concluded that they had good value for money and would highly recommend it their fellow guests. They discussed various possibilities for the following day when Fred was due to arrive, then retired to their beds.

Friday

After breakfast they started to pack up some of their belongings in readiness for their departure the following day and June phoned Fred to see how far away he was. Since he was quite close June stood outside the hotel chatting to a couple of walkers and waiting to direct him into the car park. Irene had a wander up the lane to take photos of the cottages and came back just as Fred arrived at 11.30am. After depositing his bag in the bedroom they all walked along to Rose Cottage in the village and had tea and scones in the Rose Garden Tearooms. It was a delightful interlude, the sun was shining and a young man was playing classical music on a piano under a green and white lattice work gazebo in the middle of the garden.

Strolling across to the forge June went inside to ask the lady when the horse and carriage rides started. She said that she hadn't seen any that morning and they may be on later in the day. Irene in the meantime had wandered off to take photos of the moorhens on the mill pond. They looked around the area and noticed that a group of people were assembling to catch the bus, and since they weren't able to take Fred on the horse and carriage ride as planned, they decided to catch the bus into Torquay and stroll around the harbour instead.

They got off the bus near the marina and walked back towards the Princess Theatre and looked around the gardens before going into the bistro for lunch. They sat upstairs on this occasion which afforded them an even better view of the pier and harbour than the previous day. After lunch they strolled along the pier for a while, then walked back to the bus stop by the theatre where they caught the last bus back to Cockington at 3.45pm.

Once back in the village they walked up the hill to the cricket field, trying to do a treasure hunt which Leon had given them earlier. Irene sat outside the Court checking the photos on her camera whist June and Fred went to the stables to find out why the horses and carriages were not out. The lady grooming the horses said that it had been too windy earlier on and they had decided not to take them out since one of the horses had become very skittish a few days earlier when the wind upset it. June then took Fred to see the man making rocking horses, but he had shut up shop and gone home. They stopped to watch the glass blowing for a while where Irene joined them, then went to the church to search for a clue on the murder mystery trail.

25. TORBAY 2010

Whilst they were reading the church magazine, which informed them that the famous carved wooden pulpit started life in a Spanish Armada ship *The Rosario*, which was wrecked off Torbay in a storm, they saw something which they had not spotted on previous visits. Apparently when the church was built, a heavy oak bar was inserted into a recess in the wall by the door. This was used by women who had been caught in adultery and escaping death from drowning, by claiming sanctuary in the church. Once the bar had been drawn across the doorway the accusers could not enter and the women were safe. The friends were quite indignant that only the women were punished whilst the men got off scott free. A group of people were about to enter the church as they were leaving, so they stopped to tell them about the 'sanctuary bar' and they too had not noticed it on their many visits to the church.

Leaving the church they followed the path which led to the Gamekeeper's cottage and past the pools, pausing to look for fish. Continuing on they followed the path which leads to the gatehouse archway which spans the road and looks like a bridge. This led them close to their hotel so, as it was about 5.30pm they thought that a cup of tea was in order before getting ready to go to dinner at The Drum. Back at Lanscome House they had a cup of tea whilst Fred unpacked his bag, then they washed and changed before walking up the lane to The Drum.

They had a very nice meal at the pub recounting some of their tales and before leaving they found another murder mystery clue on the pub sign outside. On the way back they looked for the answer to another clue which was on the wall of the forge near the door. It was very dark and they couldn't see the wall clearly so Irene and June aimed their cameras at the spot where they guessed the answer might be. As they took photos and their flashes went off Fred peered at the spot to see if he could discern anything, he thought he could make out some letters so they took a few more photos in the general area in the hope that one of them would reveal the mystery.

When they got back to the hotel they looked at the pictures on the two cameras and were able to decipher the initials J.F. picked out in square headed nails. These initials corresponded to a name in the murder mystery. After the obligatory night cap they retired to their beds with a sense of achievement and slept soundly.

Saturday

Knowing that this was their last day in the hotel and that they would be returning home to their cereal and toast breakfasts they made the most of the generous portions of bacon and egg whilst they could. After a leisurely breakfast they collected their bags from the bedrooms and put them into the boot of Fred's car.

They settled their bills with Leon which was made complicated by the circumstances of Mabel's illness and Buz stopping extra days. Having written very favourable comments in the visitors' book and thanking him and his wife for their hospitality they said that they hoped to return in the not too distant future. Taking their leave of him they set off for Totnes where they planned to take a boat ride to Dartmouth.

Arriving at Totnes marina they parked the car, bought their tickets and awaited the next boat. They bought 'Round Robin' tickets, which meant that they went on the boat and returned by bus, there was also an option to travel part of the journey by steam train. They were surprised at the number of people waiting to catch the boat and had to wait in quite a long queue. However there was much to see on the river, canoes, sailing boats, launches and ferry boats not to mention the antics of the passengers. Their cameras came out and it wasn't long before they were boarding the boat to take them along the Dart to Dartmouth.

There was a bit of a scramble getting on since everyone wanted the front seats, but they managed to get seats outside with a good view which was what they needed for the photographers amongst them! To their surprise as they were leaving the marina they spotted two seals travelling towards them, their little heads bobbing up and down in the swell of the boat. They were quite pleased that they appeared to be the first people near to them to spot the seals and even the man doing the commentary didn't mention them as he was pointing out places and objects of interest. This was surprising as he appeared to be very observant and they were impressed with his local knowledge and the interesting and amusing way that he related his information.

There had been a shower earlier on but as they floated along the sun was shining and they settled back to enjoy the fabulous scenery and learn about the places that they were passing along the way. The commentator pointed out the picturesque villages of Galmpton and Dittisham and the history relating to the villages and the river trade.

They passed Agatha Christie's holiday home called 'Greenway House' which is where she spent 40 years writing her plays and novels. They could just see the house nestled amongst the trees high up on the bank side. It is now owned by the National Trust and is accessible by road, but has limited parking space. Her grounds were initially just surrounding the house, but over time she acquired land reaching down to the river which is now known as her estate.

25. TORBAY 2010

There was a cormorant perched on a branch, spreading its wings out in the sun as (they were informed) after three dives they had to dry them or they would become waterlogged and unable to dive. They saw herons and shags but sadly no swans!

Arriving at Dartmouth's foot passenger ferry they alighted and June and Fred who had not been there before were immediately struck by the beauty of the place. They walked around taking photos and looking for a likely place to eat knowing that they didn't have long before catching the bus back to Totnes and retrieving Fred's car for the long journey home. There were many splendid buildings, not the least of these the Britannia Royal Naval College which overlooks the town and harbour. There was also a lovely little park where they would have liked to have spent more time and agreed that they should return to Dartmouth for a holiday as it warranted much more than a day trip to see its many attributes.

Returning to the harbour area they went into the Station Restaurant and had the carvery which was very nice. The restaurant was decorated like a boat with canoes and boating regalia covering the walls and ceiling and they had a lovely view of the river and the village of Kingswear on the opposite bank. Once replete they wandered outside to find the bus stop and caught the bus back to Totnes. Retrieving the car they set off on the journey home which happily was uneventful and they arrived safely at their destinations. On the way they regaled Fred with the week's happenings and said that they had missed Mabel in the latter days but were glad that (thanks to Buz) she had at least been able to spend a few days with them. They really loved staying in Cockington which had become their favourite village in the Torbay area and hoped that they would be able to return there in future years for more adventures!

26. Highley, Severn Valley

22nd to 26th August 2011

Mabel had not been too well on and off, so they only decided in July to go on this year's 'adventure'. They were not able to book the cabin at Highley for a full week as it was already booked, but they did however manage to get it for five days in August and were happy to settle for that. They were grateful as always that Buz offered to take them and that Fred was happy to bring them back.

Monday

Buz collected Mabel at her house at 10am and went on to pick up June. After packing up the car with their luggage and food for five days they squeezed themselves in and, waving goodbye to Fred, set off at 10.45am for Highley. They arrived at the cabin about 12.30pm and after a nice cup of tea proceeded to unpack the car.

Buz drove them to the Bache Arms in Highley, as they were hoping to have lunch there, but it was boarded up and clearly no longer in operation. Remembering a pub where they had eaten previously, they directed Buz to The Malt Shovel on the Bridgnorth Road. June went in to enquire whether they did lunches and was told that they no longer served food and the only pubs that did locally were The Ship Inn near Highley Station and The Bull's Head at Chelmarsh. Since they were already on the way towards Chelmarsh they decided to carry on and go to The Bull's Head and, happily for them, when they arrived lunch was still being served (third time lucky?).

The Bull's Head was a very interesting pub with lots of cricketing memorabilia, since the landlord was a good friend of the South African cricketer Basil D'Oliveira. He had been to many matches with him over the years and met many famous cricketers. Buz had a steak and the rest of them had cottage pie and all agreed that their meals were delicious.

26. HIGHLEY, SEVERN VALLEY 2011

From there they set off to Alveley via Bridgnorth and went to The Three Horseshoes, the oldest pub in Shropshire, and were pleased to see that it was voted the best pub in Shropshire in 2010. They had hoped to see Lianne (the landlady) and show her the chapter in their book which mentions her, however she was not there so they told the barmaid that they would try to return on Friday for lunch, and hoped to see her then.

They had a look around the lovely old twelfth century church of St. Mary's and pointed out to Buz the fox with the bird in its mouth carved into the battlements. Outside the church a rather strange young man began telling them that the church had connections with Dracula and that Jesus Christ was crucified three thousand years ago and was blonde and blue eyed. Irene sidled away from him and into the car while June and Buz made their escape as soon as was humanly polite to do so.

After a walk around the lovely old houses surrounding the church, they got back into the car and drove back to the cabin. Irene then made Buz a sandwich and a cup of tea before he set off back home. After waving Buz off they prepared and ate a light supper of ham and salad whilst watching television (something they had not been able to do there before the advent of digital TV). They retired to bed early as they were feeling tired.

Tuesday

Despite the dire forecast the weather was mild first thing and looked as though it might be a sunny day, so they decided to walk into the village and renew their acquaintance with old friends and places visited previously. After breakfast (June risked the elements and ate her 'full English breakfast' which Irene had very kindly cooked, outside on the balcony) they picked up their trusty walking sticks and set forth on their first walk of this 'adventure'.

At the station they were greeted by two familiar faces, Maureen and her Collie dog Boris. Maureen waved a friendly greeting and Boris wagged his tail and they both looked very pleased to see them. She said that she had been asking Jasmine if she had seen them this year and it sounded like they had missed them. They said that they were about to walk up to and along Smoke Alley (where she lived) so she joined them and brought them up to date with the local news.

They had already heard from Irene's friend Brenda that The Ship Inn had been refurbished under new ownership and was now serving meals. Maureen confirmed this and said that she had enjoyed an excellent meal there and thoroughly recommended it.

When they arrived at Jasmine and Willie's cottage they were surprised to see that half of their vegetable patch had disappeared and there was a lawn in its place. Jasmine and Willie greeted them as they approached and Jasmine said that they had been wondering if they would see them this year (apparently they refer to them as 'The Girls'). They looked at their lovely garden and asked what had happened to the vegetable patch and Willie explained that it was getting too much for him, so he decided to make a new lawn, which apart from anything else would not require the watering that the vegetables had. They chatted for a while about changes in the village, including The Ship Inn, which they also recommended. The friends told them that they had completed their adventures to date and that they were in a folder which was too heavy to carry about. Since they feature in the book they invited them to come to the cabin to see it and arranged for them to come the following evening. They had already invited Maureen (who by this time had gone into her house) and asked if they would mind bringing her along. They agreed to this so they bade them farewell and continued on their way to the village.

Strolling along the normally peaceful road they passed by a well-appointed detached house and were horrified to hear the racket which was blasting out from the upstairs windows. There was a boy about twelve years-old sitting on the upstairs window ledge who was shouting and waving a can about. There was another boy lying on the ground in the garden and both gave the impression of being drunk. The friends were quite distressed as their perception of Highley was that it was a crime-free peaceful village, but of course they were looking at it through rose coloured glasses. They really felt sorry for the villagers and especially the next door neighbours and it cast a shadow of gloom over their small band.

By this time their tummies were telling them that it was lunchtime, so they headed for the tea rooms hoping that they would be open, since they never had been before. Happily they were open and they were greeted by a very pleasant lady who took their order of tea and sandwiches whilst they settled themselves at a table in the window. Rejoicing in their good fortune they enjoyed their lunch before taking leave of the waitress and going on their way.

Crossing the road they walked up Silverdale Street admiring the beautiful and colourful hanging baskets, troughs and plant pots which lined the row of houses. They paused to take photos of the flowers, before turning their attention to the superb allotments on the opposite side of the street. As usual the individual vegetable plots were bursting with produce especially runner beans, carrots, beetroot, cabbages, broccoli and various salad crops. There was no-one around to talk to, so after several more photos they walked around the corner into Church Street.

Ambling along to the parish church they found a bench in the leafy churchyard for Mabel to sit and relax and wait for June and Irene to have a wander around. They checked out the old dilapidated hen house at the rear of the church, which still held evidence of its former occupants, but thankfully it was still empty. After reassuring themselves that no chickens were being held in captivity they went for a walk around the back of the church, trying to recall the route to the Donkey Bridge. There were allotments where the runner bean plants were growing to about eight feet high and they were covered in huge beans which they would have liked to 'scrump'.

Making their way back to the church after their exertions, they appreciated the cool, calm interior and walking around took photos of the beautiful stained glass windows. Irene picked up a copy of the parish magazine and they re-joined Mabel who was happily sitting in the churchyard watching the birds whirling around the stately trees.

In need of refreshments they remembered that they had promised to meet Maureen in the Parish Church Rooms for a cup of tea. So they headed off in what they thought was the general direction of the Church Rooms. Not exactly sure of where they were, they were pleasantly surprised to find them on the corner of Church Street and the main road. They tentatively pushed the side door open and wandered in where they were met by Maureen who introduced them to the ladies of the village who had assembled for a chat and tea and biscuits. One lady got up from her seat and went into the kitchen area and made them a fresh pot of tea. Once refreshed, and after being asked by one of the ladies how they began their first 'adventure' they regaled them with tales of being put in the stocks, wandering haphazardly across farmers' fields and cramming four people into a two- seater sports car. They really enjoyed the tea and the fellowship with the ladies and on reflection, wondered what on earth they thought of them taking over their afternoon tea club.

Bidding the ladies farewell and confirming with Maureen that they would see her the following evening at the cabin, they made their way down Smoke Alley to the Country Park. By the time they had reached the park Mabel was feeling a bit out of breath, so they stopped at the bottom of the hill where the miner's wheel and coal truck dominate the view, and sat on a bench for a few minutes. Once recovered, they made their way up the slope to one of their favourite places by the wheel and found a spot in the sun where they promptly lay down to do a bit of serious sun-bathing! Irene produced the crossword puzzle in the church magazine which she had picked up earlier and they spent a happy hour trying to answer the questions.

Since it was quite a step back up the lane to the cabin and the sun was still shining they decided to go straight to The Ship Inn for their dinner. So they lingered a little longer chatting and reading the newspaper until they felt hungry enough to make a move.

They strolled down to The Ship Inn and were very pleasantly surprised to see the changes that they had always hoped for had taken place. It had quite depressed them on previous visits to see the run down state of the place when it had such great potential. The outside of the building had been renovated and wooden decking had been laid overlooking the river to provide a large terraced seating area. The interior was unrecognisable, with large airy rooms and modern décor and they were very impressed with the high standard of the renovation.

As it was such a lovely evening they opted to sit out on the terrace and overlook the River Severn flowing gently past. They all chose to have fish and chips as they had been told by one of the locals that they would take some beating. They were not disappointed; their meals were not only huge but also delicious. The fish hung over the edge of the plates and the batter was light and crispy, the chips were large and golden and they soon tucked in and enjoyed them immensely. Full up and happy they slowly meandered back up the track stopping now and then to catch their breath. The rest of the evening was spent with June typing up the day's events whilst Mabel read the newspaper and Irene continued with the church crossword puzzle.

Wednesday

They awoke to a glorious sunny morning and Irene cooked a delicious bacon and egg breakfast. June sat outside and fed scraps to the robins and the blue and great tits. They had already decided that if the weather was clement they would go to Arley, as previously they had been unable to get into the arboretum there as it was closed. Irene had spotted an article in the church magazine saying when it was open.

Popping their little umbrellas into their pockets, as rain was forecast, they set off down the hill to the railway station, and took photos of the incoming train from the new bridge which now spans the track. They strolled into the attractive old ticket office with its traditional aspidistra in a green patterned Victorian plant pot, and approached the volunteer station master in his smart livery behind the counter and bought their return tickets to Arley. Shortly

26. HIGHLEY, SEVERN VALLEY 2011

2011 Highley Station

2011 River Severn at Arley

afterwards the train arrived and they sat back and enjoyed the passing scenery.

Alighting at Arley Station they walked down the hill and across the bridge where they spotted a cafe selling home-made ice cream, which was just too tempting to resist. Finding a table outside overlooking the river, Irene ordered two Worcester Plum flavoured ices for herself and Mabel and a butterscotch one for June. After a short rest they continued on their way up the road passing some very interesting buildings, one of these being a mock castle, and of course taking the obligatory photos. They thought that once they had passed through the gate to the arboretum (which was padlocked the last time they had been there) they would be near to the gardens, but it was quite a long walk to the actual entrance. They passed a grand building covered in a rich red creeper, this was Arley House and they wondered whether it belonged to the Arboretum.

Once inside the Arboretum, one of the oldest in England, and having paid their entrance fees, they set off on one of the suggested routes in the guide leaflet. It took them past numerous magnificent specimen trees and a fruit orchard. They also saw several varieties of farmyard fowl such as Silkies and Rhode Island Reds and a few birds of prey. It began to rain so they huddled around a covered stand containing a dinosaur skeleton made of wood. The sign on the stand read 'Vernon the Velociraptor'; there were several of these along a trail designed for children appropriately called The Dinosaur Trail. Trying to shelter under the edge of the stand was not really effective, so they thought that it was an opportune moment to go for lunch in the cafe. Mabel and June ordered jacket potatoes and Irene tomato soup to warm them up as the rain had made them feel a bit cold.

When the rain stopped, Mabel decided to take a rest whilst Irene and June wandered through the Italian gardens, past the fountain and on towards the maze, taking time to stop and photograph a field of hay bales (known to the two friends as mellorolls). Time was getting on and not wanting to miss the train, they didn't attempt to go around the maze in case they got lost! On the way back, after taking photos of the ornamental grasses, Irene stopped by the greenhouses to buy some Victoria plums while June carried on back to Mabel who also went to buy some plums when June told her where Irene was.

Plums purchased, they set off back to the village where they came across a cheerful group of young people who were pulling their canoes out of the river and stacking them onto a trailer, after what must have been a fun filled afternoon of kayaking. After crossing the bridge and walking up the hill to the station, they waited a few minutes for the train to arrive and relaxed chatting about the arboretum on the journey back to Highley.

Alighting from the train they saw Maureen and Boris at the station and stopped to chat, she confirmed that she was coming to visit them in the cabin with Jasmine and Willie on that evening, so she walked up the lane with them just to be sure of the cabin's whereabouts. Having established the location of the cabin she set off back home with Boris while June and Mabel went for a nap. Irene in the meantime cooked some potatoes and heated up the stew which she had prepared at home and made dumplings. Awaking refreshed from their naps Mabel and June joined Irene in devouring the delicious meal, but were too full to have Mabel's apple crumble as planned.

About 7 o'clock Jasmine, Will and Maureen arrived and were surprised at the size and cosiness of the cabin. After they declined their offer of glasses of wine they had tea and biscuits and chatted about growing vegetables and flowers and the long hot summer producing an ample yield of fruit and veg.

Once the tea was out of the way they looked at the friends' 'Adventures' book, particularly the photos and reading the sections where they and Highley were mentioned. June showed them more photos which she had stored on her laptop and which weren't included in the book. They talked about growing up during the war years and their parents growing their own vegetables and tobacco; the latter being used for pipe smoking which was the fashion in those days.

Willie talked about the years he spent down the mine at the Highley colliery and Jasmine told them about her time in the pen factory. Maureen had grown up in the Midlands and she told them about her mother's hard life there. She herself was glad to be living in such a pleasant place as Highley where she can walk Boris in safety and chat to local people every day. It was a very amiable evening and the time seemed to fly by but by 9.30pm the visitors decided it was time to go home.

After waving them off, June texted Fred, Mabel phoned Doug and Irene phoned Buz, then June wrote up the diary whilst Mabel and Irene played Scrabble and, as usual Mabel won!

Thursday

A slightly cooler start to the day so after a tasty fried breakfast courtesy of Irene; they donned warmer clothes and set off to walk to Hampton Loade. They thought that they might manage to walk there, have lunch at The Unicorn pub, and catch the train back to Highley.

In the event they bumped into Maureen again at the station with her beautiful dog Boris and she decided to walk along with them for a while. Taking the path along the riverbank from The Ship Inn they strolled through a wooded area where there were lots of fruit trees which had gone back to the wild including apples, plums and damsons. They decided that if they were more knowledgeable about wild fruits, fungi and grains they could subsidise their incomes! Coming to an area where the riverbank was covered in wildflowers, they could see through them to the river and watch the antics of the ducks, moorhens and coots ducking and diving. They also saw a pair of majestic swans, gracefully floating downstream as though the other waterfowls' antics were beneath them.

Eventually they arrived at the Highley and Alveley bridge where Mabel and Irene took the low path near to the river towards Hampton Loade, while June, Maureen and Boris took the high road and cycle path to the Halt train stop, to see how far it was in case they needed to get the train back. The signpost to Hampton Loade showed that it was one and a half miles and as it was one o'clock and getting close to their lunch time it seemed prudent to have a change of plan.

Re-tracing their steps June and Maureen re-joined Irene and Mabel who were having a rest and waiting for the other two to catch them up. After a short discussion about distances and times (and of course lunch) it was decided to abandon going to Hampton Loade, cross the river and go for lunch at the visitors centre at Alveley Country Park. After walking back to the bridge they bade farewell to Maureen and Boris, crossed the river and headed for lunch. It looked as though it might start to rain so they quickened their steps up the steep incline to the cafe. There was a limited choice of hot food, so they all settled for Minestrone soup and rolls with mugs of tea. Having given their order in to the cook, they looked around the centre whilst they awaited their lunch. Irene wandered around the wildlife displays whilst Mabel and June headed for a stand with various stuffed furry song birds for sale. They spent some time trying to decide which ones to buy, probably driving everyone else in the cafe mad by pressing all of the birds to produce their authentic bird song. They eventually decided which ones they wanted to buy just as their lunch arrived.

Having eaten their soup they purchased chocolate bars and a bottle of water for the journey back, and set out to find the pond and nature reserve where they had sheltered from the rain on a previous adventure. When they arrived at the reserve it was very much the same as they remembered it, except

26. HIGHLEY, SEVERN VALLEY 2011

that there were not as many waterfowl as previously. Also there was a hide which they didn't see the last time which overlooked a large pool, so they sat in there for a while trying to spot some wildlife, to no avail. The conservation area, the hides, benches et al, were created and maintained by local volunteers, and they sent them out a big 'thank you' for making something beautiful for them to enjoy.

After a pleasant interlude by the pond they set off back along the path to Highley and when they approached the Alveley Bridge, they saw a lady with a greyhound and three whippets which were dashing about on the bridge. She had a very pretty little blonde haired girl of about five years old with her, and as they walked across the bridge chatting to her she said that the child was her niece and that she had been badly mauled by a dog, yet showed no fear of the greyhound and whippets. She told them that the greyhound was a retired racing dog from Perry Barr in Birmingham, which of course is not far from where they all lived. They stood talking to her for a while and explained that they had been going to Highley for a few years and had got to know some of the locals. The lady's name was Carol and when they told her that they knew Jasmine she said that her husband Sean owned the pen factory where she (Carol) used to work with Jasmine.

They said goodbye to Carol and her niece as they set off to pick up her car and drive to Bewdley where she lives. They have found that one of the main pleasures of their adventures is meeting interesting and pleasant people and they affirmed this as they wandered back along the riverbank.

Clambering up the slope from The Ship Inn to Highley Station they then crossed the track and made the last push up the hill just in time, as it started to rain. The first thing they did was put the kettle on and make a pot of tea, then June set out the ham which she had cooked at home, and prepared a salad whilst Irene warmed rolls and apple crumble in the oven. They enjoyed their meal while watching a police programme on TV, then Irene and Mabel did a Crossword puzzle while June typed up the notes of the day's activities.

Friday

Using up the remainder of their supplies on a cooked breakfast they then set to cleaning and tidying the cabin and packing up the food boxes. They finished off their personal packing and were ready for when Fred arrived at 12 noon. Once revived from his journey with a cup of tea, Fred helped them to put their belongings into his car. They then packed up the rubbish sacks to be dropped into the bins by the signal box at the station. After Irene had taken photos of

THREE HAPPY WANDERERS

the cabin for the owner to put into a brochure, they set off and having dumped the rubbish drove to Alveley via Bridgnorth to return to The Three Horseshoes pub.

On Monday when they visited the pub hoping that Lianne would be there and wasn't, they planned to return today and were pleased to discover that this time she was there. They showed Lianne the book and discussed their previous visit to the pub when she was busy catering for a group of bell ringers. June asked her if she would mind reading the section about their visit and asked if the details were correct. She looked through, and told them about a couple of inaccuracies, one of them being the spelling of her name which is Lianne not Leanne. She took the book to show her husband and he pointed out the other one.

They ordered lunch and Fred and Mabel decided on haddock, whilst Irene chose scampi and June ordered cannelloni. The food duly arrived and was greatly enjoyed and as Lianne was clearing away they congratulated her upon the pub of the year award and chatted to her for a while before going on their way.

Fred drove them around to the church where he and June got out of the car and had a little walk about and June pointed out the fox carving on the balustrade of the church roof. They then drove to the Visitors Centre and walked to the nature reserve where Fred fed the fish with their leftover bread. After a short walk around the pool they availed themselves of the Visitors Centre's toilets before setting off for Bridgnorth, where they went to the Bridgnorth Antique Centre. They mooched around for a while and June bought a bedspread.

Then they drove home discussing the week's happenings including their visit to the arboretum at Arley and telling Fred how they had spent some quality time with Maureen and had invited her with Jasmine and Willie to the cabin to show them their book of adventures.

They thoroughly enjoyed their few days away together and Mabel, who hadn't been sure whether she would be able to manage the walks felt that she had benefitted from the break. Irene and June were delighted that she was able to be with them considering that she hadn't been in very good health during the past few months. They agreed that it would be great fun to go on the Severn Valley Railway's 1940s weekend and would try to do that next year, when they could look forward to spending time with the friendly and interesting people who they had come to know in Highley.

27. Highley, Severn Valley

23rd & 24th June 2012

This year they could only have a weekend Adventure as on Mondays, Wednesdays and Fridays Mabel was on dialysis. Last year when talking to Maureen and Jasmine, who had previously taken part in the Severn Valley Railway's 1940s weekend, they thought that it would be fun to dress up in war time clothes and ride up and down the line, so that was what they decided to do this year. Irene booked the train and Big Band event on Kidderminster station (which Maureen had told them about) and June booked rooms in The Ship Inn, which was just off Highley Station and overlooking the River Severn.

After much discussion they decided that they would dress up as Land Army Girls and so they rooted about amongst the dressing up clothes in June's loft and emerged looking more like 'Allotment Girls'.

Saturday

Early on the Saturday morning Fred and June collected Mabel and Irene and set off for Highley and The Ship Inn, where Fred helped them up the stairs with their bags as they were on the top floor. After waving Fred off, they got changed into their 1940s gear so that they could make the most of the day. Gathering up their sticks, flags and khaki bags they made their way up the slope and steps to Highley Station which is about 50 yards from The Ship Inn and the River Severn.

The train for Arley was shortly to arrive, so they bought Cornish pasties and beakers of tea from the kiosk on the platform and consumed them whilst admiring the wartime memorabilia and posters in and around the station. There were Union Jack flags and bunting everywhere and stacks of suitcases, milk churns, fire buckets and stirrup pumps. On the opposite side of the track there were army vehicles, tents and gun carriages, tended by men and women in military uniforms.

THREE HAPPY WANDERERS

Whilst enjoying their pasties, they spotted their friends Viv and Bob (Bob was a volunteer on the railway and had been a ticket collector for many years but has progressed to Station Master). On this occasion he was just a visitor, travelling along the line and enjoying the 1940s atmosphere with his wife Viv. They joined them in the crush on the platform and explained that they had just been to see the battle re-enactment with pyrotechnics by The Engine House, a steam museum just a short way along the track from the station.

Everywhere there were men and women dressed not only in smart military uniforms from several countries, but in very fetching 1940s civilian clothes. The women were dressed in a variety of costumes including flowered dresses, fur coats, plumed hats, fox furs, silk stockings with handbags matching their shoes and gloves. The men wore smart suits, plus fours, cravats, trilby hats, highly polished lace-up shoes and there was even a French onion seller, complete with onions, and a spiv with a suitcase full of black market goods.

The train arrived and, as in wartime, it was very crowded and they had to walk through several carriages to find seats, sitting separately wherever they could find a space. The atmosphere on the train was very light hearted and friendly, they explained to their fellow passengers that they were 'Allotment Girls' with their hair tied up in turbans and their 'Dig for Victory' badges on their khaki shirts. They thought that they looked quite authentic and people seemed to accept this.

They alighted at Arley Station and joined the crowds to wait for a 1940s wedding to take place. This was on the opposite platform but they had a very good view at the front of the throng which had gathered to watch. It was a war-time wedding with the vicar in full regalia with the groom in his American Army uniform and the bride dressed as a corporal in the Women's British Army known as The Auxiliary Territorial Service (or A.T.S.). A naval officer gave the bride away and led her through an archway of ladies holding umbrellas.

Most of the guests were dressed in formal 1940s civilian clothes but some were wearing their uniforms. Someone had baked a small sponge cake and placed it inside a cardboard replica of a three tiered wedding cake, this being all that they could manage with war time rationing. The happy couple departed through a guard of honour of soldiers holding bayonets aloft to the cheers of the assembled company.

The crowds dispersed and they wandered around the stalls, one of which was purporting to sell 1940s groceries, with the grocer wearing a brown cowgown and a bowler hat and his wife in a flowery overall with her hair in

27. HIGHLEY, SEVERN VALLEY 2012

a snood, whilst a black and white cat slept curled up on the W & T Avery scales.

A group of young musicians were assembling and getting their instruments ready to play, a policeman was 'arresting' a man for being drunk and disorderly and an armed soldier was guarding the station entrance. There were rows of pre-war British cars, American jeeps and other military vehicles in excellent condition which they admired. They were taking photos of themselves and Viv and Bob when their attention was caught by the strains of Glenn Miller's tune 'In the Mood'. They turned around to see a couple doing the Jitterbug to the music on the station platform. They were very energetic and acrobatic with the man throwing the lady around his back and both thoroughly enjoying themselves, as were the spectators.

After announcing its arrival with a shrill whistle, a steam train chugged into the station and invited them to board for their onward journey to Bewdley, where they hoped to get some lunch, with Viv and Bob. Alighting at Bewdley Station they crossed the bridge to get to the cafe which was on the opposite platform and headed for lunch. On the way to the cafe they passed stalls selling 1940s costumes and uniforms and even the small brown

2012 Jitterbugging Arley Station 1940s weekend

cardboard suitcases to carry them in! There were rows of classic cars including Austins, Morris', Singers, Fords, Morgans and even a 'Mechanical Horse' made by Scammell.

After stopping to admire them they made their way to the cafe where they enjoyed a light lunch before waving Viv and Bob off as they were on their way home. Crossing the bridge they wandered along the platform as they had a little time to kill before their train arrived, taking photos and listening to a man in RAF uniform singing ballads on the opposite platform. They all felt very sorry for him as he was singing his heart out and no-one appeared to be listening to him.

They caught the next train to Highley as they had to be back in plenty of time to have dinner and catch the train to Kidderminster for the Big Band Show in the evening. En route they passed an encampment where soldiers were erecting tents and checking their artillery, all looking very authentic to their civilian eyes.

When they got off the train at Highley Station they made their way down the slope to the river where they took a few moments to watch the antics of the ducks launching themselves into the water, before going up to their rooms to get ready for dinner. Back downstairs in the dining room, they ordered their meals and waited and waited and waited and an hour later their meals finally arrived, by which time they realised that it would be too late to catch the train for the Big Band Show once they had eaten. The meals were very nice but they didn't enjoy them as they might have, as they were increasingly nervous about missing the train. The father of a young family in the restaurant overheard them discussing this and offered to take two of them into Kidderminster but couldn't fit three of them in his car. They declined his kind offer as, at this point, they were all three of them planning to go.

When they realised that it would be too late for them to catch the train, by the time they went upstairs to change and then climbed up the hill to the station, they asked the barmaid to phone for a taxi. Sometime later she came back and said that she had tried several companies but no one had a taxi available, it being the 1940s weekend and taxis very much in demand.

While they were debating what to do, a taxi driver came to their table and asked them when they wanted to go to Kidderminster, apparently the barmaid had told him of their predicament. They said that they were more or less ready to go, they just had to go and get their coats. He then went and cleared it with the pub manager, as he was employed by him to be available to run customers home locally on Saturday evenings. He came back to their table and confirmed

27. HIGHLEY, SEVERN VALLEY 2012

that the manager had said that it was alright for him to take them, as it was early and he probably wouldn't be called upon for his services for a couple of hours.

They hurried upstairs to get their coats and get ready to go when Mabel decided that she was too tired to walk around anymore and she wanted to conserve her energy for the following day. Irene and June were reluctant to leave her on her own, but she insisted that she would be fine and would be glad to sit quietly on her bed and watch the TV or read a book. They tried to get reception on the TV but failed so Mabel said that she would be very happy to rest and read Irene's book, so the other two left her with strict instructions to ring June's mobile phone if she needed them.

June and Irene went downstairs and told the taxi driver that there were just the two of them and he set off for Kidderminster. It was a longer journey than expected but they enjoyed seeing the little villages and part of the countryside that they didn't normally see.

Alighting at Kidderminster Station they paid the taxi driver, which bugged them a bit since they had already paid for train tickets and it wasn't their fault that the meal was so late that they had missed it. Joining the merry throng of people milling around in the station's spacious entrance hall they were accosted by a member of the Home Guard who asked them if they had their identity cards, as it was illegal to be without one in wartime. They confessed that they hadn't, and he told them where to go to obtain one, so approaching a desk where a military man was seated, they were issued with cards stamped by various officials such as the Home Guard and The RAF Police Provost Marshal. They were also given a leaflet issued by the Civil Defence in July 1939 with advice on what to do if war was declared.

There were some fabulous 1940s costumes and military uniforms, both being worn and for sale, on the numerous stalls dotted about the station forecourt. There were ladies in smart suits and dresses bedecked with fur stoles, coats and jackets, completing their outfits with lisle or seamed silk stockings, high heeled court shoes, gloves and brimmed felt hats adorned with veils and feathers. The gentlemen were wearing suits with waistcoats, cravats, trilby hats or bowlers and braces to hold up their sharply creased trousers. Some wore 'plus fours', checked tweed trousers which finished below the knee worn with long woollen socks and either brogues or golfing shoes. They also had matching jackets and wore flat caps.

Girls wore short dresses or pleated skirts and blouses with smocking (embroidery) on the bodice, with white ankle socks or beige three quarter socks or black or brown machine knitted stockings. Shoes were sometimes in patent leather with a strap across the top of the foot, substantial black or brown leather lace-ups or black or white plimsolls (pumps). Boys wore short trousers with snake clipped belts and knee length socks held up with garters, which they would have worn until they left school when they went straight into long trousers. They also wore flannel shirts, Fair Isle pullovers, ties, blazers and felt caps.

Mainly the military uniforms were worn by army and air force officers with some 'lower ranks' and the occasional naval and even some German officers.

There were two mock ups of rooms set out in 1940s style, a kitchen and a living room. There were two ladies in wrap-around pinafores in the kitchen; one was washing up at an enamel sink whilst the other was hanging washing on the pulley. This consisted of striped flannel pyjamas, long-johns, vests, liberty bodices and loose shirt collars.

The living room had a three-piece suite, with antimacassars on the back to prevent staining by Brylcreem off the gentlemens' hair. There was also a man playing the pianola whilst a lady was stitching a garment on a Singer treadle sewing machine.

There was also washing hanging up on a line overhanging the vegetable patch, including pullovers, suspender belts, knickers and tablecloths, and beside it was an air raid shelter which they all explored further the following day.

As they strolled through to the platforms the Big Band struck up, playing 1940s swing music, featuring several Glenn Miller numbers and war time songs. There were 16 musicians in American army uniforms playing mainly brass and wind instruments and a blonde lady singer in a long red crepe dress with short red gloves and a fur stole. A gentleman crooner joined her wearing a dinner suit and black bow tie, and later on a man dressed as Bud Flanagan in his straw boater, long fur coat and spats on his shoes (from the Flanagan & Allen duo in the Crazy Gang show) joined her in singing 'Underneath The Arches'.

After listening to the band for a while they got a bit cold and went into the museum for a cup of tea and a warm up. The museum was packed with railway memorabilia, from station signs to telephones and they spent a happy half hour playing with the 'phones and signals.

They went back out onto the platform and listened to the band for a while, but it was getting quite cold so they boarded the train which they were travelling back to Highley on and found a window seat where they could watch people on the platform. Mostly they were in costumes and various uniforms,

27. HIGHLEY, SEVERN VALLEY 2012

milling around, chatting, drinking, dancing and generally enjoying themselves to the last strains of the music.

The train left Kidderminster Station about 11pm and they re-joined their abandoned friend by 11.30pm. Mabel said that she had been quite happy reading her book and making cups of tea, but that she had missed the chatter of the other two!

Sunday

They met up for the buffet-style breakfast in the dining room and afterwards returned to their rooms to pack their bags. They then took them downstairs and put them in a boot room, to be collected later. It was at this point that Irene spotted a wall mounted ashtray outside emitting smoke. She dashed inside to alert the barmaid who came out with a jug of water to dowse the fire, she said that this was a regular occurrence and Irene took the opportunity to snap an unusual photo.

After the fire was extinguished they set off to catch the 9.40am train to Hampton Loade, huffing and puffing their way up the slope to Highley station. They duly alighted at Hampton Loade station where they admired the rows of red fire buckets. Strolling along the platform they stopped to read the wartime adverts with recipes for making soup from potatoes and carrots. There were also propaganda posters, one depicting Winston Churchill advocating 'let them go forward together'.

They crossed the railway line and found a model railway in action and after watching the trains whizzing along the track for a while they walked along platform 2 and came across a very smartly dressed couple. The woman wore a high ranking naval uniform and the man wore an RAF uniform and they asked if they could take their photos. They got chatting to them and the man said that he was meant to be Air Chief Marshall Dowding, who, he said, was the commanding officer of Fighter Command during the Battle of Britain until he fell out of favour with other high ranking officers because he insisted on protecting the pilots and trying to lessen the risk of loss of life. He also disagreed with their views on formation flying and wanted to set up a radar defence system against night flying to stop the Germans from night time bombing of their cities. He was then sidelined to fund raising in America.

After crossing back over the track they took a few photos of the approaching train before boarding the 10.30am to Bridgnorth and making good use of their Rover tickets which enabled them to hop on and off the trains over the weekend.

When they arrived at Bridgnorth there was a workman on the track between two carriages who appeared to be coupling a carriage to an engine. They watched this for a while and then looked for a cafe to quench their thirst as they were well overdue for their elevenses (well about two minutes!).

Twenty minutes later they ambled along the platform admiring the classic cars and American Jeeps until they heard music coming from further along and so set off to find the source. There was a crowd of people gathering to watch a young lady singing wartime songs accompanied by taped music. She was later joined by a young man who was making his debut impersonating the singer Al Bowlly. They were both excellent singers and kept the friends and the group of people waiting for the next train well entertained, especially the young couples who were jitterbugging.

Once aboard the train to Kidderminster they got chatting to a couple dressed as American army officers who were sitting opposite them in the carriage. They were very pleasant, and happy to chat to them about their hobby of dressing in various costumes and travelling about the country in their campervan. They told them that they attended wartime events and helped in educating and informing school groups about life in the 1930s and 1940s. Whilst enjoying their company they also enjoyed the ever changing views of the countryside, especially the stunning poppy fields.

When they arrived at Kidderminster Station it was lunch time, so after looking at a pile of aluminium pots and pans in the station forecourt (which showed how aluminium was collected to make the bodies of Spitfires) they made their way to the cafe and assuaged their hunger with cottage pie and cups of tea. Glancing around the displays they were struck by the many and varied posters depicting war time slogans, how to make do and mend and use up bits of food and avoid any sort of waste.

There were posters showing German uniforms so that they could be identified if Britain was invaded. Often the posters were humorous with colourful catchy pictures to grab the attention, with slogans such as 'walls have ears'. There were racks of war time editions of a variety of newspapers with dramatic headlines, like the sinking of The Bismark and the raging fires after the bombing in London.

Returning to the forecourt they looked at the two 1940s rooms where in the kitchen a lady wearing a flowery wrap around pinafore was putting an aluminium kettle on the gas hob and a man was showing some young children how to use a mangle. He was feeding a sheet through the mangle's rollers whilst the children took it in turns to wind the handle.

They wandered around the forecourt and the platforms perusing the many wartime exhibits such as a vegetable patch with carrots, onions, beans, cabbages, potatoes and lettuces, with a row of marigolds around the edge to deter insects from eating the vegetables. They passed a telephone box whose windows were taped in a criss-cross pattern to prevent injury from flying glass during air raids, this was also applied to the windows in residential and commercial premises. Next to this was an ARP post which was called 'The Hotel Ritz' with an air raid warden sitting in the doorway (which was surrounded by sandbags) in his warden's uniform complete with white helmet with a large W on the front.

There was also a dummy dressed as a rescue man, complete with stretcher, gas mask, tools, ropes and stirrup pumps. Next to him was an air raid siren by a sign telling people what to do in the event of a raid. There was also a big red box containing breathing and smoke apparatus standing near to a clock showing the time of the black-out for the day. A field telephone stood beside a poster with instructions on it showing how to see in the black-out if driving a car.

They walked along to where there was an air raid shelter made of corrugated iron and before entering it they read the posters on the outside. One instructed people not to leave food in the shelters which would encourage rats and another one informed people that Anderson shelters could be obtained from their local council. If they earned less than £5 per week they were free, but if they earned more than £5 per week they had to pay between 14 shillings and 18 shillings.

On entering the shelter they saw two bunk beds made up with sheets, pillows and khaki army blankets. Under the bed was a white enamel chamber pot and next to the bed an oil lamp and a Valor oil heater. Standing nearby was a leather effect brown cardboard suitcase and a first aid box. Once outside they noticed the piles of sand bags resting against the shelter near to the doorway to protect the inhabitants from bomb blasts.

Pondering about the hardships which civilians had to endure as well as the fighting forces, they made their way to the platform and boarded the train to Highley station, admiring once again the magnificent poppy fields along the way, which seemed very appropriate, given what they had been looking at. Passing once again through Bewdley Station they felt very sorry for the RAF man who was still standing on the platform singing his heart out and being totally ignored.

When they alighted at Highley Station they crossed over the track to look at the stalls which were displaying costume jewellery, caps, clutch bags, Brownie Box cameras and a variety of knick-knacks. Alongside the signal box there was a display of military vehicles, tents and cooking utensils. Walking back across the track June pointed out a swarm of wasps that appeared to have made their nest inside a lamppost. They were very surprised by this as none of them had ever seen this before.

They strolled down to The Ship Inn by the river to wait for Buz to pick them up, where they decided to have a cup of tea whilst they were waiting. Irene brought the tea from the bar and they sat and drank it on a bench by the river watching the fishermen and canoeists.

When Buz arrived they collected their luggage from the boot room and loaded it into his camper van before setting off to Smoke Alley as they thought that they would like to see Maureen, Boris, Jasmine and Will before they left. June got out of the campervan and knocked on Jasmine and Will's door, they were quite surprised to see her and came out to say hello to Irene and Mabel, who after the day's exertions had opted to stay in the van. At this point Maureen appeared as she had just returned from taking Boris for a walk. They mentioned that they had hoped to see her at the Big Band Show and she explained that she had been visiting a sick member of her family. After telling Jasmine, Will and Maureen about the events of the weekend and taking some photos they said farewell and headed back to Birmingham.

2012 *Wardens post and air raid shelter, Kidderminster Station*

27. HIGHLEY, SEVERN VALLEY 2012

Chatting in the campervan on the way home, they all agreed that they had enjoyed their 'wartime experience' dressing up as land army girls, travelling about on the trains and admiring the costumes, vehicles and music of the 1940s. They had some very interesting conversations with people who were dressed in the costume of the time, known as re-enactors, who travel around the country recapturing the wartime spirit at festivals, rallies and steam fayres. Mabel said that she would like to take Doug there for a weekend and all of them felt that they would like to re-visit Highley and do the 1940s weekend again.

This turned out to be their last 'Adventure' as they were no longer able to do the walking that they had previously enjoyed so much. They continued to meet up on Tuesdays at Mabel's house and read out aloud from the book that they had jointly written, enjoying and re-living once again their 'Adventures'.